W9-ANG-867

TRANSITION

Transition *was founded thirty years ago in Uganda by Rajat Neogy and quickly established*
self as a leading forum for intellectual debate. The first series of issues developed a reputation
or tough-minded, far-reaching criticism, both cultural and political, and this new series carries
on the tradition.

TRANSITION

AN INTERNATIONAL REVIEW

Contents

Transition (ISSN 0041–1191) is published quarterly by Oxford University Press, 200 Madison Avenue, New York, NY 10016 and is an official publication of the W.E.B. Du Bois
Institute. Postmaster: Application to mail at second class postage rates is pending at Cary, NC, and additional mailing offices; send address changes to Transition, Journals Fulfillment
Department, Oxford University Press, 2001 Evans Road, Cary, NC 27513. © 1992 Oxford University Press

TURNING THE PAGE: AFRICAN WRITERS ON THE THRESHOLD OF THE TWENTY-FIRST CENTURY

Nadine Gordimer

In the beginning was the Word.

The Word was with God, signified God's word, the word that was Creation. But over the centuries of human culture the word has taken on other meanings, secular as well as religious. To have the word has come to be synonymous with ultimate authority, with prestige, with awesome, sometimes dangerous persuasion, to have Prime Time, a TV talk show, to have the gift of gab as well as that of speaking in tongues.

As the twenty-first century approaches, the word flies through space, bounces from satellites, now nearer than it has ever been to the heaven from which it was believed to have come. But its most significant transformation occurred for us—the writers—long ago (and it was in Africa) when it was first scratched on a stone tablet or traced on papyrus, when it materialized from sound to spectacle, from being heard to being read as a series of signs, and then a script; and travelled through time from parchment to Gutenberg. For this is the genesis story of the writer. It is the story that *wrote* you or me into being.

It was, strangely, a double process, creating at the same time both the writer and the very purpose of the writer as a mutation in the agency of human culture. It was both ontogenesis as the origin and development *of* an individual being, and the adaptation, in the nature of that individual, specifically to the exploration of ontogenesis, the origin and development of *the* individual being. For we writers are evolved for that task. Like the prisoner incarcerated with the jaguar in Borges's story "The God's Script" who was trying to read, in a ray of light that fell only once a day, the meaning of being from the markings on the animal's pelt, we spend our lives attempting to interpret through the word the readings we take in the societies of which we are part. It is in this sense, this inextricable, ineffable participation, that writing is always and at once an exploration of self and of the world; of individual and collective being.

Writers in Africa in this century now coming to an end interpreted the greatest events on our continent since the abolition of slavery, from Things Falling

Apart in the colonialist regimes, crossing the River Between oppression and liberation, passing Up in Arms through the Fog at the Season's End, Down Second Avenue, singing the Song of Lawino on the Mission to Kala, overcoming Nervous Conditions and discarding the Money Order as the price of bondage, enduring the House of Hunger, challenging the World of Strangers created by racism, recognizing we were shirking responsibility as Fools for Blaming ourselves on History, Confessing as An Albino Terrorist, telling as the Interpreters the Tough Tale of the struggle for Freedom.

There is no prize offered for correctly identifying the writers of the books whose titles you should recognize strung together to tell the story in the account I have just given, nor will it be necessary to point out that these titles and writers are only a random few of those that have made manifest in our literature the embattled awakening of our continent.

We have known that our task was to bring to our people's consciousness and that of the world the true dimensions of racism and colonialism beyond those that can be reached by the media, the newspaper column and screen image, however valuable these may be. We writers have sought the fingerprint of flesh on history.

The odds against developing as a writer able to take on this huge responsibility have, for most of our writers, been great. But as Agostinho Neto said, and proved in his own life: "If writing is one of the conditions of your being alive, you create that condition."

Out of adversity, out of oppression, in spite of everything.

Before we look forward into the twenty-first century we have the right to assess what we have come through, and what it means to be here, this particular time and place that has been twentieth-century Africa. This has been an existential position with particular implications for literature; we have lived and worked through one of those fearful epochs Brecht has written of when "to speak of trees is almost a crime." Our brothers

Engagement has been regarded as some sort of upmarket version of propaganda

and sisters have challenged us with the Polish poet Czeslaw Milosz's cry: "What is poetry which does not serve nations or people?" And we have taken up that challenge. Inevitably, the characteristic of African literature during the struggle against colonialism and, later, neocolonialism and corruption in postcolonial societies, has been engagement—political engagement.

Now, unfortunately, many people see this concept of engagement as a limited category closed to the range of life reflected in literature; it is regarded as some sort of up-market version of propaganda. Engagement is not understood for what it really has been, in the hands of honest and talented writers: the writer's exploration of the particular meaning that being has taken on in his or her time and place. For real "engagement," for the writer, is not something set apart from the range of the creative imagination at the dictate of his brothers and sisters in the cause he or she shares with them; it comes from within the writer, his or her creative destiny as an agency of culture, living in history. "Engagement" does not preclude the beauty of language, the complexity of human emotions; on the contrary, such literature must be able to use all these in order to be truly engaged with life, where the overwhelming factor in that life is political struggle.

While living and writing under these conditions in Africa, some of us have seen our books lie for years unread in our own countries, banned, and we have gone on writing. Many writers have been imprisoned: Wole Soyinka, Ngũgĩ wa Thiong'o, Jack Mapanje, Jeremy Cronin, Mongane Wally Serote, Breyten Breytenbach, Dennis Brutus, Jaki Seroke, and a host of others. Many, such as Chinua Achebe and Nuruddin Farah, have endured the trauma of exile, from which some never recover as writers, and which some do not survive at all. I think, among too many, of Can Themba and Dambuze Marechera.

What has happened to writers in other parts of the world we cannot always dismiss as remote from being a threat to ourselves, either. In 1988, what the Greek novelist Nikos Kazantzakis called the "fearsome rhythm of our time" quickened in an unprecedented frenzy, to which the writer was summoned to dance for his life. There arose a threat against writers that takes its appalling authority from something more widespread than the power of any single political regime. The edict of a world religion had sentenced a writer to death.

For three years now, wherever he is hidden, Salman Rushdie has existed under the pronouncement upon him of the *fatwa*. There is no asylum for him anywhere. Every time this writer sits down to write, he does not know if he will live through the day; he does not know whether the page will ever be filled. The murderous dictate invoking the power of international terrorism in the name of a great and respected religion is not something that happens to "somebody else." It is relevant to the themes that concern *us*, and will continue to do so, in African literature as part of worldwide postcolonial literature, for Rushdie's novel is an innovative exploration of one of the most intense experiences we share, the individual personality in transition between two cultures brought together in that postcolonial world. For the future freedom of the word, and for the human rights of all of us who write, the *fatwa* of death must be declared an offense against humanity and dealt with by those who alone have the power to do so— democratic governments everywhere, and the United Nations. The precedent of the *fatwa* casts a shadow over the free development of literature on our continent as it does everywhere, even as we believe ourselves to be moving into the enlightenment of the twenty-first century.

What do we in Africa hope to achieve, as writers, in the new century? Because we are writers, can we expect to realize literally, through our work, that symbol of change, the turning to a fresh page?

What are the conditions under which we may expect to write—ideological, material, social?

It seems to me that these are the two basic questions for the future of African literature. I think it is generally agreed that consonance with the needs of the people is the imperative for the future in our view of African literature. This is surely the point of departure from the past; there, literature played the immeasurably valuable part of articulating the people's political struggle, but I do not believe it can be said to have enriched their lives with a literary culture. And I take it that our premise is that a literary culture is a people's right.

We shall all, as I have suggested, make the approach from our experience in the twentieth century; we shall all be hazarding predictions, since we do not know in what circumstances our ambitions for a developing literature will need to be carried out. We have our ideas and convictions of how literary development should be consonant with these needs of our people; we cannot know with what manner of political and social orders we shall have to seek that consonance.

I think we have to be completely open-eyed about the relations between our two basic questions. We have to recognize that the first—what we hope to achieve in terms of literary directions—is heavily dependent on the second: the conditions under which we shall be working as writers. A literary culture cannot be created by writers without readers. There are no readers without adequate education. It's as simple—and dire—as that. No matter how much we encourage writers who are able to fulfill, according to their talents, the various kinds and levels of writing that will take literature out of the forbidding context of unattainable intellectualism, we shall never succeed until there is a wide readership competent beyond the school-primer and comic book level. And where there are readers there must be libraries

in which the new literature we hope to nurture, satisfying the need of identification with people's own daily lives, and the general literature that includes the great mind-opening works of the world, are available to them.

Will potential readers find prose, poetry, and nonfiction in their mother tongues? If we are to create a twenty-first-century African literature, how is this to be done while publishing in African languages remains mainly confined to works prescribed for study, market-stall booklets, and religious tracts? We have long accepted that Africa cannot, and so far as her people are concerned, has no desire to, create a "pure" culture in linguistic terms; this is an anachronism when for purposes of material development the continent eagerly seeks means of technological development from all over the world. We all know that there is no such workable system as a purely indigenous economy once everyone wants computers and movie cassettes. Neither, in a future of increasing intercontinental contact, can there be a "pure" indigenous culture. We see, a plain fact all over Africa, that the European languages that came with colonial conquest have been taken over into independence, *acquired* by Africans and made part of their own convenience and culture. (Whites, of course, have never had the good sense to do the same with African languages. . . .)

But we cannot speak of taking up the challenge of a new century for African literature unless we address the necessity to devise the means by which literature in African languages becomes the major component of the continent's literature. Without this one cannot speak of an African literature. It must be the basis of the cultural crosscurrents that will both buffet and stimulate that literature.

What of publishing?

We write the books; to come alive they have to be available to be read. To be available, they have to be competently distributed, not only through libraries, but also commercially. Many of us have experienced trying to meet the needs of the culturally marginalized by launching small, nonprofit publishing ventures in African literature. We find ourselves stopped short by the fact that the distribution network, certainly in the Southern African countries (I don't imagine there is much difference in countries in the North), remains the old colonial one. Less than a handful of networks makes decisions, based on the lowest common denominator of literary value, on what books should be bought from publishers, and has the only means of distributing these widely to the public, since they own the chain bookstores that dominate the trade in the cities, and are the only existing bookstores in most small towns. In South Africa, for example, in the twentieth century, there have been and are virtually *no* bookstores in the vast areas where blacks have been confined under apartheid.

Another vital question: what will be the various African states' official attitude to culture, and to literature as an expression of that culture? We writers do not know, and have every reason to be uneasy. Certainly, in the twentieth century of political struggle, state money has gone into guns, not books; literature—indeed, culture—has been relegated to the dispensable category. As for literacy, so long as people can read state decrees and the graffiti that defies them,

that has been regarded as sufficient proficiency. As writers, do we envisage, for example, a dispensation from a Ministry of Culture to fund publishing in African languages, and to provide libraries in rural communities and in the shanty towns that no doubt will be with us, still, for a long time? Would we have to fear that, in return for subvention, writers might be restricted by censorship of one kind or another? How can we ensure that our implicit role—supplying a critique of society for the greater understanding and enrichment of life there—will be respected?

Considering all these factors that stand between the writer's act of transforming literature in response to a new era, it seems that we writers have, however reluctantly, to take on contingent responsibilities that should not be ours. We shall have to concern ourselves with the quality and direction of education— will our schools turn out drones or thinkers? Shall we have access, through our writing, to young minds? How shall we press for a new policy and structure of publishing and distribution, so that writers may write in African languages and bring pleasure and fulfillment to thousands who are cut off from literature by lack of knowledge of European languages? How shall we make the function of writers, whose essential gesture, the hand held out to contribute to development, is in the books they offer, something recognized and given its value by the governing powers of the twenty-first century? We have to begin now to concern ourselves with the structures of society that contain culture, and within which it must assert its growth.

And there is yet one more problem to be faced by the naked power of the word, which is all we have, but which has proved itself unkillable by even the most horrible of conventional and unconventional weaponry. Looking back, many well-known factors inhibited the growth of a modern African culture, and African literature, in the century whose sands are running out through our fingers. One hardly need cite the contemptuous dismissal of all African culture by frontier and colonial domination; the cementing-over of African music, dance, myth, philosophy, religious beliefs, and secular rituals: the very stuff on which literary imagination feeds. The creativity of Africa lay ignored beneath the treading feet of white people on their way to see the latest Hollywood gangster movie or to pick up from the corner store a comic with bubble text in American. And soon, soon, these were joined by black people in the same pursuit, having been convinced, since everything that was their own was said to be worthless, that this was the culture to acquire. The habit of

Surely the great adventures that writers explore in life can offer a child something as exciting as the cumbersome battle between Japanese turtles?

chewing cultural pap is by now so deeply established among our people, and so temptingly cheaply purchased from abroad by our media—including the dominant cultural medium of our time, television—that literature in Africa not only has to express the lives of the people, but also has to assert the beauty and interest of this reality against the mega-

subculture that, in my revised terminology in a vastly changing world, is the opium of the people.

Surely the powers of our writers' imaginations can be exerted to attract our people away from the soporific sitcom, surely the great adventures that writers explore in life can offer a child something as exciting in image and word as the cumbersome battle between Japanese turtles? We do not want cultural freedom to be hijacked by the rush of international subliterature into the space for growth hard-won by ourselves in the defeat of colonial cultures. That is perhaps the greatest hazard facing us as we turn the page of African literature and write the heading: twenty-first century.

Albert Camus wrote: "One either serves the whole of man or one does not serve him at all. And if man needs bread and justice, he also needs pure beauty, which is the bread of his heart." And so Camus called for "Courage in one's life and talent in one's work." We shall need courage in our lives to take part in transforming social structures so that African literature may grow.

Gabriel García Márquez wrote: "The best way a writer can serve a revolution is to write as well as he can." That goes for the peaceful revolution of culture, as well; without talent in our work, without ourselves writing as well as we can, we shall not serve African literature as we should.

I believe that the statements of Camus and Márquez and Neto (remember his words: "If writing is one of the conditions of your being alive, you create that condition") might be the credo for all of us who write in Africa. They do not resolve the conflicts that will continue to come, but they state plainly an honest possibility of doing so, they turn the face of writers squarely to their existence, reason-to-be, as a writer, and the reason-to-be, as a responsible human being, acting like any other within a social and political context. Bread, justice, and the bread of the heart, which is the beauty of literature: these are all our business in Africa's twenty-first century.

POSTCOLONIAL CULTURE, POSTIMPERIAL CRITICISM

W. J. T. Mitchell

The humanities in the United States today is a profession that sees itself in crisis. This "crisis" has been going on long enough now to become absolutely banal, to become, in fact, something of a professional institution in itself. The basic assumptions and terms of literary study, in particular, are undergoing radical revision in an utterly systematic, encyclopedic, and professional way. Notions of intentionality, authority, textuality, the purpose of reading and writing, and the value of literary or "humanistic" education are in question, both from within, in the skeptical gestures of advanced theory, and from without, in the reactionary jeremiads of the New Right. For those committed to the continuity of the professional humanities, one way of defusing the crisis is to frame it in the terms made familiar by Thomas Kuhn, as "paradigm change" or "scientific revolution." This framework offers us a revolution without tears, terror, or radical disruption: we are simply moving from one model of normal science to a new, presumably better model, replacing the phlogiston theory of authorial intention

with the Second Law of Thermodynamic textuality, or the NewtonianCartesian model of artistic space with the relativity theory of multicultural practices. Some individual careers based in outmoded paradigms of literary history may suffer, but the profession as a whole will survive quite nicely.

I think we should be uneasy with the Kuhnian paradigm, if only because it tells us what we, as professional humanists, want to hear. It reinforces our somewhat tarnished self-esteem as poor but respectable contributors to the knowledge-industry—underpaid relatives of the scientists, producing a *kulturwissenschaft* that will contribute, as Kuhn's own work did, to an "International Encyclopedia of Unified Science"; and it allows us to hold onto our cherished self-image as guardians and transmitters of something called "culture," a body of values and valuable texts that we "profess" as exemplars of an abstract "humanity." The myth that professional humanism is "more humane" than other professions (law, medicine, advertising, politics, science) is kept intact at the same time.

Who, after all, could be more humane than a professional humanist?

Another reason to be suspicious of the paradigm of paradigm change is a development that was anticipated (and later retracted) in Kuhn's own works, and that is the temptation to metaphoric totalization, the transformation of paradigm change (a feature of internal professional traditions and discourses) into shifts of "worldview." There is no doubt some connection between these local, specialized "revolutions" in scientific models, and larger transformations at the level of what Foucault called the "episteme," but there seems good reason to be skeptical that one can simply be mapped onto the other. When Kuhn conflates his paradigm with the notion of "worldview," and equates the unified "world of the scientist" with "the paradigm-embodied experience of the race, the culture, and, finally, the profession," we see an all-too-familiar image of the traditional temptation of the humanist: the profession's internal history becomes the microcosm of a totality, often conceived (as Kuhn's remark suggests) in terms of culture and race. I won't rehearse here the obvious dangers of these rhetorical moves. I recommend a reading, however, of Simon During's brilliant demonstration of the intricate routes by which "the discourse of philological culture flows into fascism," a "flow" which "is generated by the practices of professionalisation and *Wissenschaft*." The recent attempts of the New Right to mobilize a campaign of "cultural literacy," to institutionalize English as the official language of the United States, and to return to an approved canon of white Western literature ought to provide vivid reminders of the ideological uses of "culture." They also remind us, I suggest, that affirmations of "professionalism" are never a sufficient answer to "professor bashing," and arguments over "disciplinarity" are conspicuously short on attention to the powers that discipline. Paradigm change serves only to keep us within the "institutional framework," to circle the professional wagons. We need a stronger alternative, one that addresses the public sphere, not simply asking it to take it on trust that we know what we're doing—producing real knowledge and value for our nonprofessional clientele.

What should we be talking about, if not paradigm change? The other temptation is to work from the top down, from a global, epistemic shift down to the paradigm shift, to see the professional microcosm as a reflection of a cultural macrocosm. This is the strategy of "global mapping" that parades under the banner of "Postmodernism," and exalts (or attacks) our own epoch with a totalizing, dialectical master-narrative that treats the present as a negation of the Modernist past. This alternative is better insofar as it gets us out of the professional circuit and into some contact with a public sphere. But it does so, I fear, at the cost of a loss of precision, and an overgeneralization that is likely to simply mirror the sort of result we derive from a close examination of the professional sphere. The "public sphere" it addresses, moreover, is likely to be confined to the culture industries (media, advertising, architecture, and "art worlds") of the First World. My suggestion is that we shift the whole inquiry about "changes" in something called the "humanities" to a middle or "border" region, somewhere between the the Foucauldian episteme and the Kuhnian paradigm. This middle region I will call the "scene of *translatio*," or "transference," and by this I mean simply instances of reconfiguration and relocation of cultural and critical energy, reversals of center and margin, production and consumption, dominant and emergent forces, reversals even in traditional divisions of cultural labor such as "criticism" and "creative writing." These patterns, I hope to show, do not locate themselves exclusively within any profession or academic structure—though they pass through and affect these structures—and they have a global circulation without straightforwardly lending themselves to totalizing images.

I'm speaking, as you will have guessed from my title, of the process of "decolonization," a term that suggests as its necessary corollary some related transformations in the corresponding centers of empire, a "deimperialization." The basic tropes of this process are as old as the Roman Empire, which saw (as Horace put it) a "translatio studii" or transfer of arts and learning as the consequence of the "translatio imperii," the transfer of empire. The Enlightenment version of this *translatio* is aptly summarized in Bishop Berkeley's "Verses on the Prospect of Planting the Arts and Learning in America":

The Muse, disgusted at an age and clime
Barren of every glorious theme,
In distant lands now waits a better time
Producing subjects worthy fame:
. . . .
There shall be sung another golden age,
The rise of empire and of arts,
The good and great inspiring epic rage

The wisest heads and noblest hearts.
. . . .
Westward the course of empire takes its way;
The four first Acts already past,
A fifth shall close the Drama with the day
Time's noblest offspring is the last. (1752)

Berkeley constructs the relation between imperial center and colonial outpost as a straightforward dialectic: as Europe degenerates, the American colonies will thrive, developing a new culture and a new imperial destiny. Empire continues in its inexorable westward path, from Greece to Rome to Europe to England (the first four acts) to its final act in America.

This scenario of *translatio* is remarkable for several features, not the least being its (probably unintentional) shifting of the literary shape of empire from epic to the (tragic) five-act drama. America, the final frontier to the West, the potential soil for the "wisest heads and noblest hearts," is also the "last" of the empires. The destiny of the "Western empire"

The "West" never designates where it is, but only where it hopes to go

equivocates between a western location and a westward imperative: the imperial consciousness is thus always displaced from its location, always oriented toward an occident not yet attained. This is the central paradox of "the West" as the rubric for an imperial civilization and for our own identity as the bearers of "Western Civilization": the name never designates where it is, but only where it hopes to go, its "prospects" and frontiers. For some time, however, it has been evident that the Western empires have nowhere to go. We live not just in a "postmodern" but a "postcolonial" world, where the "westering" imperative makes no literal or concrete sense, and must be displaced in various figurative substitutes: outer or inner space, Star Wars or Self-Actualization. The most powerful of the emergent empires is located in the Orient, not the West, and its power derives from the electronic marketplace, not gunboats or ICBMs.

How do we translate Berkeley's dialectics of empire into our contemporary scene? The United States presents special problems, of course, because (despite Berkeley's explicit prediction) the frank acknowledgment of imperial identity has always been anathema to American exceptionalist ideology. The United States may well be the first nation in history to realize that it has been an empire only as it ceases to be one. Americans are less disturbed by the idea of imperial decline than with the notion that the term "empire" could ever apply to the United States. Our national self-concept has always been resolutely anti-imperialist, from our origins in a colonial rebellion against the British Empire to our most recent stands against the "Evil Empire." Even the Monroe Doctrine, an imperial manifesto if ever there was one, represents itself as an anti-imperialist policy, a shield for "free" countries in the Americas from the threat of European imperialism. The apparent redundancy, "America for the Americans," conceals a potent equivocation. Citizens of the United States have no name for themselves other than "Americans"; there are no "United Statesians" as there are Nic-araguans and Brazilians and Canadians. Other inhabitants of the Americas are thus not quite "Americans *proper*": they are South, North, Central, Afro-, Native, or Latin Americans. Citizens of the United States are the only Americans unmodified or unhyphenated, the only Americans pure and simple.

Let us bracket, for the moment, the possibility that the United States, along with the rest of the "First World," could acknowledge its imperial identity. What sort of *translatio* or cultural reconfiguration seems most overwhelmingly evident in the global cultural relations of the First, Second, and Third Worlds? I want to put this in the form of a massively general and oversimplified impression to be argued out and qualified, and which I think of, not as a professional scholarly discovery, but as a commonplace that is now emerging into general public consciousness. The commonplace is simply this: the most important new literature is now emerging from the former colonies of the Western empires—from (for instance) Africa, South America, Australia, New Zealand; the most provocative new criticism is emanating from research universities in the advanced industrial democracies, that is, from the former centers of the "Western empires"—Europe and the United States.

Before I begin qualifying this commonplace, let me document its currency. In 1988 the Nobel Prize for Literature went to the Egyptian novelist Naguib Mahfouz, the first Arab ever to win the award. The *Los Angeles Times* story on this event (Friday, October 14, 1988) did not treat it as a surprise or anomaly, but as something that could have been predicted, noting "a recent trend . . . to seek

[Nobel] laureates outside the mainstream of European and American literature." Actually, Wole Soyinka of Nigeria, the 1986 laureate, is the only other non-European to win in recent years. William Golding (1983) is the last Englishman to win, and Claude Simon, the French novelist, won in 1985. The other winners, Czeslaw Milosz (Poland, 1980), Elias Canetti (Bulgaria, 1981), Jaroslav Seifert (Czechoslovakia, 1984), and Joseph Brodsky (Soviet exile) show a pattern that is not so much "non-European" as non-*Western* European. They are what we might call "Second World exiles." What is striking is that the "trend" noted by the *Los Angeles Times* is not quite empirically accurate; it is a half-truth, a premature generalization, an impression. In a word, it is a commonplace. And a similar commonplace might be documented in the trends perceived within the literature of the English-speaking world. The *Encyclopedia Britannica Book of the Year* for 1987 strikes a characteristic note: "On the whole, British fiction had a wan despondent air in 1986," and the winner of the Booker Prize, Kingsley Amis, is given only half a cheer, "for in latter years Amis's novels had not been considered respectable enough for prizes." When *Britannica* turns to the "other contenders in the shortlist for the Booker prize," however, it notes that they "were mostly of overseas extraction," and discusses with some enthusiasm the Canadian writers Robertson Davies and Margaret Atwood, and "British educated Asians" like Kazuo Ishiguro and Timothy Mo. Indeed, the "overseas contenders" are now doing even better than making the shortlist. When Keri Hulme, a Maori-Scottish feminist mystic from the

remote west coast of New Zealand's south island, wins Britain's most prestigious literary prize with her first novel (*The Bone People*), we know that familiar cultural maps are being redrawn.

The literary map of the Americas is in even greater flux. A mere recitation of the familiar names—Carlos Fuentes, Maria Vargas Llosa, Gabriel García Márquez, Jorge Luis Borges, Julio Cortazar—is enough to suggest a literary *translatio* from South to North, from Spanish to English. And within the borders of the United States it is now possible to assemble an anthology entirely composed of "modified" Americans—African, Arabic, Spanish, Asian, and "Native." Here is a partial list from the table of contents of a new freshman anthology edited for Norton by J. Paul Hunter: Jamaica Kincaid, Luis Cabalquinto, Ray Young Bear, Cathy Song, Agha Shahid, Leslie Silko, Mitsuye Yamada, Bharati Mukherjee, Lorna Dee Cervantes, and Mary TallMountain. Paul Hunter asks: "What is a professor of *English* supposed to do with such a list?" More, I suspect, than apply a new paradigm, though that will certainly happen.

If one commonplace is that the balance of literary trade has shifted from the First to the Second and Third Worlds, its corollary perception is that the production of criticism has become a central activity of First World culture industries, especially those located in institutions of higher education. "Ours is an Age of Critics and Metacritics," notes Gene Bell-Villada, an American professor of Spanish, "theirs an Age of Literature." The observation is not exactly news. Over thirty years ago Randall Jarrell mournfully declared that Europe and the United States were entering an "age of criticism." One wonders how he would have greeted the literary developments of the 1980s: issues of *Time* and *Newsweek* devote space to deconstruction; the *New York Times* covers critical movements at Yale and Duke in full color; academic critics write best-selling books on "cultural literacy" and "the American mind," and become instant talk-show celebrities. Even the most ordinary academic critic can now aspire to participate in a global network of what Edward Said has called "Travelling Theory," flying between conferences on semiotics, narratology, and paradigm change in places like Hong Kong, Canberra, and Tel Aviv.

Most literary critics are familiar with David Lodge's *Small World*, a marvelous satire on this global critical culture. What they may not recall is the opening metaphor in Lodge's book: "The modern conference," says Lodge, "resembles the pilgrimage of medieval Christendom in that it allows the participants to indulge themselves in all the pleasures and diversions of travel while appearing to be austerely bent on self-improvement." But the comparison of "Travelling Theory" to the medieval pilgrimage has a serious implication as well. It suggests that the global circuit of intellectual exchange in modern criticism is a cultural system just as significant to us as the pilgrimage was to the Middle Ages. The "holy places" where the pilgrims gather are universities and conference centers; spiritual regeneration of the individual believer has been replaced by professional and intellectual advancement; and the collective goal of reuniting Christendom has been replaced by a secular notion of the reunification of human understanding in new paradigms of knowledge. A full exploration of travelling criticism as a cultural phenomenon would, of course, take into account other precedents such as the missionary, the explorer, the trader, the tourist, the colonial administrator, and the subaltern, traditional bearers of "Western culture" from the imperial centers to the colonial peripheries.

If criticism has to some extent muscled in on the territory of traditional cultural exports of the Western empires, it has done so in an odd and unpredictable way. Traditional cultural exports (literature, history, philosophy, the fine arts) tended to support the authority of the imperial center. English culture was transported to the "natives" and the colonial settlers in the full confidence that it would have a civilizing influence while serving as a continual reminder of where civilization was really located—in the imperial center. Contemporary criticism, by contrast, tends to subvert the imperial economy that supports it, "decentering" the very structure of discursive authority. Skepticism, relativism, and "antifoundationalist" modes of thought such as pragmatism and deconstruction may come to the Third World from the First, but they conspicuously lack the authoritative address of traditional imperial culture. Critical movements such as feminism, Black Studies, and Western Marxism may offer stronger assurances of authority and purpose, but they can hardly be said to speak with the authority of the imperial center. On the contrary, they are in the paradoxical position of bringing a rhetoric of decolonization from the imperial center. Perhaps this is why so many imaginative writers of the Third World (J. M. Coetzee in South Africa, Ian Wedde in New Zealand, Toni Morrison in "African America") look with wary fascination on contemporary criticism, unsure whether it is a friendly collaborator in the process of decolonization, or a threatening competitor for limited resources.

What is the relationship between First World critical movements and literary developments in the Second and Third Worlds? Clearly the situation is too complex to be reduced to any simple formula. We ought to resist, for instance, the notion that this relationship merely reflects the traditional economic relations of imperial centers and colonial peripheries. It is surely wrong to say that cultural "raw materials" are coming from the colonies to be turned into "finished products" by the critical industries of

The best evidence for a positive relation between postimperial criticism and postcolonial literature comes from those who feel most threatened by it

empire. If one thing is striking about Latin American writers like Carlos Fuentes and Gabriel García Márquez, it is the total absence of colonial provinciality in their work, and the presence of a sophisticated, cosmopolitan awareness, including an awareness of contemporary criticism. At the same time, one should not minimize the dissonance between postimperial criticism and postcolonial culture. Criticism may find itself preach-

ing a rhetoric of decentering and de-essentializing to cultures that are struggling to find a center and an essence for the first time; conversely, it may find itself bringing an imperial theory of culture into a situation that resists any conceptual totality: structuralism and post-structuralism may, in a word, be equally unwelcome guests at the table of postcolonial culture. The strategic location and historical timing of a critical idea may be as important in a period of global reconfiguration as any transcendental truth-claims it might want to make.

The best evidence for a positive, collaborative relationship between postimperial criticism and postcolonial literature comes, curiously enough, from those who feel most threatened by it. The common rhetorical thread that runs through recent right-wing jeremiads on the "decline of American culture" is precisely that of the fall of empires and the emergence of new, threatening centers of cultural power. When the neoconservative National Association of Scholars reacts to the emergence of ethnic and women's studies by declaring that "the barbarians are in our midst," we recognize the hysterical (or is it "testerical"?) rhetoric of an empire in decline. Allan Bloom's characterization of Afro-American studies as "the Little Black Empire" plays on similar buzz-words, simultaneously denigrating the value and inflating the threat of the barbarians by projecting imperial ambitions onto them. E. D. Hirsch's *Cultural Literacy* promises a "quick fix" for an empire whose appetite for diverse cultures has outstripped its ability to digest them into a single national identity. Hirsch offers lists of terms, names, great books, and authors as an alternative for critical method and as a substitute for cultural community. Lynne Cheney's report on the "Humanities in America" sounds the alarm to defend "American(=)Western(=)Universal Human" values from the depradations of ethnic and women's studies, and her position as director of the NEH would seem to place her on the front lines, at least with regard to funding for research projects.

The neoconservative attack on contemporary criticism may well be a blessing in disguise for those who hope for an alliance between postcolonial culture and postimperial criticism. For one thing, it should produce some solidarity among academic humanists by providing a clear sense of the common threat to standards of literary excellence and scholarly responsibility. Genuine conservatives in the academy should be the first to welcome the production of new literary forms among emerging nations and peoples, a development that fulfills (albeit in an unsuspected way) the ancient imperial dream of the *translatio studii,* a trope that can (and already is) being absorbed as a professional paradigm for research. Conservatives should also be the first to resist what Barbara Herrnstein Smith has aptly called the "querulous populism" of the New Right, its attempt to impose by political coercion and appeals to an uninformed mass audience views that it has been unable to make convincing in the context of professional debate. The pretense of the academic New Right that it is only concerned with eternal, human values while others are reducing everything to politics is now wearing so thin that even academic administrators should be able to see through it.

Even more important than these negative effects of the neoconservative reaction is the challenge it poses for those who work in the criticism of culture to move beyond professional paradigms to address the public sphere. The challenge is to articulate a comprehensive vision of the humanities, one that is sensitive to the innumerable local particularities of the global decolonizing process and yet capable of identifying common interests, opportunities for alliance and collaboration. We must have stories, if not as simple, at least as compelling as the gloomy jeremiads rehearsing the "decline of the west," the "fall of the American empire," and the "destruction of the white races." Perhaps an outline for one such a story might be found by retracing the American ideology of anti-imperialism, and connecting it with the great Western models of more or less graceful imperial decline. France, England, ancient Athens all had the advantage of knowing and acknowledging themselves as empires from very early on. The acknowledgment of *decline,* when it came, tended to 'be grudging because it went against the grain of an expansionist national identity.

For Americans, perhaps, the difficult move is the acknowledgment that we are and have been for some time an imperial power, and the easier task might be the acceptance of graceful decline (this, I think, was the official, though unpopular, message of the Carter administration). The unique gift of the American empire might be to combine the sober realism of these acknowledgments with a serious commitment to the idealism—as distinct from the self-deluding ideology—of our anti-imperialist traditions. George Washington showed us how to read the history of empire when he invoked the example of Cincinnatus, and refused the wrong kind of power at the right time. Only after Athens lost its navy did it become in fact what Pericles had, at the height of its power, hoped for it to be—"the School of Hellas." Perhaps American higher education can aspire to some such role in the next century, a world school for intelligent, peaceful, and productive decolonization. The idea of a "university" might then live up to its name.

MALCOLM'S MYTHMAKING

David Bradley

John Brown's body lies a-mouldering
  in the grave,
His soul goes marching on.
                    — *Thomas Brigham Bishop*
                    John Brown's Body

One balmy night in September 1991, I was in Newark, New Jersey, dining at the home of Amiri Baraka. It was not primarily a social occasion—he, Toni Cade Bambara, Thulani Davis, and I were scripting a documentary film about W. E. B. DuBois: this was a working meal—but it was convivial as could be, due to the rich supply of food, wine, and culturally concerned folk. And it was almost inevitable that eventually conversation would turn to the Malcolm X movie, which the redoubtable Spike Lee was supposed to start shooting the next week.

Baraka, of course, had already started shooting. In early August he had held a rally in Harlem and charged that Lee was trashing the story of Malcolm's life "to make middle-class Negroes sleep easier." The charges were hard to verify, as they were based on a "leaked" script; Lee had, supposedly, classified the thing Top

**Discussed in
this essay**

Malcolm: The Life of a
Man Who Changed
Black America, *Bruce
Perry, Barrytown, NY:
Station Hill Press*

Secret. Reliable sources said that the camera operators had only seen the shooting script a day or so before, and Baraka wasn't showing his copy around, but reliable sources said the script emphasized Malcolm's youthful days as "Detroit Red"—which is to say, it was full of big band music, drinking, doping, and hustling, and that may have been what Baraka had been alluding to in Harlem. Now he just shook his head and said, "The script is terrible." I'd heard that before. I'd been hearing it since another balmy September night, back in '84, when I agreed to write the script.

Not *this* script. Actually, not *the* script. *Another* script. I was not the first writer on the job. Nor was I the last; two drafts and a set of changes later the producer, Marvin Worth, and the studio, Warner Brothers, "brought in another writer"—Hollywoodese for, I got fired. I don't know when this happened—nobody called up and fired me, that's not how it works—but I heard about it in early 1988, at a cocktail party in Philadelphia, from another writer who said he had been offered the job.

He took it. And got fired from it. And

thereby no doubt hangs a tale or two, just as a tale or two depends from my own hiring and firing, and no doubt from those of the writers who came before. Lately a lot of journalists have been trying to find out what those tales are—the Malcolm X movie has by now generated more publicity without getting made than most films that do get made. They've gotten frustrated and a mite discouraged—"Perhaps we'll never know what went down with the script," lamented Playthell Benjamin, in *Emerge Magazine*.

Probably not if you don't know any more about Hollywood than Benjamin apparently does.

Few do. The General Public has an idealized notion of how the Motion Picture Industry operates—a notion derived mostly from movies and MPI publicity. As a result, the GP consistently misapprehends MPI events. For example, emotional outbursts on the set. A nuclear exchange that has rocked all Tinseltown? Hardly. Usually it's just a firecracker in a tin can. Or maybe a smokescreen over contract negotiations. For another

Malcolm X at Kennedy Airport upon return from abroad, November 24, 1964.

Photo: Robert Parent/ Courtesy of Pathfinder Press

example, firings. When I tell people I was fired off the Malcolm X movie they often get a half-compassionate, half-embarrassed, "Gee, what can I say?" look on their faces. One reporter marveled that I wasn't "bitter" about getting fired.

It's hard to be bitter when you're living in—not on—your severance pay.

People think getting fired in Hollywood is like getting *fired*. It's more akin to ending an *affaire du cœur*. At worst it's like breaking up with someone you love. Usually it's like breaking up with someone you hate. At best it's like getting divorced from somebody you married for money anyway—you always get alimony, and sometimes you get joint custody and child support; if the writer they bring in uses a lot of your material and the Screen Writers Guild decides you ought to get credit, your name ends up on the silver screen, and you get paid even more. People also think that if they see three names in a writing credit, the writers worked together. More likely they never *saw* each other, except at cocktail parties. And when they hear that a writer got fired, people think it's because there was something wrong with the script.

From the point of view of the producer and/or the studio something *is* wrong—only they can't say what. Legally, they have to tell the writer what it is—there's boilerplate in the contract about notes. I know writers who claim to have seen notes—numbered, neatly typed on studio letterhead—but I never have. I once got two handwritten (back-slanted, purple ink, little circles over the "i's") pages (yellow lined paper, letter-, not legal-size), but that was on another project, and besides the wench is now an "independent producer" and working

out of her house in suburban Oxnard, which is to say, dead. Most producers won't put *anything* on paper, and get nervous if the writer takes notes (or, God forbid, brings a tape recorder to a meeting) because they're afraid somebody will find out the stupid ideas were theirs.

They probably weren't; producers' ideas are rarely coherent enough to be translated directly into dialogue and action. In fact, producers don't have ideas; they have instincts and gut-feelings. They're right a lot of the time—you don't have to make sense to make movies—but it's not like they can *explain*. . . . That's why they solve "script problems" by bringing in another writer, who, they hope, will understand what's wanted without being told in words. But that doesn't mean the old writer didn't do the old script right; it just means the producer and/or the studio (not the same thing, usually not the same people) didn't like it.

You don't have to be a Hollywood insider to "know what went down with the script" on the Malcolm X movie. All you have to do is know a little bit about the business and apply a little logic—which Playthell Benjamin doesn't have and surely didn't do when he listed the candidates for writer credits thusly: "Worth commissioned the distinguished Afro-American novelist James Baldwin to write the script . . . after a year of 'livin' large in Tinseltown at studio expense, he failed to come up with a usable and finished script. Two other novelists tried their hand at it and failed: David Bradley, a black college professor and author of the celebrated novel *The Chaneysville Incident,* and Calder Willingham, author of the novel *Eternal Fire.* Two Pulitzer Prize–winning dramatists also bit the dust trying to produce a viable script: Charles Fuller and David Mamet. . . . A brilliant playwright who has taken us on marvelous excursions into the soul of African American culture [Fuller] seemed destined for the project. But alas, zilch."

First of all, no writer produces "zilch," because if he does he doesn't get paid, and maybe gets sued. So whatever happened, every writer produced something that looked like a script. And all the scripts told pretty much the same story. Now any writer can produce something that is—in the words of Mr. Benjamin, "unusable and unfinished" or not "viable"—but *all* the writers couldn't have screwed up the same story so badly—remember, we're talking not only drafts but producer- and studio-influenced redrafts—for so long—we're talking a quarter of a century here—that a talented director—both Sidney Lumet and Norman Jewison were involved at some point—couldn't have come up with a shooting script.

Especially not these writers.

Leave me and Willingham out of it—everybody knows novelists can't write scripts. But Mamet and Fuller surely can—Pulitzer Prize–winning plays and scripts for films that get mentioned at Oscar time. You really think *neither* one of those guys could come up with a "viable" script? As for James Baldwin, he was a novelist, sure, but he was also a playwright and, while the man admittedly wasn't afraid to spend his expense allowance (which is written into the contract; it's not like the studio got taken by either Baldwin or surprise) if he "failed to come up with a usable and finished script" how come Worth brought in another writer, the late Arnold Perl, to fin-

ish the unusable? And how come Spike Lee—as he told Benjamin—"thought it was a great script except for the last third" and is using the "unusable" script to make the movie? I mean, nobody would be so cynical as to suggest that the unusable script became usable once both the writers were dead. . . .

It's not so terrible that the General Public doesn't do the logic, or that Playthell Benjamin didn't. What was terrible is that *I* didn't, back in 1984 when I flew into LAX (first class; it's in the Guild's Minimum Basic Agreement) to take my first meeting on the Malcolm X Project. I was both naive and egotistical—perfect qualifications for a young scriptwriter—so when the producer told me (as he apparently told Benjamin) that the only reason the film hadn't been shot was because all the writers before me screwed up, I believed it.

I kept on believing it until the spring of 1986 (It doesn't usually take that long to do a script, but there was a Guild strike in there) when I was taking another meeting on the project and one of the studio executives expressed a certain discomfort about the content of one of the speeches I had the Malcolm character making. I explained that those particular lines came directly from one of Malcolm's actual speeches. The executive said she understood that, but still wanted me to tone it down, because it made Malcolm sound too anti-Semitic. I can't swear that quote's exact, but it's close. And as I sat there not-screaming I had a flash of Socratic lucidity: Why do these people want to make a movie about Malcolm X?

The old Malcolm X, I mean.

Not Malcolm as he now appears—neutralized by death, sanitized by time,

Malcolm X leading Nation of Islam pickets February 13, 1963, in Times Square protesting police harassment of *Muhammed Speaks* salespeople.

Photo: Robert Parent/
Courtesy of Pathfinder
Press

and legitimized by the failure of the social programs he denigrated. Nor Malcolm as he appeared in 1968, when his advocacy of self-defense was vindicated by the assassination of Martin Luther King. (Might as well get violent, homey, 'cause they blew Mr. Nonviolence's ass *away*.) And not Malcolm as he appeared in 1967, when even Roger Wilkins, Mr. Blue Chip Nigger himself, admits he "thought of Malcolm X and understood him better than I ever had before." Nor even Malcolm as he was at the end of his life—exiled from the Nation of Islam, broke, homeless, hunted like an animal.

I mean Malcolm in 1959. When Mike Wallace's documentary *The Hate That Hate Produced* gave white America its first look at a black leader who wasn't marchin' and singin' and keepin' a-humble and talkin' 'bout Jesus, but who was standing up and shouting and preaching pride and a warrior religion that had been killing Christians (and vice versa) for thirteen hundred years. I mean the Malcolm whose political credo was a lot more American than the *agape* love songs of Martin Luther King (the American Revolution was *not* a nonviolent demonstration) and whose potential appeal was therefore greater—you didn't have to convert anybody to self-defense, it's the hallmark of every American founding document. I mean the Malcolm who was as handsome and young and vigorous as Jack Kennedy, Mr. Youth and Vigor himself—and more charismatic by some folks' measure. I mean the Malcolm whose personal morality, unlike Marcus Garvey's, or Adam Clayton Powell's (or

King's or Kennedy's), was above re-proach. I mean the Malcolm who was liberal America's second worst night-mare—a powerful black orator who preached hate and made sense—and who became liberal America's worst night-mare, because when he stopped preach-ing hate he didn't start preaching love,

They didn't keep firing writers because the scripts were wrong. They kept firing writers because the *story* was wrong

he just started making more sense, to more people. That Malcolm frightened the feces out of damn near everybody. Why would these people want to make a movie about him?

Answer: No reason.

Conclusion: They didn't keep firing writers because the scripts were wrong. They kept firing writers because the *story* was wrong.

And not just because Hollywood numbers among its denizens a number of folk with ethnically identifiable sur-names who might have legitimate con-cerns about portraying as a hero some-one who during most of his life mouthed sentiments that Adolph Hitler would have found extreme. *Everybody* in Hol-lywood does not have an ethnically iden-tifiable surname, even if they haven't changed it. And the Malcolm X story is more wrong than that.

It did not conform to a three-act structure—a real life almost never does. But if a writer doesn't conform to it, pro-ducers and studios have a fit. (No, they never heard of Shakespeare.) It was too

long, because if you start when Malcolm is young (to get in the bits about the white supremacists burning down his childhood home and putting his father on the trolley tracks so the streetcar can crush his skull), you've got to deal with thirty-five years—and some of the most powerful events of the century: the Selma March; not one Harlem riot but two; the assassination of John Kennedy; the March on Washington . . . the list goes on. Only the writer can't—in script form you've got one hundred and twenty pages, most of it white space.

But that's just formal stuff. The con-tent of the story was also wrong. All wrong. Malcolm was a victim of racism—but in Michigan and Massachu-setts, not Mississippi. Even *publishers* know *that* won't play; that's why Rich-ard Wright's editor said Wright's auto-biography "would break much more logically with the departure from the South." Malcolm attended integrated schools—and came out a semi-illiterate because some of his teachers were racist bastards who humiliated him in class. Can't have that, when the legal basis of the modern civil rights movement rested on the Supreme Court's decision in *Brown v. Board of Education,* and that said, "Segregation of white and colored chil-dren in public schools has a detrimental effect upon the colored children . . . for the policy of separating the races is usu-ally interpreted as denoting the inferior-ity of the negro group. A sense of infe-riority affects the motivation of a child to learn. Segregation with the sanction of law, therefore, has a tendency to [retard] the educational and mental development of negro children and to deprive them of some of the benefits they would receive in a racially integrated school system . . . ." Malcolm was a stone-crazy, brutal, drug-addicted, no-good nigger on the express train to hell via the violent death route, but during his predictable layover in maximum security he sho' nuff rehabilitated his ass—taught himself to read, learned to argue like Socrates and Cicero, all those Greek and Roman cats—because he got religion. But it was the wrong religion—wrong scripture, wrong God, wrong devil, wrong imagery. *The Cross and the Switchblade,* now that's right; *The Scimitar and the Switchblade,* now that's . . . not. And if any director or producer or star—such folks have more clout than writers—pitched that concept over lunch at the Tribeca Grill, the studio exec would have made him pay the check.

Because we're not just talking prejudice or politics. We're talking losing money. Consider: Malcolm got off drugs. Not just the illegal ones—*all* the drugs: tobacco, alcohol, white women. So, if the movie doesn't make money in the theaters, what are you going to do? You can't sell it to TV, because who'd sponsor it? RJR Nabisco? The Miller Brewing Company? Maybe Maxwell House—Malcolm did drink a lot of coffee. But not Ford, or GM or Chrysler. Because Malcolm kicked the habit of thinking white women were beautiful just because they were white—he kicked the *image.* Which meant he rejected the fundamental icon of American advertising—the Caucasian T & A used to sell the tobacco and the alcohol and the new car (how old *was* Malcolm's Oldsmobile?) and almost everything else. Malcolm did not become a Communist, but he ceased to be an uncritical consumer.

Malcolm even kicked Hollywood. Once he sat for hours watching gangster movies. Then he turned into a bookworm.

Want to hold that up as a model for the "Underclass"?

Well, yes. *I* did. Because back in '68, when I first read *The Autobiography of Malcolm X,* I had been right on the verge: smoking a pack a day, drinking bad Scotch but wanting better, conforming to the primary stereotype of the black male—the one Clarence Thomas *didn't* mention—and thinking that it was morally superior to work through the system, and that liberation lay in the goodwill of my fellow man. Malcolm, through *The Autobiography,* made me wonder why. Did I want the cigarette or did I just want the woman? Did I like the taste of Scotch or did I just think it would help me get the woman? Did I want the woman—or just her skin under my hand? And did it make sense for you to work through the system when the system wasn't working for you? And did I really want my liberation to depend on liberal goodwill and/or guilt?

And back in '84 I agreed to write the script because it seemed that The Black Community (I love that term) was all caught up in symbolic agitations about Martin Luther King (Should the city name a freeway or a street or a convention center after him, and should his birthday be a national holiday?) while fewer and fewer young black people were being made aware of Malcolm— and his rational and philosophically legitimate alternative to nonviolence. There was a joke floating around about a kid who asked, "Who is this Malcolm the Tenth, anyway?" I didn't think it was funny.

None of the people at that meeting thought it was funny when we'd first talked about the script. Then, in '84, they'd shaken their heads as I had, and said that that was terrible. And now, in '86, whatever else they said, they were talking about the Malcolm X story as if they *liked* it. But they didn't like it. They hated it. And they hated Malcolm, just as most of America had hated him. Statistically speaking, when he died almost no one—white folks, black folks, folks with ethnically identifiable surnames, folks who had changed their ethnically identifiable surnames to something more generic (like Smith or Jones), and folks who would one day change their generic surnames to something ethnically identifiable—wanted him alive.

I'm not saying they wanted him dead—although somebody surely did. They just wished someone would rid them of this troublesome priest. And were relieved when it happened and happy about how it happened—King intoned that those who live by the sword shall die by it; Malcolm's death legitimized nonviolence—temporarily. A lot of tears were shed for Malcolm in the Inner City, but people in the geographical and political and philosophical suburbs—Hollywood is one big suburb— heaved a sigh of relief when Malcolm breathed his last.

But a movie would breathe life back into his corpse. Because that's what movies *do:* bring things to life. And Hollywood has always done it better than anybody in the world. Forget European cinema—maybe it's artistic but you think any French *auteur* could do the Bible like Cecil B. De Mille? Forget Japanese cinema. Even their *monsters* can't

act—that's why they have to buy Hollywood—and their greatest production, Pearl Harbor (Mitsubishi-Sansui– Sony, 1941), didn't have the punch of John Ford's remake. And today Hollywood can do it better than ever. So you take even a semigood actor and give him strong lines (you don't *need* a writer, just crib from "The Ballot or the Bullet") and put him on that big screen with the sixteen-speaker SurroundSound. Let some people sit there in the dark and the Dolby, and you CLOSE UP: MALCOLM'S FACE and CONTINUE VOICEOVER as you DISSOLVE TO: MONTAGE—full-color and sound of the boys in the 'hood gettin' strip-searched at bayonet-point by the National Guard and what you've got is . . . well. Malcolm said he didn't know that he could start a riot, but Hollywood can, and has. I don't mean some silliness like breaking shop windows in Westwood or on Chestnut Street—I mean what happened after *Birth of a Nation.*

I don't know what else was said in that meeting. I stopped listening. I never reviewed the tape. Because by then I'd figured out I was going to get fired.

Right then I *deserved* to be fired. The script was a mess. It fell apart after act one. The first act was a natural—the producer loved it—because there were plenty of opportunities for music and dancing and sex. But in act two, while Malcolm hadn't yet become the man the studio hated, he also had not yet become the man I loved. In act two he was a guy who hadn't escaped drugs, only gotten on a Methadone program of hate, half-baked religion, and addictive loyalty to a murderous little mulatto who looked like he escaped from the organ grinder. And he was *boring*—you want to watch forty minutes of somebody *not* drinking, *not* dancing, *not* fornicating, and making crazy speeches about a Judgment Day on which a big flying saucer loaded with hundreds of fighter planes would descend and destroy the white folks? This was maybe what the producer and the studio were trying to say.

But even if I got fancy with the flashbacks and got some music into act two and some hint of the man Malcolm would become into act one, I was still going to get fired. Because the studio wasn't going to like act three and because the producer wasn't going to like anything but what went on in act one. The only thing I could do was make sure I got fired for purely Hollywood reasons.

So—to make the story conform to the three-act structure—I went home and got my head screwed on straight and stopped thinking that Jimmy Baldwin and David Mamet had screwed up and

Hollywood finds novelists annoying. They're tolerated because they add an air of class and they work cheap

did what they did—captured what I could of Malcolm's life in script form. And I sent it in, billed for the work, spent the money happily on a house in Southern California—but a hundred miles from Hollywood. FREEZE FRAME. ROLL CREDITS.

The trouble with the three-act structure, though, is that it makes you leave things out. Like how I felt when I sent the script in: scared. Because once I'd figured out they didn't really want to make a

movie about *my* Malcolm, I had to wonder why they wanted me.

Well, let's see. I was an award-winning novelist. And I'd written an article about Malcolm for *Esquire.* And I had academic credentials—grad school, college professor. And I had one (unproduced) screenplay to my credit. . . .

Let's get serious.

Hollywood finds novelists annoying. They're tolerated because they add an air of class and because they work cheap, but eventually the Industry chews them up and spits them out—or turns them into scriptwriters. Hollywood finds academics amusing. Screen *Bringing Up Baby* or *Teacher's Pet,* or one of those Flubber movies starring the late Fred MacMurray. And *everybody* in Hollywood has an unproduced screenplay—including the guys parking the Benzes at Trumps.

So maybe they brought me in to fire me. I mean, let's say a studio that owns a property that a lot of popular actors—who are complaining loudly that the industry makes very few movies with major parts for them—think would be a good vehicle, so you want to look like you're trying, but don't want to succeed. Maybe you scrape somebody off the bottom of the scriptwriter barrel, turn him loose, and stand back and say, "See, we're trying."

Or maybe they brought me in to take the blame. Because one thing was certain; if a movie got made, there were going to be compromises—some for reasons that were technical or dramatic, and perfectly honorable, and some for reasons that were not—and a lot of people who revered the memory of Malcolm were going to be displeased, and likely to make accusations of racist exploitation.

They'd have at least a *prima facie* argument, because none of the Hollywood people was a black person. Marvin Worth was not a black person. (Still isn't, so far as I know, although Hollywood makeup men are notoriously brilliant.) Sidney Lumet—the only director who had then been mentioned—was not a black person. (He'd been married to Lena Horne's daughter, though.) None of the Warner Brothers executives were black persons. (There were two black guys at Warner who read the script, young comers, two doors up from the mail room, but one young comer opposed the project and the other young comer went.) Ah, but if there were a black writer involved, the producer and the studio (and a white director, too) could shrug and point and say, hey, hang him. (You think Hollywood doesn't think that way? Why do you think Steven Spielberg wanted Alice Walker on the set of *The Color Purple,* even though he rejected her script?)

Not that whatever happens in a movie is the writer's fault. A script is just the basis for a lot of other artistic decisions, over which writers have no control at all. It's right there in the contract boilerplate: "Writer will defer to Producer in all matters of taste and judgment." And that's just on the script. Writers don't agree to defer on choice of director, or casting, or cinematography, or music—or any of the things that give film its awesome power—because writers rarely have anything to say about any of those things to begin with. Being a scriptwriter—unless you're a writer-producer, or a writer-director—is like being the navigator on the *Titanic:* you lay out the course, but somebody else says full speed ahead

and damn the icebergs. But the GP doesn't know that. The GP will lynch a writer for the studio's decisions. The GP will lynch a black writer for a white studio's decisions. You don't believe me? Go ask Alice.

As I worked through the process of script changes—mostly cutting a hundred and forty-six pages down to a hundred and twenty-five—I was really scared. Because by that time I'd gotten around to reading *Cultural Literacy,* the book that made E. D. Hirsch a bugbear of liberal intellectuals back in 1987. After I brought my brain back on line—cutting fifteen percent of a script is best done without cerebration—I looked into the controversy.

Unlike many of my colleagues, I didn't think Hirsch was all that bad; he pointed out some things that were at worst obvious and often subtle and profound. One chapter I found intriguing described nation-making; in Hirsch's terms a conscious and artificial process. Hirsch's argument linked the establishment of what is an obviously artificial entity, the geographic border, to the less obviously—but equally—artificial entity, a standard language. Then he argued: "Every national culture is similarly contrived. . . . For nation builders, fixing the vocabulary of a national culture is analogous to fixing a standard grammar, spelling, and pronunciation."

Hirsch went on to give an example of creating part of a national culture:

> *One American culture maker who was driven by the aim of doing well by doing good was Mason Weems, the author of numerous popular works, including an edition of Franklin's* Autobiography *expanded by anecdotes.*

. . . His . . . main contribution to the American tradition was his biography of George Washington, wherein could be found the original legend of the cherry tree. . . . If this legend had been left to languish in Weems's book, it might have been forgotten. For the sober later biographers of Washington, anxious to discriminate between fact and what Weems openly called romance, were successful in discrediting Weems's book, the popularity of which waned greatly in the later nineteenth century. But with a sure instinct, the compilers of textbooks took up the Weems stories. McGuffey included a sterner version of the cherry-tree episode in his Second Eclectic Reader *and thus assured it a place in many other readers, and in our permanent lore. Abraham Lincoln relates in his* Autobiography *how he educated himself by carefully reading and rereading a few books . . .* Weems's Life of Washington, *the Bible . . . the* Autobiography *of Benjamin Franklin (possibly the expanded version by Weems). . . . This typical frontier education itself became part of American national mythology after Lincoln's assassination. . . . In the early stages of a nation's life, its traditions are in flux. But with the passage of time, traditions that have been recorded in a nation's printed books and transmitted in its educational system become fixed in the national memory. They become known by so many people over so long a time that they enter the oral and written tradition, where they tend to remain through generations.*

The first thing that struck me about this description was that truth seemed to be an option. While the aim of culture-making was the inculcation of morality and values, it didn't seem to matter whether the cultural icons had actually exemplified those values—only that

eventually everybody thought they had. Maybe it worked in the short term, but I wondered if a culture based not only on myths, but on lies—the Big Lie, maybe—could be viable in the long term. The question seemed not to have occurred to Hirsch. It occurred to me, because the second thing that struck me was that description of Mason Weems as "driven by the aim of doing well by doing good." That pretty much described my motivations for taking on the Malcolm X project. Weems introduced the biography thusly:

> *Give us his private virtues! In these every youth is interested, because in these every youth may become a Washington—a Washington in piety and patriotism—in industry and honour—and consequently a Washington in what alone deserves the name, SELF ES-TEEM and UNIVERSAL RESPECT.*

With only minor caveats—like a clarification of the word "patriotism"—that could have been my declaration of intent. The trouble was, I knew I didn't like what had resulted from Weems's efforts. I wondered if, in the end, I could like what would result from mine.

Because, even absent any politics—and what is?—the Malcolm X story is a risky one to tell in a medium that imposes some genuine limitations with regard to length and structure. (Playthell Benjamin quotes two "film pundits," one of whom "confided 'If Spike makes this film anything less than four hours long he's doomed.' " and the other of whom "assured me . . . 'The only way you can tell Malcolm's story effectively is with two movies of about three hours and ten minutes each.' " Both may be right, but neither one knows Sunset Boulevard from the Sunset Marquis when it comes to the economics of commercial filmmaking. A ticket to a four-hour movie would have to sell for maybe twice as much as normal; how would you end a three-hour movie to get folks to come back for a three-hour sequel—the next day? The simple fact is that the Malcolm X story is not a natural. It has colorful parts and dramatic parts and parts that are historically significant, but they aren't the *same* parts, and they don't always come at the "right" time, and Malcolm was often at the "wrong" place.

For example, the Harlem riot of July 1964. It started as a nonviolent protest orchestrated by CORE, but it turned violent and spread to Bedford-Stuyvesant and it went on for six days, and in the middle of the looting and burning young blacks started shouting: "We want Malcolm." So you've got this great sequence: cops beating journalists, looters running down 125th Street with TV sets, traditional civil rights leaders in suits riding around in limos with bullhorns trying to quell the riot and getting pelted with bricks and doggie doo, and Malcolm standing at the window of his headquarters at the Hotel Teresa, smoke from the fires swirling around him, listening to the gunshots, sirens, rioters chanting his name, and he's tortured by the sudden realization of his rhetoric. . . .

Too bad he was in Europe at the time.

Or take the confrontation in Selma, Alabama. There had already been some minor violence, so the SCLC had a fit when Malcolm arrived, because the young folks in SNCC wanted him to speak but Martin Luther King was in jail so he couldn't counterbalance Malcolm

with that big soothing Baptist baritone. So Andy Young tries to get him to keep it cool, but Malcolm told him (politely) to go to hell and stands up and says that white people better make sure Martin Luther King gets what he's after, because there are "other forces waiting to take over if he fails." Great stuff. So then you CUT TO: THE PETTIS BRIDGE, five hundred nonviolent marchers come over the rise and two hundred cops go at them with tear gas and billy clubs and whips, and Malcolm . . .

Was dead by then. And Martin Luther King had long since bailed out of jail and gone off to Norway and come back with the Nobel Prize. It's a beautiful ironic finish—for a movie about King.

But you can deal with those little historical problems. You don't have to lie, just adjust the timing a little—so Malcolm rides through the riot-torn streets on the way to the airport, maybe. And you cut straight from the scene at Malcolm's funeral to the Pettis Bridge—so what it was two weeks later? Film is a discontinuous medium.

Now, I don't think anybody in Hollywood is crazy enough to turn Malcolm X into a Martin Luther King clone (although I did once hear a producer seriously suggest that the role of Otis Redding be played by Neil Diamond. Well, he did blackface in *The Jazz Singer*, didn't he?) but somebody might suggest that Malcolm ought to privately say something positive about nonviolence just before he goes out on stage the last time, just to give the blow-off an ironic twist. You throw in enough ironic twists and you've got just about any story you want. Or rather, any story the studio wants. (What, you won't do that? Bring in another writer.) But the thing is, maybe you did do it, because, hey, the Malcolm X story promotes a sense of self-esteem. And you did it because you wanted to do well while doing good.

So when I heard my fellow Philadelphia writer had taken the job, I sighed with relief, because my fellow Philadelphia writer was a fellow black person (so at worst I'd end up with shared credit—which is to say, shared blame) and also because my fellow Philadelphia writer had intelligence and integrity. When I heard he'd gotten fired—actually, I heard he'd walked off the project, but who knows—I was neither surprised nor disappointed. But then somebody said they'd spotted Marvin Worth in Manhattan, doing lunch with Spike Lee, even though Norman Jewison supposedly had the directing job, and then there was Lee saying the life of Malcolm could only be treated properly by an African-American director, and Jewison voluntarily (maybe) resigning, and then I got a call from a reporter at *Mother Jones* who wanted to talk about Spike Lee's "cultural" controversy (which is merely a racial controversy—last I looked, Spike Lee wasn't a Muslim).

But by that time I wasn't worried at all. Because it was January of '91, and America, the most powerful Judeo–Christian nation on earth, was studying war with the most powerful Islamic nation on earth. Saddam Hussein said he was going to kill 'em all and the forensics guys in Dover were going to have to sort 'em out because nobody knew if God was Jehovah or Allah. Winter trees were blooming with yellow ribbons, the media was downplaying any hint of antiwar dissent, and this lady thought Hollywood—those wonderful people who gave us *Hellcats of the Navy*—were going to make a movie about a black guy who finds salvation in being a better *Muslim?*

More likely a remake of De Mille's *The Crusades.*

I still suspect that, had hostile fire been as effective as friendly fire at taking out Allied armored personnel carriers, the Malcolm X project would have suffered the fate of that Baghdad bomb shelter. But Desert Storm made Americans look like heroes and Muslims look . . . non-threatening. So I was only mildly surprised when another reporter—*Newsday? Washington Post?* I can't recall—tracked me down in California to talk about Baraka and his class controversy, which I hadn't heard about, but which I figured was really just a way to make headlines for somebody, although I couldn't say for whom. Some say Baraka, who admittedly has never shunned a spotlight. But there ain't no such thing as bad publicity, and having your project in the public eye might keep an antsy studio from killing a project on the eve of principal photography, which has been known to happen—ever wonder what happened to the movie version of Sherley Williams's *Dessa Rose?* I'm not saying Spike Lee is in cahoots with Amiri Baraka—although you have to wonder who "leaked" the script, and why they "leaked" it to Baraka, especially since Baraka's daughter was Lee's longtime collaborator. I'm just saying that if you were making book on the Malcolm X project's ever hitting the theaters, you'd have shortened the odds the day Baraka held his Harlem rally.

And as we sat in Baraka's dining room that September, the odds looked good that they'd actually get the thing shot. I found myself with conflicting feelings about that. For I surely understood that Baraka's concerns were essentially valid—although the excesses of Barakan rhetoric tend to obscure the validity of Barakan concern. But I also understood that the nature of the processes, creative and commercial, made his focus on Lee wrong. Lee asked for it, by making himself sound like a bigger shot than he is—he told Playthell Benjamin he would have final cut, but that's nonsense. The studio always has final cut—in more ways than one. The studio can cut the budget. The studio can fire Spike Lee. (Oh, yes, directors get fired, too.) The studio can screw up postproduction—not allow enough time or money for editing, reshoots, or dubbing. The studio can insist on a shorter running time because the theaters can't get in enough showings per day to make a profit. The studio can gerrymander distribution (ever wonder how come some films *never* seem to be showing at a theater near you?). The studio just keeps the thing in the can. Maybe they'll lose money, but maybe not; sometimes not distributing a film is the only way to make a project pay off . . . for the studio.

I was also reminded of another night in Newark. Not a night that I personally remember, because I wasn't there. But Arnold Perl was.

He was working on some aspect of the Malcolm X project—completing Baldwin's script, or writing the script for the documentary version (a powerful, funny film that may be the only one we need about Malcolm X). In any case Perl had gotten into the ill-advised business (for a scriptwriter) of running around trying to find people who (a) knew Malcolm and (b) would talk to a guy named Perl about Malcolm. When he found them, sometimes he'd tape an interview, but a lot of people had problems with that, so sometimes he'd take notes, but some people had problems with that too, so sometimes he'd wait until he got back to his apartment and sit up late scrawling down notes—which I ran across while going through Marvin Worth's files looking for material for my version of the script—and trying to remember what he'd been told and trying to figure out if he was being lied to, and if so why, and how to find the truth, and how to be sure he'd found it, and how to tell the truth if he had found it. It was obviously a tricky and frustrating business, and his notes kept trailing off in some fairly maudlin musings.

But then he finds somebody—I can't recall the name—who had been in the Newark Temple, and who had known not only Malcolm but Talmadge Hayer, the only man who (almost) everybody is (almost) sure was a member of the team that assassinated Malcolm. Perl is a little shaky about coming face-to-face with this guy, especially since the meet is set for midnight at what Perl thinks is a bucket of blood in Newark. But it turns out to be a clean, well-lighted diner, and the informant is a typical, conservatively dressed polite Muslim; he apologizes for the lateness of the hour, but he works three-to-eleven, and he wasn't sure he could make it before midnight, and he didn't want to keep Perl waiting around.

So he talks and Perl listens, and they drink coffee and eat donuts, and then the guy gives Perl a ride back across the Hudson. And Perl is totally confused. Because the guy was forthcoming, and he *seemed* to know a lot of things, but in fact, he didn't know anything about Malcolm—he just knew what he'd been told about Malcolm, either by Malcolm himself or by somebody else who got it from Malcolm. So Perl starts going back through his notes and realizes that almost all the interviews are that way, and he starts wondering if maybe a lot of people who won't talk to him because they say they don't know anything really *don't* know anything—except hearsay, mostly from Malcolm.

So Perl sits there in the dark of night in an apartment on the Upper West Side of New York, and I'm sitting there in a file room on Sunset Boulevard in LA, a continent apart, a decade apart, and we have the same horrible thought. And we both ignored it. Because if we didn't ignore it we'd have had to quit. But we didn't forget it; and one of us wrote it down. I don't know which one—Arnold Perl and I will have to share credit—but even now I can see the image in my memory of words scrawled in black ink on yellowed or maybe just yellow paper.

All we know of Malcolm is what he wanted us to know—and not one damn thing more. So . . . what if he lied?

The form I used to see
Was but the raiment he used to wear . . . .
—John Pierpoint
"My Child"

One chilly morning in October 1991, the mailman brought a book. I knew it was coming. The author, a guy named Bruce Perry, had sent me a note of thanks because apparently I'd encouraged him about writing it a long time back, and he'd needed the encouragement; he'd devoted more than a decade to research— the interviewing of more than four hundred people, the perusing of hundreds of

documents, the careful comparing of transcripts to tapes—and nearly as long to finding a publisher. The book was subtitled: *The Life of a Man Who Changed Black America*. It was titled: *Malcolm*.

When first I'd heard it would be published, I was happy. A biography would in a sense legitimize what I had done, what was, presumably, at that very moment happening in Harlem with the lights, camera, and action. The theory was that somebody would see the movie and want to know more of Malcolm, and it was good that there would be some factual reference, something with . . . an index, which *The Autobiography* doesn't have. But now the book was here before me, and I hated it on sight.

Unfortunately, in a moment of insanity, I'd agreed to review the thing. "When I was a young college student in the early seventies, the book I read which revolutionized my thinking about race and politics was *The Autobiography of Malcolm X*," wrote Bell Hooks in "Sitting at the Feet of the Messenger: Remembering Malcolm X." She is not alone. Ask any middle-aged socially conscious intellectual to list the books that influenced his or her youthful thinking, and he or she will most likely mention *The Autobiography of Malcolm X*. Some will do more than mention it. Some will say that, back in the sixties (by which they really mean the late sixties and early seventies), when they were young and earnest but callow, and oh, so confused, they picked it up—by accident, or maybe by assignment, or because a friend pressed it on them—and that they approached the reading of it without great expectations, but somehow that book . . . took hold of them. Got *inside* them.

Altered their vision, their outlook, their insight. Changed their lives.

In that there is some irony. For while Malcolm had in the early sixties achieved national prominence as the national representative of the Nation of Islam—what some called the Black Muslims—by the end of 1964 he had been expelled from that post with extreme prejudice, had left the Nation "voluntarily," and was the official leader of nothing but the Organization of Afro-American Unity, an insignificant, insolvent, and hyperbolically apellated handful of blacks, mostly refugees from the Nation. By most measures he was politically impotent and in all probability he would have gone gentle into the good night of the seventies, for despite talents that should have destined him for leadership—tough-minded managerial skills, an incredible intelligence, an encyclopedic knowledge of history, a brilliant flair for rhetoric, an incredible combination of integrity, dignity, and discipline—Malcolm's political positions ethically and practically cut him off from the sources of money and influence that might have led to some legitimate power. His one (dim) hope seemed to be for the congressional seat held by Adam Clayton Powell who, in 1964, seemed to be on the verge of retirement. Powell did not retire.

But in February of 1965 Malcolm became the victim of the sixties' second (and most brutal) domestic assassination. Some would say that martyrdom rescued Malcolm from obscurity. Bruce Perry does not, but he is aware that in death Malcolm became that most attractive of things, a dead hero. Worse, from a biographer's perspective, the myth was mostly self-made, as Malcolm told his story again and again, in public speeches, magazine interviews, and finally *The Autobiography,* over which he exercised great control despite the fact it was written with the assistance of Alex Haley and published posthumously. Worst, in this case the myth is a highly constructive one; *The Autobiography* tells a tale of personal development that is in many senses a desirable model for the black urban masses—the modern equivalent of *Up From Slavery.* Which means that a lot of folks who prefer their idealism untainted by realism are going to be a wee bit upset by a factual—which is to say, non-mythic—treatment, which could be seen as, at best, a willingness to sacrifice a positive force for the sake of a little picky accuracy, and, at worst, as a blatant attempt to sully an African-American hero, when the demand for such is great and the supply of same short.

Perry well knows this: "The story of Malcolm's life," he writes in his Introduction, "will comfort neither his detractors nor his idolaters. Nor will it please those who allow heroic myths about him to obscure his real heroism." Real heroism, for Perry, is less visionary leadership than "transforming youthful weakness into political strength," a definition that leads him to write "far more about the subject's childhood than one does in most biographies. . . . One cannot thoroughly understand the adult, political Malcolm without thoroughly understanding the youthful Malcolm."

This is not basically an onerous notion; Malcolm himself subscribed to it. But Perry goes beyond basics to suggest that Malcolm's entire career was less the result of a growing political, intellectual, religious, or moral concern consciousness than a set of compensations. "This biography," Perry writes, "is a narrative about one man's struggle to liberate himself inwardly by liberating his people politically."

Supporting such a thesis requires Perry to emphasize childhood conflicts, and some of the emphasis is questionable. It probably is significant that Malcolm's father beat his wife and children, but to note that when he was a child "darkness terrified Malcolm . . ." is to imply significance by merely noting the norm; to ascribe childhood avoidance of fistfights to a "fear of combat" is a bit grandiose. To assert that "his unhappiness and his youthful delinquency . . . originated largely in his loveless, conflict-ridden home" is to deemphasize the dysfunctions of the welfare system of which Malcolm became both ward and victim. And to say that Malcolm "was a man in conflict—a living microcosm of the racial discord that corrodes American life" in that he was torn by an "inner struggle to decide what color he wanted to 'be' " is to ignore the possibility of change. There is no question that the youthful Malcolm fell prey to a physical aesthetic that glorified the European, and that he was hardly alone in this—in *The Autobiography* he offers himself as an example of what is wrong with the black masses in this regard. But there is little evidence that, as Perry insists, the adult Malcolm continued to have such ambivalence, that in public utterances he altered facts of his mixed ancestry because his "black self-image was so fragile" or that he called moderate leaders Uncle Toms "in an effort to purge himself of his ambivalence about skin color." This ignores explanations that are less patholog-

ical and more political and rhetorical. (Also more accurate; Uncle Tom, one must note, was "a large, broad-chested, powerfully made man, of a full glossy black, and a face whose truly African features were characterized by an expression of grave and steady good sense.")

Perry's emphasis seems all the more distorting because his psychology is Freudian. He therefore tries to demonstrate this fragility of Malcolm's black self-image by citing a series of "slips"—so labeled by psychologist Kenneth Clark—and takes obsessive interest in the functions Freudians love best. While in prison Malcolm suffered from headaches that "frequently responded to placebo treatment" and "had recurrent bouts with hemorrhoids . . . and suffered from constipation" which Perry speculates resulted from "harsh toilet training . . . his mother had responded to her children's lapses of sphincter control with beatings." Similarly, the causes of symptoms Malcolm experienced later in life—splitting headaches, stomach cramps—Perry labels "not physiological" or "psychosomatic." In the latter instances, stress-related would be a more accurate diagnosis; at the time Malcolm had a pregnant wife and three children and was being evicted—and the Nation of Islam was trying to blow him up with car bombs.

Even if one lacks the concept of stress-related illness, one would hardly suggest that a man whose life had been threatened publicly and privately was overly concerned with his personal security. Perry does, though—the index lists entries under "Malcolm X, paranoia of." One passage so indexed relates how Malcolm "secured the hood of his Oldsmobile with a lock and chain," even though Perry elsewhere describes, and independently documents—that "Langston X, a NOI [Nation of Islam] member who had done demolition work" was asked "to wire Malcolm's automobile ignition with a bomb. Langston warned Malcolm of the plot." The other passage indexed as paranoia says that "as time passed Malcolm appeared to put increasing stock in the thesis that he was the target of an international conspiracy." The suspicion was hardly unjustified, since Malcolm had recently been denied entry to France. Nor was it even false; Perry's own research documents that "State Department functionaries" including William Atwood, the American ambassador to Kenya, "received instructions to keep tabs on Malcolm"; that one of Secretary of State "Dean Rusk's assistants, Benjamin Read, asked the Central Intelligence Agency to help," and the CIA, which, Perry notes, "later tried to cover its tracks," did attempt "to ascertain what funds Malcolm was receiving from abroad."

While a concerned and conscientious biographer—and Perry is surely that—has a right to develop a paradigmatic interpretation, Perry's psychological emphasis unfortunately supports a reductive, mechanistic, and ultimately behavioristic interpretation of Malcolm's career, an interpretation that cannot be divorced from the same liberal-racist attitudes that caused Dorothy Canfield Fisher to describe Richard Wright's *Native Son* as a "report in fiction . . . from those whose behavior-patterns give evidence of the same bewildered senseless tangle of abnormal nerve-reactions studied in animals by psychologists in laboratory experiments," and which, a century earlier, caused Harriet Beecher Stowe to aver that only "the desperate horror" of being sold South "nerves the African, naturally patient, timid and unenterprising, with heroic courage" necessary to running away.

Although Perry cannot be accused of such extremes, the connection is problematical, because his pushing of the paradigm affects what is usually clean and readable prose, and pollutes otherwise insightful statements with irrelevant neo-Freudian nudges. Malcolm's "oratorical prowess . . . soon surpassed his father's," for example. Similarly: "The black preachers he castigated for failing to practice the Christianity they preached—and for sponging off their gullible followers—bore a striking resemblance to his own father." And: "Malcolm was no more able to halt [corporal punishment] which was practiced throughout the Nation of Islam than he had been able to put a stop to the beatings his parents had administered in his boyhood home."

This emphasis is unfortunate because in general Perry scrupulously restrains himself to opinions that are firmly based on fact and evidence. Indeed, it is possible that his psychological emphasis might have seemed more justified had he been able to quote fully from unpublished materials—specifically Malcolm's letters—which current law prevented. (Perry notes that "in one letter, Malcolm declared that his imprisonment had enabled him to recapture the contentment he said he had known as a child" and rather cryptically laments that legal concerns dictated that he "delete substantial amounts of material from certain chapters." And psychology in a generic sense does explain the undeniable and admitted pain of Malcolm's childhood and some of the contradictions of his complicated adulthood. When Perry's most extreme interpretations are discounted, Malcolm emerges as a subtly altered figure—more intriguing, more intelligent, certainly more human.

Alas, subtlety may be the first casualty when the cold waters of fact encounter the molten lava of myth. There's likely to be a steam explosion when the "idolaters" read that during his first sojourn in New York in his incarnation as Detroit Red, Malcolm "arranged a 'party' in the six-by-nine foot YMCA cubicle of a man who called himself 'Reverend Witherspoon' . . . " involving friends whom he encouraged by saying, "It's not so bad, they suck dick," or that later, in Boston, Malcolm "actively participated" in sessions involving a white "bachelor," talcum powder, and full-body massage. In fact, these and other sensational details merely augment *The Autobiography* and other of Malcolm's statements which alluded clearly, albeit in less detail, to the degradations of the hustling life. But on other, more significant points, Perry challenges *The Autobiography* directly.

One is the 1929 fire that destroyed the Lansing, Michigan house which Malcolm's parents had purchased in good faith but from which they were about to be evicted under a covenant forbidding sale to blacks. *The Autobiography* claimed the fire was arson and the work of whites, but "one interviewee suggested [Perry] examine the records of the 1929 fire." He did so, and concluded the fire

was indeed arson, but done by Malcolm's father, Earl Little. Perry also examined the records of the 1965 firebombing that destroyed the house from which the adult Malcolm's family was about to be evicted. *The Autobiography* implied this was the work of the Nation of Islam; Perry concludes the arsonist was Malcolm himself.

Many other points have to do with the image of Earl Little, who is presented in *The Autobiography* as a brave and independent thinker, and a staunch Garveyite, who was driven out of Omaha, Nebraska by the Klan and murdered in Lansing, Michigan by a Klan-clone called the Black Legion. But Perry's informants describe Earl as a "natural whoremonger" and two-bit hustler who "worked hard when he worked." The Nebraska Klan incident was denied by Malcolm's mother, Louise, who, in *The Autobiography*, confronted the Klan with a shotgun. Perry says the Black Legion was never active in the Lansing area; indeed, it may not even have existed at the time of Earl's death. And Earl's skull was not crushed; he was conscious when help reached him, able to tell a police officer how the accident had occurred, and the coroner's report made no mention of head injuries.

Perry reveals that Malcolm was not as much of a career criminal as *The Autobiography* implied. The supposedly highly professional Boston burglaries "were amateurish and unplanned. . . . There was no reconnoitering . . . none of the specialized burglary tools . . . no glass cutter or lock pick . . . Malcolm did not even know how to pick a lock." In one of its most dramatic scenes, *The*

Autobiography had a supposedly wild and dangerous Malcolm caged in court; but Perry implies this was routine; the "cage was reserved for prisoners who were unable to make bail." *The Autobiography* portrayed Malcolm as "a tough convict who had refused to respond when his prison number was called, dropped his dishes in the dining hall, cursed his guards, and spent considerable time in solitary confinement. But prisoners were addressed by name, not by number. There was no dining hall . . . each prisoner ate locked in his cell . . . no evidence that he cursed any guards or spent more than his first day of prison in solitary confinement."

Perry typically makes too much of the possible psychopathological explanations for these discrepancies, but some kind of psychological process does seem to have been at work in Malcolm's hear-no-evil relationship with the Nation of Islam in general and with Elijah Muhammad in particular. Perry demonstrates quite convincingly that Malcolm "learned about Elijah's philandering in 1957, after two of the Messenger's secretaries became pregnant and gave birth." Indeed, the whole business of Elijah's sexual escapades and Malcolm's reactions to them takes on a different twist, for Perry reveals that two of the women who eventually filed paternity suits against Elijah—one of whom claims her liaison with the Messenger began as rape—had been romantically interested in Malcolm, a fact which *The Autobiography* entirely omits. Perry even suggests that Malcolm in essence pimped for the Messenger by "sending additional secretaries . . . to Chicago in the hope they would induce 'stronger' men to join the Nation."

But the challenge that those who revere *The Autobiography* will probably find most disturbing is Perry's assertion about Malcolm's change of heart regarding whites. Most readers would say that the moral and spiritual climax of *The Autobiography* comes when Malcolm, ousted from the Nation of Islam, makes his pilgrimage to Mecca and discovers, even as he becomes a true Muslim through the rituals of the *hajj,* that true Islam is a brotherhood that transcends race. According to Perry, the pivotal experiences were nonmystical and took place during an earlier trip to the Middle East; that "*The Autobiography* devotes forty-three detail-studded pages to his April 1964 trip to the Middle East and only one short, unrevealing paragraph to his 1959 trip there" was part of a determined and remarkably successful deception. "Louis Lomax," Perry asserts, "was not fooled. . . . Nor were Philbert or Wallace Muhammad fooled. Nearly everyone else accepted Malcolm's assertion that the scales had suddenly fallen from his eyes that morning in Jedda. Even his wife was apparently fooled, for it would have been political suicide for him to admit that, despite his pronouncements about white devils, he had known for years that white-skinned people are no worse than anyone else." Perry suggests that Malcolm may never have believed it ("Privately," he writes, "Malcolm admitted that he did not believe everything he said publicly."), but during those five or more years of deception, Malcolm concealed his new attitude from the faithful by using a careful locution: " 'The Honorable Elijah Muhammad teaches us that God taught him that the white race is a race of devils,' " a sort of verbal Simon Sez that he increasingly used to conceal other serious doctrinal disagreements between himself and Elijah.

Political disagreements followed. "Mr. Muhammad," Perry writes, "was reluctant to allow his ministers to engage in political activity. . . . Muhammad's position on political involvement was so rigid that the members of the Nation of Islam . . . were even forbidden to vote. . . . Yet Malcolm, who reportedly found it embarrassing to have to sit on the sidelines while others risked their lives, had been trying to nudge the Nation of Islam in the direction of political involvement for some time. There is evidence that suggests he unsuccessfully tried to secure Elijah Muhammad's permission to boycott Harlem stores that refused to hire or promote black employees." On at least two occasions this disagreement was publicly apparent. Once "the Messenger made Malcolm apologize publicly for organizing a protest demonstration in nearby Newark." And in May of 1963, two days after the nonviolent protest in Birmingham, Alabama turned violent in response to the peace-keeping tactics (K-9 dogs and high-pressure hoses) of Police Chief Bull Conner and cross-burning and bombings by the Klan, the head of the Birmingham temple announced that Malcolm "would soon arrive in Birmingham to hold a series of public rallies." This was reported in the *New York Herald Tribune,* but the next day, Malcolm denied he had plans to go to Birmingham. Perry concludes that the idea was instigated by Malcolm, who su-

pervised the Birmingham temple, but was vetoed by Elijah. "Malcolm," Perry writes, "kept pressing Mr. Muhammad for permission to engage in demonstrations. The Messenger instructed him not to raise the subject again. Malcolm obeyed." But Malcolm's obedience, as Perry describes it, was more a matter of letter than spirit, and the net result of the conflict suggests that Malcolm's silencing by Elijah, the event that supposedly produced a major crisis in his life, could hardly have been as great a surprise as *The Autobiography* implies.

Those whose experience with *The Autobiography* was intensely personal and emotional, perhaps even spiritual, will want to reject Perry's challenges and his book angrily, perhaps violently. I speak here from personal experience—a wall of my study has a small hole in it, and the spine of my copy of Perry's book shows traces of matching paint. As I picked the thing up (a few hours and several curses later) I found myself feeling sorry for Bell Hooks, whose excellent essay is organized around precisely those critical turning points in the story—as Malcolm told it—that Perry insists occurred at other times or in less dramatic fashion and assumes that, like herself, "most readers of *The Autobiography* are moved by his quest for self-realization, by the frank and direct way he communicates his rage, and profound commitment to black liberation struggle." I've never met Bell Hooks, but I can't imagine that she could read Perry's book without . . . well, let's just say I can't imagine that she could read it without feelings of extreme displeasure.

But all the legions of the displaced— and anyone who recalls *The Autobiogra-*

phy with fondness and some accuracy is likely to be a little displeased—would do well to begin reading *Malcolm* on page 382, the first of more than one hundred twenty-five pages of citations, references, and notes. They should begin there not only because Perry has there included "material that . . . could not be fitted into the narrative without transforming it into a tedious debate with other published works" and not only because the extent and detail speaks eloquently of Perry's concern for details and accuracy (Malcolm's eye color, mentioned *en passant* on page 4, has two full paragraphs of citation, and the additional notation: "see additional note on eye color, supra.") but mostly because, when one is not grappling with dramatic debunkings (and Perry's psychology) one realizes that Perry's research overwhelmingly confirms *The Autobiography;* in general and, in specific, it corroborates some of the most bizarre and poignant particulars.

Details of Malcolm's humiliation in public school, for example, were confirmed by three classmates. Malcolm's acting crazy for draft board psychiatrists was something he did not once, but twice. His prison sentence was unusually long. Malcolm was under constant surveillance—by the FBI, the State Department, the CIA, the New York Police. The biography confirms that, as Malcolm charged, Elijah Muhammad tried to enlist the aid of the Ku Klux Klan in obtaining land for a black homeland. Perry adds that the meeting, at which Malcolm represented the Nation, took place in Atlanta, probably on January 28, 1961, and was reported by an informant to the FBI. Ultimately, Perry confirms

what most readers of *The Autobiography* have known in their bones—that it is a fundamentally true document.

But Perry's research also supports the conclusion that *The Autobiography* is not truly a document at all. For Perry establishes that Malcolm did alter the facts. If Perry's treatment has a fundamental flaw, it is that he ascribes the alterations to psychological compensations but gives only passing consideration to other possibilities. For example, on entering prison, Malcolm was not as thoroughly illiterate as *The Autobiography* reported. "The reasons Malcolm later exaggerated his reading difficulties are not altogether clear. . . . Perhaps it was also due to his desire to inspire his ghetto followers to educate themselves as he had educated himself."

Fact is, a comparison between Perry's facts and Malcolm's tale reveals that Malcolm changed those facts in a remarkably precise and consistent way. And the striking thing about the alterations is that they are not particularly self-serving, at least not in conventional terms. Perry insists, generally, that Malcolm was uncertain of his manhood, yet *The Autobiography* makes no reference to women in his life between the time he entered prison and the time he married, and states explicitly that during that time he was celibate. Perry shows that there were women interested in Malcolm, and for whom he had strong romantic feelings. The omission of these women from *The Autobiography* certainly did not create a macho image, but rather the reverse— and that impressed many readers. Bell Hooks, for example, wrote that "undoubtedly there are many individuals who would question that a public male figure as charismatic and dynamic as Malcolm X could have remained celibate for so many years. But unlike other significant black political figures, no one has uncovered a past that would cast doubt on the truth of this assertion. Those twelve years exemplify the depth of Malcolm's emotional and spiritual engagement with Elijah Muhammad." Perry

Malcolm turned a two-bit wife-beater of a father into a political and religious visionary

does not suggest that Malcolm was anything other than celibate, but in identifying women who were interested in Malcolm and pointing out that "the tall, lean, muscular celibate was the movement's most eligible bachelor" he could be said to have uncovered a past that would cast doubt. That only suggests that Malcolm had his reasons for not mentioning it.

Perry shows that Malcolm lived a life. But he also shows that, in public utterances and expressions, Malcolm consistently transformed his life. He turned a two-bit wife-beater of a father into a political and religious visionary who was killed because of his beliefs and defiance; he transformed his youthful self into a dangerous and hard-nosed criminal; he made the process of conversion seem sudden and powerful and inescapable. He made the bottom deeper so the top could be higher. He did just what a novelist or a scriptwriter would have done; tightened up the action, combined characters, gave the thing a better act structure and more dramatic impact—more punch.

Anyone who feels cheated by that might well reflect that at the time he was writing *The Autobiography,* although at the zenith of his rhetorical power, he was at the nadir of his political power. Full in the knowledge that he was in real danger, he consciously crafted a myth of struggle and uplift. On the eve of his death he read and approved it. Perry, in documenting the reality, allows us to see *The Autobiography* not as a social document but as a literary expression, and provides a standard by which the mythmaking of *The Autobiography* can be judged.

And the judgment has to be that Malcolm was a writer as great as any who has turned his or her hand to a quintessentially American form that includes the autobiographies of Booker T. Washington and Frederick Douglass, Abraham Lincoln and, as prototype, the *Autobiography* of Benjamin Franklin. Some may find this Malcolm, less the political animal, more a literary lion, unsatisfying. Not I.

• • •

We the living have a complaint: ignorance

—David Rosenberg
"Lamentations"
A Poet's Bible

On a cloudy afternoon in November 1991, I got off a train at Pennsylvania Station in New York City. My errand in the Apple was slightly unusual. Some months earlier a fellow writer named David Rosenberg had completed *A Poet's Bible,* a new translation of fifteen of the most moving and poetical biblical books not only into contemporary language, but into modernistic poetical form and imagery. As the book neared publication, someone had decided it would be a good idea to invite a number of writers to appear publicly, read from the translation, and speak briefly about their personal connections with a particular book. The aim was, I suspected, to secure a subtle and sorely needed referendum on Rosenberg's work which, while brilliant, was sure to offend some readers and outrage many nonreaders who would reject the very thought of tampering with the Scripture—and Rosenberg's concurrent notion that some of the Hebrew poets who wrote these books had been women.

I'd agreed to appear for a number of reasons, but the oddest of them grew out of thoughts and feelings that had been occasioned by the hoopla over Spike Lee's movie, the synchronicitous appearance of Bruce Perry's biography, and early reaction to some writing I myself had been doing. Basically, I felt concern and a kinship for any writer who could be called a revisionist—especially one who revised what could be called the Holy Writ.

I arrived at five in the afternoon. The reading was not till eight, so I strolled through the drizzle to my hotel, getting myself in the mood for my offering, which was from the Book of Lamentations, and thinking about what personal reflections I would offer. I'd assumed that I would talk about my father, a minister of the Christian Gospel, who, toward the end of his life, when he was afflicted with diabetes, partial blindness, and several other ills, had often preached from what I'd always called the Downer Books—Lamentations and Job. But as I

approached the Hilton Hotel on Sixth Avenue and 54th Street I thought of someone and something else: Malcolm X and my artistic failure in writing the script for a film version of his life.

On the night before his murder—February 20, 1965—Malcolm checked into the New York Hilton, probably in an attempt to draw his pursuers away from his family. He ate supper in the hotel dining room and later met with several of his aides. At ten o'clock Talmadge Hayer and two unidentified black companions entered the Hilton lobby and questioned bellmen about the location of Malcolm's room. They were given no information, but the attempt to ascertain Malcolm's room number was repeated by an unidentified black man at seven the next morning.

At eight o'clock that morning—February 21, 1965—Malcolm answered the phone in his room and heard an unknown voice saying, "Wake up, Brother." A few minutes later he telephone his sister, Ella, and told her of the call. At nine he called his wife, Betty, told her of the call, and asked her to attend the rally at the Audubon Ballroom that afternoon—something he had forbidden her to do the previous day. He dressed in long johns, a white shirt, a dark brown three-piece suit. At one in the afternoon he checked out of the Hilton, got his car out of the hotel garage, and drove uptown. He parked at 146th Street, possibly to avoid arriving at the Audubon Ballroom in his trademark Oldsmobile. He was spotted at a bus stop by one of his followers, who gave him a ride to 166th and Broadway. At approximately two p.m. he arrived at the Audubon. The rest, as they say, is history.

In the summer of 1986 I pieced together most of that timetable to help me organize the ending of the first draft of my version of the script. I saw immediately what any experienced writer would see: that the hours between Malcolm's meeting with aides and that cryptic, threatening phone call offered a natural dramatic opportunity—the doomed tragic hero, a man of contemplation and faith, aware of his impending fate, cut off from friends and family, alone in the still watches of the night. Moreover, I realized it was a way to sell the story to a culturally Christian audience.

Because the facts of Malcolm X's last night fit almost perfectly into the Christian paradigm, the last night of Jesus Christ. I mean, you've got that dinner at the hotel—all you have to do is shift it from the public dining room to a private room. Make it Malcolm's room, to cut down on the number of sets, and combine it with the meeting with the aides and you've got . . . the Last Supper. And then, dramatically speaking, it gets better than the Gospel, because you have the martyr alone—you don't have to fool around with Peter and James and John being close to him and falling asleep, and you don't have to deal with Judas. . . .

But you do have to deal with what he did all night. And that was the problem.

It was a problem the Gospel writers couldn't solve. Luke offers the most detailed version of the hours of prayer in the Garden of Gethsemane (only he doesn't say anything about Gethsemane, or a garden, it's just the Mount of Olives) and gives Jesus those great lines about "removing this cup" and "not my will but thine," but he takes up only four or

five verses. Matthew and Mark do set the scene at Gethsemane and they give it twice as much space, but most of what's described is process—Jesus going off and coming back and finding the three disciples who were supposed to be keeping watch asleep. Their dialogue isn't any better than Luke's (in fact, it's a lot flabbier) and both of them leave out the nifty part about the angel appearing and giving Jesus strength (which is a bad move, because all you're left with visually is a guy on his knees). Even so, they did a better job on the scene than John, the only one of the Gospel writers who was also among the Favored Three who went further into the garden with Jesus. Only he doesn't say that. He has everybody going to a garden across the brook Cedron, but doesn't mention disciples sleeping, or Jesus praying, at all, much less angels.

So, as I'm looking over the garden scene in the Gospels to get some idea of what to have Malcolm X doing in the scene at the Hilton, it occurred to me that the Gospel writers who did the best job on the scene (Luke was first hired, but the studio thought the angels were a bit much, so they brought in Matthew and Mark) were the ones who were farthest from it; their material was based mostly on hearsay—indeed, hearsay from guys who were nodding off. And not hearsay from John, who wasn't talking.

So I tried the Qu'oran. It wasn't much help. Mohammed wasn't really into agonized contemplation; he was more a vision man. Neither was the Muslim caliph Omar, whom some likened to Malcolm, and to whom some said Malcolm likened himself; according to legend, Omar, sensing he was about to be assassinated, climbed on a horse and tried to get out of Dodge. (He didn't make it.)

In the end, I talked myself out of writing the whole Hilton Hotel sequence. I told myself there'd have to be too many one-use sets—hotel room, garage, lobby

Maybe young people do need role models, but I am not a young person anymore

—and minor characters—Hayer and his associates, at least one bellman, a desk clerk—and all the phone calls and intrigue were going to make the movie look like a thriller. But if I left it out I was going to have nothing but a guy praying, and there were already two strong prayer and contemplation scenes, one in the jail cell when Malcolm—"Satan" at that point—has to fight to bend his knees, and one in Jedda, where he gives up on the "white devil" theory. . . . Nah. It was too complicated. You could do it in a novel, but there wasn't enough action for a movie. So I set the phone calls at the Teresa Hotel headquarters, and CUT TO: THE AUDUBON.

Which is to say, I copped out, artistically. Not that the producer ever noticed. And in the end it didn't matter anyway, except that from time to time I would think about it, about what would have happened in that room, in Malcolm's mind. About how a man faced death, what he thought, what he did— and why I had been able to come up with so many excellent reasons (rationalizations) for not writing (avoiding) the scene.

Most recently, I had thought about it as I read Rosenberg's translation of the third chapter of Lamentations. Because in Rosenberg's version the writer— female—is suffering an almost clinical depression because she feels Jehovah has deserted her and her people. The poet begins by lamenting the abandonment in symbolic terms, but then the lament evolves into a midnight recollection of the suffering that resulted from having been forsaken:

> Memory the weight on my back
> and deep in my breast every crushing
>   detail
>
> I cannot close my eyes before it
> I cannot rise from my bed.

The tone changes;

> and yet I do each day
> and I rouse my heart

and the poet goes on to say:

> The Lord's mercy brings a new morning
> each day awakens the thought of him
>
> though I'm buried in nights of doubt
> day returns faithfully—he's always there.

As I read that I thought: this was what those last hours were for Malcolm. A final rejection of Elijah Mohammad and a final acceptance of the One True God. Not something you could put in a script, but a hell of a passage in a novel. A beautiful passage anywhere.

And that was what I was thinking as I walked up Sixth Avenue toward the

Hilton. It came to me that this was the tale I would tell that evening, at the Ethical Society.

But then I remembered Bruce Perry. And I started wondering if all this dramatic agonizing stuff wasn't really a problem. Maybe Malcolm was tired and fell immediately into satisfying and dreamless sleep. Or maybe he turned on the Late Show and spent his last night watching one of those old gangster movies that he'd once so loved. And maybe, if that was the story, it wasn't dramatic, and maybe it wouldn't play, but in my heart of hearts, I kind of liked it better. I kind of liked *Malcolm* better. And maybe young people do need role models, but I am not a young person, any more. I am older than Malcolm ever got to be.

Now, if I were writing a movie—or a myth—I'd tell you that that resolution came to me after I'd checked into the Hilton, and while I was sitting in a lonely room preparing for the reading and agonizing over . . . well, whatever. It didn't. I didn't. I checked into the Dor-

set, half a block away. And I met a friend for drinks in the bar, and then we strolled on uptown to the Ethical Society. And while I did tell the audience a short version of the Malcolm story, I cut right to the text.

But as I read I did think of Malcolm. And of Bell Hooks. And Bruce Perry. Of Charlie Fuller, and Jimmy Baldwin, and me. Of all the folks who, for whatever reason, love what they know of Malcolm. And I prayed that all of us would find it in our hearts and minds to keep on loving him, no matter what we learned. The Hebrew poet (after the rewrite by David Rosenberg) exhorted:

> *open your heart on the rough path of knowing*
> *open your mind on the hard road of under-*
> *standing*
>
> *the solid ground supports*
> *firm trust.*

Selah.
Insh'allah
Amen.

MARTIN AND MALCOLM

Michael Eric Dyson

Opposite: Martin
Luther King, Jr.,
and Malcolm X

AP/Wide World Photos

Martin Luther King, Jr., and Malcolm X are the towering icons of contemporary African-American culture. Of course, King has transcended the boundaries of race. His iridescent image has been seized upon to illumine an astonishing array of social projects—and commercial products—whose humanitarian pedigree is thought to be vouchsafed by symbolic solidarity with an American hero. But the international fame and nearly universal respect he now commands have not diminished his appeal among common black people who will never know either. Millions of black homes continue to display portraits of King, his graceful humility radiating a perennial blessing to their domestic space. For many blacks, King's progressive civil protest, in which American ideals of justice engendered civil disobedience and social compromise, has become the definitive model for social transformation.

But for a generation of black youth reared on sound bytes of history that mimic the rap culture that has shaped them, the voice of Malcolm X supplies the authentic timbre of social rebellion.

Discussed in
this essay

Martin & Malcolm &
America: A Dream or
a Nightmare, James H.
Cone, Maryknoll, NY:
Orbis Books

And his serene but ominous countenance peering from countless posters forms the perfect portrait of black anger at American pride and prejudice. Unlike King, however, the hues of Malcolm's charisma have for the most part remained dark and radical. His reputation is shaped by the specific appeal to racial identity and cultural pride, heroic gestures in an era of political surrender and resurgent racism.

• • •

Rap artists, black youth culture's self-styled postmodern urban griots, dispense social criticism and history lessons with Malcolm's hot breath sampled between their fiery lyrics. Radical and black nationalist intelligentsia employ Malcolm's words as the touchstone of an independent and critical black cultural consciousness. And even black people for whom King's example provides an ideological north star draw solace from Malcolm at moments of uncertainty about the sanity of American culture or the sincerity of American democracy.

That Martin and Malcolm, therefore, represent two distinct traditions of response to home-grown American racism is undeniable. Captured in the useful but imprecise shorthand developed to distinguish the ways black people have resisted racism for more than two centuries, King's position represented an integra-

King's and Malcolm's strategies seem the fragmented components of a narrative whole of racial redemption

tionist approach to the American dilemma, advocating equal inclusion of blacks in the drama of national privilege. And for most of his life Malcolm X advocated a separatist and nationalist strategy for black survival, seeking a space free from white racial violence. But what is even more intriguing, though more subtle and complex, is the way in which King's and Malcolm X's strategies, ideologies, and principles of racial combat seemed at *crucial points* to be of a piece, the fragmented components of a narrative whole of racial redemption.

This is a complicated point to make without homogenizing King and Malcolm X into a mythic unity, without creating consonance where there is none, and without imposing a grid on racial experience. The challenge to anyone who would interpret King and Malcolm X is to appreciate both overlap and opposition, but only after tracing the contours of their ideologies; exploring the nuances of their respective visions of racial transformation; and investigating the varied

intellectual and social resources they brought to bear on the traditions in which they took part.

To this task James H. Cone seems particularly well suited. Born and reared in the Deep South, Cone has spent most of his career as a teacher and scholar in northern institutions. Educated as an undergraduate at a historically black college, Cone gained his doctorate at a white university, where he was trained in the thought of neo-orthodox German theologian Karl Barth. Soon thereafter, Cone came to reject many of the premises of white Western theology. In its place, he articulated a theology that reflected black religious experience and reshaped theological language in light of the guiding principle of black liberation and resistance to oppression. Indeed, Cone is widely regarded as the father of black theology.

In his incipient expression of intellectual dissent from traditional theology, the groundbreaking *Black Theology and Black Power* (1969), Cone proved to be the angry young man of the religious academy. He took traditional theology to task for its vicious complicity in the oppression of blacks by supplying theological comfort and philosophical justification to white racism. Though he failed to take seriously the important exceptions to his theological diatribe (a failure duly noted by equally blind white theologians), Cone's often shrill tone struck a highly responsive chord in important sectors of the theological academy.

But more importantly, Cone made theology suddenly attractive, and in some cases irresistible, for a whole generation of black religious intellectuals and church persons who questioned the power of their discipline and faith to facilitate social transformation after King's death. Cone integrated elements of traditional black church life (discourse about justice, God, and judgment) with radical social ideas (black power, a black

Here was a black man trained like Martin who spoke like Malcolm, an X in King's clothing

God, and trenchant criticism of white racism). Here was a black man trained like Martin who spoke like Malcolm, an X in King's clothing.

In more than twenty years and several books since then, Cone has refined his vision of the scope and tasks of the black theological enterprise. He has introduced a vibrant idiom in theological language from his academic base as Charles Briggs Distinguished Professor of Systematic Theology at New York's Union Theological Seminary. Cone has lectured across the hemisphere, his books have been translated into several languages, and his ideas have spawned dissertations, conferences, and books in many parts of the world.

Like King and Malcolm X, Cone is a revolutionary figure, and like them, he has endured the pain and risk of growth. He has integrated new strands into his arguments over the years to address his former weaknesses, particularly on issues of gender and social theory. Each new book has reflected his continuing dialogue with an expanded group of in-

terlocutors. Cone's latest book, *Martin & Malcolm & America: A Dream or a Nightmare,* takes us forward by looking backward. He examines two figures who have influenced black Americans, and more specifically, the shape and character of his own thought. In a sense, his book is a public reckoning with his own intellectual and personal heritage. It is, in many ways, an impressive achievement and perhaps his best book.

Cone's book is organized in a methodical fashion with his characteristic clarity of expression on generous display. While obfuscatory and insular jargon hold sway in so many academic disciplines, Cone never lets the language he is using get in the way of the story he is telling. Other fine studies have compared King and Malcolm X, along with other black religious and intellectual figures, such as Peter Paris's *Black Leaders In Conflict* and Robert Franklin's *Liberating Visions.* With the exception of Louis Lomax's *To Kill a Black Man,* Cone's is the only book-length study devoted exclusively to comparing the two figures.

Though the trajectory of their social acceptance has been wildly different, King and Malcolm X scaled the heights of cultural popularity only after their apocalyptic martyrdoms. Though he is now shrouded in myth and legend, King's popularity plummeted in the years prior to his death because of his opposition to the Vietnam War, the rise of black power, and his turn toward matters of class inequality. And when he was assassinated, Malcolm was diligently redefining his ideological identity, and winning increasing popularity among an audience previously denied him because of his role in the Nation of Islam. But it has taken nearly a quarter century for his appeal to fully emerge, and for his image, voice, and message to find a new place in the black cultural imagination. As Cone observes,

Twenty-five years after his assassination, there is a resurgence of interest in him, especially among the young who were not born when he died. Malcolm's name, words, and face appear on buttons, T-shirts, and the covers of rap records. His life has become the basis of films, plays, and even operas. He is now being quoted by mainstream black leaders, who once despised him. Conferences, seminars, and parades are being held in his honor, and streets, schools, and organizations are being named after him. People are making annual pilgrimages to his birthplace and grave site.

Though research on King is voluminous and growing daily, the literary attention paid to Malcolm is only now swelling to match his renewed popularity. Bruce Perry's recent biography of Malcolm X and Spike Lee's upcoming film about him will most certainly stimulate more interest in the man's legacy, as will Cone's fine comparative study.

Cone's text also deftly explores the differences between King and Malcolm X, which upon cursory glance appear conspicuous. After all, their differences from birth might be considered a study in suggestive polarities: South/North; middle-class/poor; dark-skinned/light-skinned; short/tall; educated/autodidact; and slow southern cadence/rapid-fire oratory. And Cone goes to great lengths to show how substantial their differences were. He shows us how the

social, political, and economic forces that produced them, as well as the geographic regions that were the scene of their major contributions, reveal a great deal about the character and limitations of their respective contributions. King was reared in a comfortable, middle-class home in Atlanta that nurtured his sense of self-worth in the bosom of a vibrant black religious faith. Malcolm X's first memory in 1929, ironically the year of King's birth, was a nightmare, a terrifying remembrance of the burning of his family home in Lansing, Michigan, by white vigilantes.

Cone's introductory chapter shows how King and Malcolm X participated in venerable traditions of integrationist and nationalist social thought and practice, and hence were neither completely nor finally the inventions of mass media or white society. Each was fundamentally a creative and singularly gifted political and social actor within a rich and particular ideological heritage. Though Cone delineates the specific marks of each tradition on King and Malcolm X, he also concedes that the rhetoric of nationalism and integrationism was used to express complex beliefs that were sometimes combined by black leaders and intellectuals in their struggles against slavery and oppression.

Of course, no black thinker has been a pure integrationist or a pure nationalist, but rather all black intellectuals have represented aspects of each, with emphasis moving in one direction or the other, usually at different periods of their lives. . . . When blacks have been optimistic about America—believing that they could achieve full equality through moral suasion and legal argument—they have been

integrationist and have minimized their na-
tionalist tendencies. On the other hand de-
spair about America—believing that genuine
equality is impossible because whites have no
moral conscience or any intention to apply the
laws fairly—has always been the seedbed of
nationalism.

Cone's abbreviated genealogy of conflicting and sometimes converging black ideological traditions provides a helpful schema for comprehending continuities between past advocates of resistance to racist oppression and his twin subjects. It may also result in closer attention to the significant and suggestive dissimilarities between King and Jesse Jackson, Malcolm X and Louis Farrakhan—dissimilarities that are often overlooked in the avid search for successor messiahs in our era of racial desperation.

Cone skillfully contrasts the impact of their early lives on the development of their thought in sketching a kind of existential ecology of the origins of King's dream and Malcolm X's nightmare. King's embrace of crucial elements of a Booker T. Washington version of accommodationism and a Frederick Douglass version of integrationism, supported by his father's and grandfather's philosophies, found expression in his early leadership style. And his absorption of the ideals of Christian brotherhood and universal love preached in the black church shaped his understanding of acceptable forms of protest and resistance to racism.

Cone's point here, set against the stream of one school of King interpretation, is that the black church was the primary influence on King's life and thought, and that only later did white

Protestant liberal theology, Gandhi, Niebuhr, and strands of the social gospel play a role. In intellectual biographies of King such as Kenneth Smith and Ira G. Zepp's *Search for the Beloved Community* and John J. Ansbro's *Martin Luther King, Jr.: The Making of a Mind,* the latter influences have been accorded primacy. Other recent studies of King have acknowledged the decisive role of black church faith and culture in shaping King's thought, such as Lewis Baldwin's *There Is a Balm in Gilead* and Fred Downing's *To See The Promised Land.* And in a few scattered essays, Cone has argued for the preeminence of black Christian values and practice in understanding the moral vision and social protest of King, an argument he elaborates in the course of this book:

> *The* faith of the black experience *began to shape King's idea of God during childhood, and it remained central to his perspective throughout his life. This point needs emphasis because many interpreters have failed to acknowledge the* decisive *role of the black religious tradition upon King's thinking. Without denying other important influences —liberal Protestantism, Gandhi, Niebuhr, among others—we still must emphasize that no tradition or thinker influenced King's perspective as much as the faith which blacks created in their fight for dignity and justice.*

Moreover, King's virtually unlimited optimism about the possibilities of interracial coalitions defeating racism developed only after he conquered his "antiwhite feeling" in college, where he encountered whites in interracial organizations. As Cone points out, King's desire to explore the merits of integrationism almost blinded him to the necessity for addressing racism in his graduate work.

It is important to note that he did not even mention racism in most of his graduate papers that dealt with justice, love, sin, and evil. In six years of graduate study at Crozer and Boston, King never identified racism as a theological or philosophical problem or mentioned whether he recognized it in the student body and faculty. . . . Like most integrationists of his time, and in contrast to Malcolm and the nationalists, Martin appeared to be glad merely to have the opportunity to prove that Negroes could make it in the white man's world.

Here, and throughout his book, Cone gives the sharpest criticism of King's psychological disposition toward white society articulated since John A. Williams's *The King God Didn't Save* and David Lewis's *King: A Biography*. While avoiding the more exaggerated effects of Williams's self-conscious debunking of the King myth, and supplying a more nuanced reading of the black religious roots of King's thought than found in Lewis's treatment, Cone vigorously challenges and critiques King's weaknesses.

He is just as balanced toward Malcolm X. Cone discusses Malcolm X's origins in Omaha, tracing the influence of his parents' nationalist activity on his worldview. Like King, Malcolm X's father was a Baptist preacher, though on a much more modest scale, preaching as an itinerant or "jackleg" minister. Malcolm X's father was president of the Omaha branch of Garvey's UNIA, while his mother was the group's reporter. During his childhood, Malcolm X was subject not only to white violence but also to a vicious cycle of domestic violence as his father beat his mother, and they both abused their children. Malcolm lost his father early, and it is not clear whether his death was accidental or murder. What is clear, though, is that Earl Little's death had a traumatic effect on Malcolm X's family, leaving mother Louise Little to rear eight children during the Depression. She eventually suffered a mental breakdown, and the children were placed in several foster homes.

After experiencing the ravages of integrated schooling, Malcolm dropped out of high school to live with his half-sister in Boston. Malcolm had already begun to steal in Nebraska because of extreme hunger, and he expanded his hustling repertoire in Boston. He used cocaine and established a burglary ring to support his expensive habit. After he was caught and sent to prison, Malcolm X displayed a resentful attitude until his conversion to the teachings of Elijah Muhammad, founder of the Nation of Islam.

As Cone explains, Malcolm X was drawn to the Nation because of its definition of the white man as the devil, and its strong emphasis on pride in black culture and history. Malcolm's many difficulties with whites in adolescence, and his experiences in Boston's ghetto, prepared him to reject nonviolence and integration, and to accept a strong separatist philosophy as the basis for black survival in racist America.

Malcolm's experience in the ghetto taught him that the black masses could be neither integrationist nor nonviolent. Integration and nonviolence assumed some measure of political order, a moral conscience in the society, and a religious and human sensitivity regarding the dignity and value of all persons. But since the masses in the ghettos saw no evidence of a political order that recognized their humanity or a moral conscience among white people, an appeal to integration and nonviolence sounded like a trick to delude and disarm poor blacks, so whites would not have to worry about a revengeful response to their brutality.

In the first section of his book, Cone gives us a good sense of how King and Malcolm X were formed, and what differences their respective social origins made on the way they thought about race and American society.

Cone devotes two chapters to exploring King's and Malcolm X's understanding of America through the metaphors of dream and nightmare, metaphors that would define their different approaches to racial justice. Cone probes the social sources of King's American dream, linking King's vision to the white public, "because he believed they had the material resources and moral capacity to create a world based on the principles that they claimed to live by." Cone also explains that King urged black people to enact their redemptive roles in American society by pursuing self-respect, high moral standards, wholehearted work, leadership, and nonviolence. Despite severe challenges to King's faith in the plausibility of American democracy, especially after the bombing of a church in Birmingham that killed four innocent black girls, he continued to believe that the American dream would soon be fulfilled.

From the very beginning, however, Malcolm X understood that the conditions of black Americans were a nightmare of racial injustice, urban poverty, and drug addiction, all presided over by the negligence and hypocrisy of white liberals and unprincipled racists. Here and throughout, Cone makes clear that Malcolm X's unbridled anger toward white racism provided a strong counterpoint to King's integrationist philosophy, making King's views, once deemed radical, seem acceptably moderate by comparison. Once Malcolm X left the Nation, however, he discovered that many integrationists were more radical and militant than he had formerly believed. Still, Malcolm continued to enliven the role of the angry black in order to provide a sharp enough contrast to King that white people would gladly listen to King's demands.

For most of Malcolm's life, King avoided him. Of course, Malcolm had developed a side career of verbally assaulting "so-called Negro" leaders, taking special delight in tagging King with a jumble of colorful but caustic monikers, including "religious Uncle Tom,

King believed that violence as a tactic of survival was suicidal

traitor, chump and the Reverend Dr. Chickenwing." For his part, King believed that Malcolm X's promulgation of black anger, and his statements about the "reciprocal bleeding" of whites and blacks, were irresponsible and morally wrong. King also believed that violence as a tactic of survival was suicidal in light of the fact that blacks were only ten percent of the population, and therefore grossly overmatched and underarmed.

Cone probes Malcolm's conception of divine justice, predicated upon a philosophy of an-eye-for-an-eye, and explores his advocacy of self-knowledge, self-love, self-defense, racial separatism, and most of all, racial unity, "the dominant theme of his ministry." After he examines the impact of King's and Malcolm X's faith and theology on their versions of the American dream and nightmare, Cone details the unraveling of King's faith in American justice and Malcolm X's reexamination of a strong version of separatist black nationalism after his break with Muhammad.

King's confrontation with persistent racism caused him to reject his former optimism about the capacity or willingness of whites to practice social justice. Though Cone details King's growing pessimism about the structural racism and economic inequality of American society, he doesn't tell us that this prompted King to advocate "nonviolent sabotage," which included blocking the normal functioning of the government as a sign of deep social frustration and moral outrage. Cone reveals that King also began to ponder the virtues of "temporary segregation" as a means of reconstituting the economic health of black communities, since American society had not shown serious interest in reordering social priorities and redistributing wealth.

In his mature stride, King also increased his emphasis on black pride, appealing to a theme that had been implicit in much of his work but now, because of the challenges to nonviolence posed by black power, required an explicit articulation. Such moves caused David Halberstam to call King a "nonviolent Malcolm X," a characterization King rejected. Nonetheless, his later thinking is detailed by Cone in a way that leaves no doubt that King's shift to progressive and radical social thought was a permanent feature of his mature civil protest.

But, as Cone shows, Malcolm X too was changing. His break with Muhammad had freed Malcolm to become publicly political, an opportunity that Malcolm X used to attempt to join forces with King and progressive elements of the traditional civil rights community. But Malcolm's reputation of advocating violent self-defense had been so deeply entrenched that even his move away from Muhammad didn't prevent the white media from viewing Malcolm as a rabid racist and destructive demagogue. As Cone notes, this troubled Malcolm X, who had a genuine desire to forsake his recent past and articulate his racial demands to a wider audience. Rebuffed and scorned, Malcolm entered into a phase of

Shared suffering due to racism is no guarantee of unanimity on the means to racial justice

radical rabble-rousing, still specifying the absurdity of white racism, while displaying a newfound openness to limited white support of black freedom. Even after his journey to Mecca, however, Malcolm never surrendered his advocacy of black unity as a precondition to black freedom, a unity that could never result if even well-intentioned whites participated in black organizations.

Malcolm X's stress on unity is a theme that resonates with Cone's own thinking, and shapes his understanding of King and Malcolm X throughout his book. It also limits his understanding of the two figures. In a discussion of the impact of the faith of the black experience on King's idea of God, Cone says:

As different as Martin's and Malcolm's religious communities were, Martin's faith, nonetheless, was much closer to Malcolm's than it was to that of white Christians, and Malcolm's faith was much closer to Martin's than it was to that of Muslims in the Middle East, Africa, or Asia; that was true because both of their faith commitments were derived from the same *experience of suffering and struggle in the United States. Their theologies, therefore, should be interpreted as different religious and intellectual responses of African-Americans to their environment as they searched for meaning in a nation that they did not make.*

But is this accurate? Is it true that the experience of black suffering and struggle is the primary basis of unity, even when the differences between black people are strong and persistent? While Cone may be right to suggest that King and Malcolm X were closer to one another than they were to white Christianity and orthodox Islamic belief, this must be proved by citing historical evidence. As Cone has so convincingly shown us, King and Malcolm X were deeply divided not only about their tactics of social protest, but about their anthropological, social, and psychological understanding of human beings.

It is, therefore, conceivable that a white person who embraced King's understanding of human community, love, interracial coalition, and the limitations and injustice of white racial practices might indeed have more in common with King than a black person who held highly divergent views about such issues, despite a shared experience of racial suffering. The case of Supreme Court Justice Clarence Thomas and other black conservatives proves that there is no necessary or automatic similarity in the interpretation of the "black experience," and that shared suffering due to racism is no guarantee of unanimity on the means to achieve racial justice. Thus, King would have had (and I believe he did have) more in common with, say, Michael Harrington than he would have had with George Schuyler when it came to issues of racial and economic justice.

Cone himself provides ample support for the belief that King and Malcolm X, as a result of their concrete set of historical experiences, were indeed converging on a similar, though by no means identical, view of racial justice and economic health for black people. But as Cone also makes clear, they had enormous and longstanding barriers to overcome to achieve even limited ideological parity. For instance, Malcolm's earlier views of violence, as Cone points out, "were hardly different from [those] of the whites he criticized." And in criticizing King and Malcolm X for their abominable views on women, Cone points out how they had more in common with white men than with black women.

While Martin and Malcolm challenged white values regarding race, their acceptance of black male privilege prevented them from seeing the connection between racism and sexism.

While both differed sharply with most white men when it came to matters involving race, they shared much of the typical American male's view of women. Martin's and Malcolm's views regarding women's place were not significantly different from those of men of other races.

The call for racial unity is usually premised on the assumption that the experience of black suffering will itself guarantee similarity of perspective. But the complexity and diversity of racial experiences cautions against advocating racial unity based on the presumption of homogeneity. Neither does it bode well for trying to explain the genuine and irresolvable differences between King and Malcolm X, no matter how much we appeal to their same experience of suffering and struggle. Besides, other dimensions of struggle to which King and Malcolm X became more sensitive, such as class inequality, mean that the experience of suffering, though crucial and certainly central, is not the exclusive or exhaustive basis of racial unity.

Because Cone believes that both King and Malcolm X promoted self-knowledge and respect for one's history and culture as the basis for unity—without which there could be no freedom—the view of unity based on sameness of experience fails to capture other enabling forms of racial solidarity. Furthermore, it imposes a narrow view of their uses of history and culture, especially in King's case. Such a view leads Cone to stress the necessary and crucial ingredients of self-esteem in combating black disunity and the corrosive racism that destroys black culture, without supplying a trenchant criticism of the social forces that help construct and define self-regard. Regarding the latter, Cone concludes:

> *It is not easy to survive in a society that says that you do not count. Many do not survive. With the absence of black pride, that "I am somebody" feeling, many young African-Americans have no respect for themselves or for anybody else . . . . Malcolm X is the best medicine against genocide. He showed us by example and prophetic preaching that . . . we can take that long walk toward freedom. Freedom is first and foremost an inner recognition of self-respect, a knowledge that one was not put on this earth to be a nobody. African-Americans can do the same today. We can fight for our dignity and self-respect.*

While Cone's claims are undeniable, what is needed at this point is a complex and detailed cultural criticism in light of the social vision and religious values that King and Malcolm X promoted, values that Cone has expressed in his own work. It seems odd that Cone prescribes self-respect and self-esteem without giving a sharp or substantial analysis of the social resources for such qualities, and the political and economic reasons that prevent their flourishing in many urban black communities across the country. It is precisely here that we want the full analytical power of black theology, and the best available insights of progressive social theory brought to bear upon the various crises that confront black Americans in tracking a path for those who take the mature King and Malcolm X seriously. Here Cone's treatment falls noticeably short.

Nevertheless, Cone's study of King and Malcolm X is admirable. Cone gives a life-sized portrait of two figures who have grown larger than life. And with the phenomenal resurgence of interest in Malcolm, Cone has not been afraid to criticize him for his often lethal sexism, his advocacy of impractical strategies of violence, and his almost exclusive focus on race, which was only decentered after his break from the Nation of Islam.

The imaginative virtue of Cone's book is that he has shown that Martin and Malcolm needed each other, that their ideas and social strategies brought them to a strange but effective symbiosis. His title, employing his subjects' first names, is a symbol of the first-name familiarity we feel with these great men, and a striking emblem of their genuine humility. As we struggle to take measure of their extraordinary accomplishments, Cone's book will be indispensable in charting how two supremely human and heroic figures occupied and defined their times with empowering vision and sacrificial action.

BAD COMPANY

Stanley Fish

One of the things that has been left out of the current debates about the canon and multiculturalism is history. Few have paused to inquire into the relationship between the present controversy and controversies that have erupted in the past. The only exception to this silence about history has been the oft-repeated assertion that the proponents of revised and enlarged curricula are left-over sixties revolutionaries who have traded in their beards and beads for tweed jackets and tenured positions in the universities. So we have this rather thin account of where the multiculturalists come from, but we have had no account at all of where the antimulticulturalists come from, and my intention here is to provide one.

Let me begin by rehearsing some of the main tenets of the antimulticulturalist argument, an argument that has been recently given a concise and forceful exposition by Arthur Schlesinger, Jr., in his book *The Disuniting of America: Reflections on a Multicultural Society*. Schlesinger begins by sounding a call of alarm, a kind of 1991 Paul Revere warning that

not the British (or the Russians) but the multiculturalists are coming, and that they threaten the American way of life. He finds the threat in what he calls the "ethnic upsurge," an "unprecedented . . . protest against the Anglocentric culture" that "today threatens to become a counterrevolution against the original theory of America as . . . a common culture, a single nation." Schlesinger deplores the rejection of what he calls "the old American ideal of assimilation"—the ideal that asks immigrants and minorities to "shed their ethnicity" in favor of the Western Anglo-Saxon tradition. That tradition, says Schlesinger, is the "*unique* source" of ideas of "individual liberty, political democracy, the rule of law, human rights, and cultural freedom," and he contrasts the virtues of Western individualism with the "collectivist cultures" —the cultures based on group or ethnic or religious identity—of Africa and Islam, cultures that, he says, "show themselves incapable of operating a democracy . . . and who in their tyrannies and massacres . . . have stamped with utmost brutality on human rights." Given the practices of what he calls "tribalist" cultures, cultures based in his view on "despotism, superstition, . . . and fanaticism," Schlesinger finds it absurd that people are now arguing that we should accord those cultures dignity and respect, and that "in this regard the Afrocentrists are especially absurd." "White guilt," he declares, "can be pushed too far," and he predicts that the multiculturalist ethnic upsurge will be defeated by the fact that "the American synthesis has an inevitable Anglo-Saxon coloration."

It is clear from these quotations that for Schlesinger the danger of multiculturalism is not confined to the classroom, but extends to the very fabric of our society. The message is that unless we beat this challenge back and reclaim the educational process for the mainstream values upon which America was built, the unity of the American experience will be replaced by the balkanization and barbarism characteristic of the alien cultures of Africa and Islam. "The debate about the curriculum," says Schlesinger, "is a debate about what it means to be an American," and "what is ultimately at stake is the shape of the American future."

Now when Schlesinger utters these statements, he does so with a sense that the challenge to the American way is a new one; he calls it "unprecedented," a recent phenomenon invented in his view by a group of self-serving intellectuals who really don't speak for the communities they pretend to champion; and he implies that until this self-authorized group began its rabble-rousing efforts, the national business of forging and maintaining an American identity had not been threatened. But in fact that

threat—if it is a threat—is a very old one, and old too are the arguments Schlesinger uses against the threat. When he declares that at this moment what is at stake is the shape of the American future, a future that will be lost if we do not reject policies and agendas that are simply un-American, he echoes, knowingly or unknowingly, a series of essays and books written between 1870 and 1925. These books and essays had titles like *The Melting Pot Mistake* (by Henry Pratt Fairchild), *Our Country* (by Josiah Strong), *The Passing of the Great Race* (by Madison Grant), and *A Study of American Intelligence* (by Carl Campbell Brigham). Although they have different focuses, they share a set of attitudes and arguments. First, they are all anti-immigration tracts that identify immigration, especially from countries other than those that provided the original "American stock," as a great and imminent danger. Here is a typical quote: "The most significant unity of the American people is national unity, and the outstanding problem involved in immigration has been the problem of preserving national unity in the face of the influx of hordes of persons of scores of nationalities" (*Melting Pot*). In the mind of this writer the chief peril comes from Southern Italians who have a "very small proportion of Nordic blood" in their veins and the "Alpine stock" which "appears to be essentially mongoloid in its racial affiliations," thus raising the fearsome prospect "of introducing into the American population considerable strains of Mongoloid germ plasm."

In addition to being anti-immigration, these tracts are often anti-Catholic or, as they put it, anti-Romanist:

Catholics, they argue, are loyal not to this country but to the pope of Rome; and not only do Catholics owe their allegiance to a foreign power, but in allying themselves with this power, they reject the ethos of "free inquiry" and substitute for it the ethos of blind obedience to authority. Nor can one take comfort in the fact that many fall away from Catholicism, for not having been nurtured in the right Protestant virtues, lapsed Catholics react to their newfound freedom by falling into "license and excess" (*Our Country*). It is because license and excess are thought to be the opposite of the Anglo-Saxon virtues of restraint and moderation that these same books are temperance tracts, and indeed in the eyes of these authors, the growth of immigration, the unchecked breeding of Catholics, and the rise of what one author calls "the liquor power" are seen as manifestations of the same threat.

At bottom, that threat is a racial one. Invoking a popular belief that the path of civilization was moving ever westward, these authors identify that path with the emergence of a pure Western type drawn from Anglo-Saxon stock. The fact of this emergence is explained by reference both to God, who is seen as guiding this adventure with his "mighty hand" (*Our Country*), and to Darwin, who tended to see in the American "race" a strong confirmation of the theory of natural selection. Indeed, at one point in *The Descent of Man,* Darwin quotes approvingly this statement made by a Protestant minister: "All other . . . events . . . only . . . have purpose and value when viewed in connection with, or rather as subsidiary to, the great stream of Anglo-Saxon emigration to the West."

When all of these ingredients—anti-immigration, anti-excess, anti-Catholicism, and out-and-out racism—are mixed into one brew, the result is something like this:

> *It seems to me that God . . . is training the Anglo-Saxon race for an hour sure to come in the world's future. . . . Then this race of unequaled energy—the representative . . . of the largest liberty, the purest Christianity, the highest civilization . . . will spread itself over the earth . . . this powerful race will move down upon Mexico, down upon Central and South America, out upon the islands of the sea, over upon Africa and beyond. And can anyone doubt that the result . . . will be the survival of the fittest?* (Our Country)

And what happens in this grand vision to the indigenous peoples of these lands? The answer is as inevitable as it is chilling: "Nothing can save the inferior races but a ready and pliant assimilation." Significantly, the triumph of Anglo-Saxon superiority will also be a triumph of language. Here is the Reverend Nathaniel Clark sounding just like those who today defend the traditional canon: "The English language . . . gathering up into itself the best thought of all the ages, is the great agent of Christian civilization throughout the world"; and another minister also speaks with 1991 accents when he prophesies that "the language of Shakespeare would eventually become the language of mankind" (*Our Country*). One sees again how comprehensive this vision is: it is informed by a sense of history; it declares a social program and argues for its political implementation; it boasts a theory of language and at least one sacred text; and it is shadowed by dangers—often called perils or menaces—that must be withstood so that a glorious past may flower into an even more glorious future.

In linking these late nineteenth- and early twentieth-century tracts with the recent essay by Arthur Schlesinger, I may seem to be practicing guilt-by-association, just as the McCarthyites did in the fifties when they condemned anyone whose writings or speeches could be shown to include phrases that were also used by Communists. The difference, however, is that where the members of the House Un-American Activities Committee seized on isolated sentences taken out of context, I am arguing for a match at every level, from the smallest detail to the deepest assumptions. It is not simply that the books written today bear some similarities to the books that warned earlier generations of the ethnic menace; they are the same books.

Consider, for example, Laurence Auster's *The Path to National Suicide: An Essay on Immigration and Multiculturalism.* Published in 1990, the book warns, in familiar apocalyptic terms, that "we may be witnessing the beginning of the end of Western Civilization as a whole"; the principal villain is the 1965 immigration act, which shifted immigration priorities from those Nordic European peoples who had furnished America with its original stock to Asian and African peoples from Third World countries. The result, if we do not reverse this policy, will be the end of American culture: "Like ancient Greece after the classical Hellenes had dwindled away and the land was repopulated by Slavonic and Turkic peoples, America will become literally a different country." And what evidence does Auster cite for this dire prediction?—multiculturalism in our schools, which he describes as "an attempt . . . to tear down, discredit and destroy the shared story that has made us a people and impose on us a new story." In that story, which is taught to our children, "the contributions of the American Indian, African, Hispanic (and even *Asian!*) cultures are as important to our civilization's heritage as the Anglo-Saxon contribution." What is obscured is "that the United States has always been an Anglo-Saxon civilization" and that previously immigrants, largely European, tended only to "augment the . . . mix of minorities in our predominately white society." It is this white society that must be preserved in the face of the twin evils of immigration and multiculturalism. Anticipating the objection that demographic projections indicate that in some places like California, whites will soon be a minority, Auster responds that this is just the trouble: "If it is the sheer *number* of Non-Europeans . . . that obligates us to abandon 'our' cultural tradition, is it not an inescapable conclusion that the white majority in this country, if it wishes to preserve that tradition, must place a rational limit on the number of immigrants?"

Now it would be easy to dismiss Auster as a fringe voice. His book is published by something called "The American Immigration Control Foundation" —its financing would no doubt make an interesting story—and his vocabulary is much too blunt to be attractive to mainstream audiences. This is less true, however, of another book, published in 1991, Richard Brookhiser's *The Way of the WASP: How It Made America, and How It*

Can Save It, So to Speak. Brookhiser is a senior editor of the *National Review,* a contributor to *Time* and the *New Yorker,* and a former speech-writer for then Vice President Bush. He begins his book by identifying the key white Anglo-Saxon Protestant virtues—Conscience, Anti-sensuality, Industry, Use, Success, and Civic Mindedness—and contrasts these to a set of non-WASP, presumably African or Asian or Mediterranean, characteristics: Self, Creativity, Ambition, Diffidence, Gratification, and Group Mindedness. (Interestingly, this contrast, which elevates Nordic populations at the expense of populations living in temperate or tropical zones, is an inversion of the much-ridiculed distinction between "ice people" and "sun people" put forward by Leonard Jeffries.) "The *WASP* character," says Mr. Brookhiser, "is the American character" and without it, America "would be another country altogether." Without it, America "is sure to lose its way." It follows then that non-WASPS, and especially immigrants, must submerge their native character in the American one, and this is why "the only price even the most exclusive WASPS exacted was that newly arrived others should become exactly like themselves." This is the strong form of assimilation which produces not a mixture but a surrender and it is exactly the message trumpeted by Henry Fairchild in *The Melting Pot Mistake:* "The true member of the American nationality is not called upon to change in the least. The traits of foreign nationality which the immigrant brings with him are not to be mixed or interwoven. They are to be *abandoned."* Unfortunately, according to

Brookhiser, that message has not been heeded, and today the WASPS, rather than demanding the assimilation of alternative cultures, are deferring to them, and "the cumulative effect of multiple acts of deference—to other standards, cultures, even species—is insecurity, uncertainty, sheepishness." Brookhiser concludes by urging a return to the older model: "The best favor America can do its newcomers is to present them with a clear sense of what America is, and what they should become . . . the people we want aren't permanent immigrants, but future WASP's."

Auster, Brookhiser, Schlesinger—three very different authors—one a xenophobic nationalist, the second a neoconservative well placed in the corridors of power, the third a moderate progressive identified with the policies of the Kennedy administration; and yet all three tell the same story about the formation of the American character, the necessity of preserving it, and the threat it faces from ethnic upsurges: a story that continues in every respect, from words and phrases to large arguments, a tradition of jingoism, racism, and cultural imperialism. Moreover, that tradition has been implanted into the educational process by a mechanism designed to enforce its assumptions. I am referring to the SAT tests, often put forward as the objective measure of the true merit that is being undermined by the erosion of standards. What most people don't know (in addition to the facts that the tests are culturally biased, statistically unreliable, and easily vulnerable to manipulation by expensive crash courses that teach tricks rather than content) is that the test was devised and administered by an out-and-out racist, indeed by one of the authors I alluded to earlier.

Carl Campbell Brigham's *A Study of American Intelligence,* published in 1923, is an amazing document, even in the context of this particular tradition. It advertises itself as the "first really significant contribution to the study of race differences in mental traits." Brigham announces that he begins by accepting the classification of races found in Madison Grant's *The Passing of the Great Race,* an unashamed racist tract that identifies the Nordic as the superior race and classifies the others in a descending order from Alpine, to Mediterranean, to Eastern and Near Eastern, with the Negro race at the bottom. Clearly Brigham expects to find confirmation of Grant's hierarchy in his data and—surprise, surprise—he is not disappointed. First he finds that army officers are more intelligent than enlisted men, and then he finds that within the enlisted ranks whites are clearly superior to blacks. Turning to immigration he uncovers "a gradual deterioration in the class of immigrants . . . who came to this country in each succeeding five year period since 1802," a deterioration that corresponds to the increasing number of non-Nordic immigrants, whose intelligence is found to be more than five times less than that of immigrants from England and Scotland. "In a very definite way," he concludes, "the results which we obtain by analyzing the army data support Mr. Madison Grant's thesis of the superiority of the Nordic type."

Happily these results not only corroborate "the marked intellectual inferiority of the negro," but also "tend to disprove the popular belief that the Jew is highly intelligent." Conclusions from these "results" quickly follow: "The average negro child cannot advance through an educational curriculum adapted to the Anglo-Saxon child." This is a warning against any form of integrated education, and there is inevitably a warning against the mixing of the races by marriage. If the Nordic type makes the mistake of blending with the other types, "then it is a foregone conclusion that this future blended American will be less intelligent than the present native born American." Unfortunately, Brigham reports, there is a tendency in this direction already, but the "deterioration of American intelligence is not inevitable" if the appropriate "legal steps" are taken. These steps, he assures us, should be dictated by "science"—that is, by his results—"and not by political expediency." In this last paragraph, Brigham looks back at the several places in his book where he considers the possibility that environmental conditions rather than simple native racial ability might account for his statistics, but he insists, without any argument or documentation, that all studies "agree in attributing more to original endowment than to environment," an insistence that has been repeatedly echoed by SAT testers who are today administering the test he devised; for, two years after the publication of *A Survey of American Intelligence,* Brigham became director of the College Board's testing operation and set in motion the procedures to which, only slightly modified, many of us have been subjected. There has not even been an official repudiation of Brigham's racism, merely a declaration that it did not compromise his scientific objectivity; the library at the Educational Testing Service compound still bears his name.

What does it all mean? Does it mean that Auster, Brookhiser, and Schlesinger are racists? Well, if you mean by racist someone who actively seeks the subjugation of groups thought inferior to his own, none of these qualify. If you mean by racist someone whose views about race, if acted upon in a political way, will lead to the disadvantaging of certain groups, then Mr. Auster is a serious candidate; and if you mean by racism the deployment of a vocabulary that avoids racist talk but has the effect of perpetuating racial stereotypes and the institutions that promote them, then Mr. Brookhiser is in the running; and Mr. Schlesinger, with his talk of the inevitable Anglo-Saxon "coloration" of the American character and the necessity of sublimating ethnic strains in a true American amalgam, is a shoo-in.

Of course none of these men would consider themselves racists, and they are concerned in their writings to distance themselves from that label, usually by presenting themselves as the champions not of the Anglo-Saxon race as such but of the political and cultural values given to us by that race two hundred years ago. The appeal, in short, is not to prejudice but to national unity in the face of the danger posed by ethnic balkanization. Auster goes so far as to cast a retroactively benign glow over the entire tradition I have examined: "The concern common to all the historical stages of anti-immigrant sentiment was not race as such but the need for a harmonious citizenry, holding to the same values and political principles and having something of the same spirit." Similar statements can be found in the pages written by Schlesinger, C. Van Woodward, and others, but the distinction begins to blur when one realizes that in order to produce a harmonious citizenry the traditions and values associated with non–Anglo-Saxon races must be ruthlessly sublimated; "the people we want are future WASPS." There is, to be sure, a difference between a sense of racial superiority that takes the form of legal and political oppression and a sense of racial superiority that issues in a noncoercive call to national unity and common values; but in the end the result is the same, even when it is reached by softer means. Schlesinger, Auster, Brookhiser, etc. may not be racists in the manner of their predecessors, but in the absence of the real thing—although we must always remember David Duke—they will do. "Common values," "national unity," "American character," "one people," a "single nation," the idea of "assimilation"—these are now code words and phrases for an agenda that need no longer speak in the accents of the Know Nothing party of the nineteenth century or the Ku Klux Klan of the twentieth.

Of course there are many who resonate to those words and phrases and who would be horrified to think of them as alibis for a racist politics. To them I would give the advice that has often been given to me when I was taken by a piece of rhetoric I later disavowed: consider the source. I know that this advice goes against the assumption, so strongly embedded in liberal thought, that ideas are to be evaluated on their merit and not on the basis of the historical condition of their emergence, but that assumption itself assumes that ideas exist in some eternal realm or depoliticized marketplace of ideas, and that assumption seems to me to be wrong: ideas are only intelligible within the particular circumstances that give rise to them, and it is within those circumstances that ideas are put to purposes and do work. The ideas that are the stock-in-trade of the argument against multiculturalism originated in bad purposes and have traditionally done bad work, and to those who find them congenial today, I say they will make bad company.

I cannot end without saying one more word about Arthur Schlesinger, or rather about a picture of him that appears in his book. The picture is without any apparent relationship to the facing text, but there is a relationship to be teased out of it nevertheless. Schlesinger's figure in half torso fills the foreground of the picture; his back is toward us, but his head is twisted around so that he faces the camera and looks directly at us, seeming almost ready to step out of the frame. The face is a young one—the year is 1958—and unformed; the features are ethnic, Semitic, even a bit negroid; the look is quizzical, as if he were asking, "what will I become?" The answer he hopes for is represented in the picture by a figure in its middle ground—elegantly dressed, erect, self-contained, finished, looking not at us but at the far horizon. It is Arthur Schlesinger, Sr., a man fully and safely framed, obviously at home in the landscape which just happens to be Harvard Yard. Harvard is the national University, the true symbol of Protestant America; the picture suggests that Protestant America has not yet enclosed the younger Schlesinger in its bosom and that it is not yet certain that he will be able to complete the passage from the heritage of his Jewish grandfather to total assimilation. By the evidence of this book, which nowhere makes mention of that heritage, he has made it.

DEMOCRACY AND DUALISM

Richard A. Posner

Some years ago, Bruce Ackerman, a professor of constitutional law at the Yale Law School, advanced the startling—to legal professionals, the incredible—thesis that the constitutional turmoil of the 1930s—the Supreme Court's invalidation of key New Deal programs in the name of the Constitution, Franklin Roosevelt's Court-packing plan, and the "switch in time that saved nine," which presaged the retirement of the older justices and their replacement by New Dealers—had actually *amended* the Constitution. Ackerman's new book, and the entire planned trilogy of which it is the first volume, extend and defend this thesis and embed it in a larger view of constitutionalism.

Ackerman begins by outlining rival approaches that he seeks to supplant. One, which he calls "monism," sees the task of constitutional theorizing as one of reconciling the authority of unelected, life-tenured judges to invalidate legislation with America's commitment, seen as primary and fundamental, to democracy. The usual monistic solution is a presumption of legislative validity. One

leading monist, however, John Hart Ely, ingeniously dissolves the tension inherent in judicial review of legislation by arguing that constitutional rights are designed to make democracy work better, as by removing obstacles to the franchise and to free debate. A second approach, which Ackerman calls "rights foundationalism," sees the task of constitutional theorizing as that of identifying principles worthy of preempting democratic choice. A leading rights foundationalist is Ronald Dworkin, and he ingeniously dissolves the tension with democracy by arguing that American democracy just *is* the political regime prescribed by the Constitution, whatever that regime may be; since the Constitution implicitly authorizes judicial review of the validity of legislation, such review *can't* be anti-democratic—nothing allowed by the Constitution can be.

Ackerman's approach to the tension between judicial review and democracy, an approach he calls "dualism," is to posit two sorts of democratic political activity, a higher and a lower. That is why he called the first approach to this issue

Discussed in this essay

We the People, Vol. I: Foundations, *Bruce Ackerman, Cambridge, MA: Harvard University Press*

I thank Lawrence Lessig for his extremely helpful comments on a previous draft.

Bruce Ackerman, author of We the People.

"monistic." Its supporters believe that democracy is primary, and so does he; the difference is that they think democracy is one thing and he thinks it's two things. The "higher lawmaking," as he repeatedly calls it, occurs in periods of revolutionary self-consciousness, as he believes the founding period, the period of the Civil War and Reconstruction, and the New Deal all to have been. It is the expression of a deep, broad, genuine, and unimpeachably legitimate popular will, when people are thinking and acting as private *citizens*. It is "the considered judgment of a mobilized majority of American citizens." The lower form of political activity occurs in normal times, when people are thinking and acting as *private* citizens; it expresses the quotidian horse-trading and intrigue of ordinary politics. (An analogy to Thomas Kuhn's distinction between "revolutionary" and "normal" science is apparent.) The approach generates principles that judges can use to invalidate the legislative products of ordinary politics. When they do this the judges are not being undemocratic; they are being faithful to a deeper conception of democracy than mundane representative democracy. One might call them Rousseauans, except that Ackerman insists that the popular will be tested and refined in the crucible of public debate and earnest deliberation before it can be elevated to constitutional dignity.

Ackerman thinks it a detail whether the authentic popular will that emerges in periods of revolutionary consciousness is embodied in a document that complies with the prescribed formalities for a legally binding enactment. Some perfectly regular amendments, such as the amendments creating and repealing Prohibition, are mere "superstatutes," with no radiations beyond their language, while some informal or even invalid amendments have transformative force because they are manifestations of the "higher lawmaking." He points out that both the original Constitution and the Reconstruction amendments were adopted irregularly, even illegally: the constitutional convention of 1787 exceeded its terms of reference from the Continental Congress, and the United States Army forced the southern states to ratify the Reconstruction amendments against their will—making those amendments, in Ackerman's words, merely "amendment-simulacra." So it hardly matters, says Ackerman, that the third great constitutional revolution, that of the 1930s, produced no piece of paper to tack on to the Constitution as an amendment (except the repeal of Prohibition). The only thing that matters is that by invalidating New Deal statutes the Supreme Court forced the populace to think hard about what kind of constitutional structure it wanted, making the reelection of Roosevelt by a huge plurality in 1936 a genuine expression of the popular will—the will to big government dedicated (in Ackerman's interpretation of that tumultuous era) to equality. Ackerman insists on the parity of these constitutional revolutions. "The Republican Reconstruction of the Union was an act of constitutional creation no less profound than the Founding itself," while in the New Deal, the Supreme Court "began to build new [not rediscover old] constitutional foundations for activist national government."

The wicked Reagan tried to precipitate a fourth constitutional revolution by nominating Robert Bork—who "could supply the intellectual firepower necessary to write judicial texts that would shape the law as fundamentally as had the great New Deal opinions"—to the Supreme Court. The effort failed, as have many similar efforts throughout the history of the nation, such as William Jennings Bryan's populism and Joseph McCarthy's lumpen anticommunism. Bork, as an "originalist," would have tried to restore the founders' constitution—a restoration that would be revolutionary because it would overturn the second and third constitutions. Ackerman overlooks the fact that Justice Scalia has the same basic beliefs as Bork and adequate intellectual firepower to embody them in transformative judicial opinions.

Between periods of revolutionary excitement, the Supreme Court, Ackerman believes, plays and should play only a preservationist role—preserving the structure created in the preceding such period. To play this role requires great interpretive skill, because what is to be interpreted is not a text but a revolution that need leave no documentary traces, at least in the form of constitutional amendments. The modern judge, moreover—the judge of the New Deal era, which is our era because there has been no successful constitutional revolution since the New Deal—must interpret three revolutions rather than just one, because numbers two and three didn't sweep number one away entirely. Ackerman calls this interpretive challenge, grandly, "the problem of multigenerational synthesis."

His analysis of the judicial function enables him to rescue the notorious decision in *Lochner v. New York*—which over a stirring dissent by Justice Holmes ("The Fourteenth Amendment does not enact Mr. Herbert Spencer's *Social Statics*") invalidated as a violation of due process a state law limiting hours of work—from the traditional charge of usurpation. Although the decision went far beyond the founding fathers' understanding of national power, it reflected the Supreme Court's awareness that the Civil War and Reconstruction had created a new constitution, one in which states no longer had a free hand to curtail liberty. No longer could they countenance slavery—that much was clear. But in addition (so Ackerman interprets *Lochner* as deciding) no longer could they permit those lesser but still significant interferences with freedom of property and contract brought about by paternalistic laws, such as laws fixing wages or hours of work.

Ackerman discusses two decisions that in his view interpreted the New Deal constitution. *Brown v. Board of Education,* which invalidated public school segregation, he thinks pivots on the expanded importance that the New Deal gave to public school education, while *Griswold v. Connecticut,* in invalidating a state law forbidding married persons to use contraceptives, transformed the contract and property rights that had been important in the first and second constitutions into a right of privacy responsive to the altered balance between governmental power and personal liberty that had been brought about by the third, the New Deal, constitution.

I have sketched Part One of Ackerman's book—the first 162 pages. The rest (Part Two) begins the process, to be completed in the remaining volumes of the trilogy, of substantiating the thesis sketched in Part One. Part Two of the first volume focuses on the *Federalist Papers* and the modern commentary on them, and argues that the Founding Fathers believed both that there was a difference between revolutionary and normal politics and that they were practicing the first sort. Part Two also defends the possibility of genuinely public-spirited politics—the sort Ackerman finds, and for his thesis to persuade must find, in the nation's revolutionary periods—against public-choice theorists who argue that free-rider problems prevent democratic politics from expressing a genuine, informed popular will. (Ackerman is derisive about what he terms the "economistic" thinking of these theorists.) The subsequent volumes of the trilogy, we are promised, will discuss in detail the Reconstruction and New Deal revolutions—showing that they were genuinely such—and will evaluate the full range of judicial responses, preservationist and otherwise, to all three revolutions.

The first volume is relatively short (about 140,000 words) and not tightly written. There are frequent pauses for unnecessary summarization, lapses into plethoric diction (such as "ongoing dialogue over time"), and characteristically Ackermanian pomposities such as "Thesis, antithesis, synthesis—each generation's dialogic activity providing in turn the new historical thesis for the next generation's ongoing confrontation with the constitutional future of America." Ackerman could probably have squeezed the entire trilogy into a single volume and I wish he had done so, or at least had waited till he had finished the last volume and then published all three at once. For as it is, a final verdict on Ackerman's ambitious project is impossible until we read the remaining volumes—so why are we asked to read the first volume *now?* It's not as if Ackerman were writing linear history and pausing every century; he is propounding a thesis, using historical evidence that this first volume asks us to take on faith.

And a bold and (notwithstanding its unacknowledged debt to Kuhn) original thesis it is, as well as an ambitious one, but it is also deeply problematic, both in gross and in detail. To begin with, Ackerman never makes clear why he thinks we should bestow legitimacy on revolutionary excitement. Suppose that in some future period of economic crisis, such as that which spawned the New Deal, a Hitler-style demagogue is elected president and persuades Congress to en-

act plainly unconstitutional statutes sweeping away basic civil liberties, and the courts duly invalidate these statutes but the demagogue is reelected anyway on the crest of a wave of public indignation at judicial obstructionism and within a few years is able to pack the courts with judges who share his views. This sequence would for Ackerman create a constitutional revolution that the next generation of judges would be *legally* obligated to preserve—even though it entailed their disregarding the written Constitution, which had never been amended—until another constitutional revolution erupted. Why would one want to encourage judges to behave this way by telling them that otherwise they would be acting lawlessly? Ackerman does not answer this question but he is sufficiently alert to the concern behind it to propose that the Constitution be amended to forbid amending it to repeal the Bill of Rights. He wants, in short, to "entrench" the Bill of Rights against a future Hitler. In so proposing he both flinches from the implications of his approach and contradicts it, for he forgets his basic point that an amendment does not have to conform to the constitutionally prescribed procedure for amending the Constitution in order to bind the judges. All entrenchment can do is prevent formal amendments; but on Ackerman's own account the most important amendments are informal, and it is profoundly unclear what form of words could rule them out. Entrenchment presupposes—what he denies—the legal paramountcy of formal amendments.

Legal positivism is controversial enough. Ackerman is proposing that we bestow the mantle of legitimacy on something far more questionable: positivism without positive law. "During both Reconstruction and the New Deal, the Court recognized that the People had spoken even though their political leaders refused to follow the technical legalities regulating constitutional amendment." He thinks it is a good thing (as distinct from a merely prudent thing) that the Court did this, but he does not defend his radical position. He should at least have asked *why* the leaders refused to follow the amendment process. Because it would have taken too long? Because a proposed amendment would have failed of enactment? Aren't these reasons for doubting whether "the People" really *had* spoken? As these questions suggest, Ackerman is on weak ground in asserting the parity of his three constitutional moments. The original Constitution is a detailed and comprehensive document and the *Federalist Papers* explained the meaning of the various provisions and the political theory behind them in considerable detail. The antifederalists set forth their objections in great detail too. As a result, the people who elected delegates to the state ratifying conventions had the benefit of a comprehensive and explicit debate, and no one could have doubted the importance of the issues debated. So if the restricted nature of the eighteenth-century franchise is ignored (women, slaves, and the unpropertied could not vote), the original Constitution can fairly be thought a considered expression of informed public opinion. Not so Ackerman's two subsequent "constitutions." To a casual, and indeed to a careful, reader of the Reconstruction amendments, they do not revolutionize the relation between the national government and the states; they outlaw the racial caste system of the southern states. The amendments were vague enough and their interpretation by some supporters ambitious enough to enable aggressive judges, without being laughed out of court, to transform the amendments from a protection of the freedom of black people against oppression by the governments and people of the southern states to a protection of economic freedom from state regulation; but Ackerman has yet to show (maybe he will in a subsequent volume) that this diversion actualized the popular will expressed in the amendments.

As for the third revolution, the New Deal, there was, granted, strong popular support for the New Deal programs. But there also was strong popular support, expressed in the successful opposition to Roosevelt's Court-packing plan, for allowing the Supreme Court to invalidate New Deal programs. The popular support for the New Deal, moreover, was not well informed. Much of the support was motivated by the confused and mistaken belief that the New Deal would bring the country out of the Depression, which it did not do. Some of its programs, such as the cartelizing codes promulgated by the National Recovery Administration, probably prolonged the Depression, as did the restless experimentation characteristic of Roosevelt's pre–World War II presidency. Others, we now know, were merely unsound, such as the separation of commercial and investment banking, the breaking up of public utility holding companies, the attack on chain stores, the creation of farm-price supports and acreage restrictions, and the regulation of truck and airline routes and fares. Perhaps the nation could have done no better in the circumstances; but beginning with the Administrative Procedure Act and the Taft-Hartley Act, and continuing to this day, much federal legislative activity has had to be devoted to pruning the excesses of the New Deal. Ackerman finds running throughout the welter of New Deal programs a steady theme of using Big Government to promote an egalitarian redistribution of income and wealth (national socialism, might one call it?). Others might prefer to characterize those programs as partisan, ad hoc, opportunistic responses to a frightening but poorly understood economic crisis and to relentless interest-group pressures. Is it really true that the last time the American people thought straight was when they re-elected FDR in 1936?

All that this shows, though, is that the popular will can be mistaken; and the fact that it *was* the popular will might be enough to confer legitimacy upon it. Or might not. You need an argument that democracy is normative, and Ackerman doesn't make one. No doubt, under modern conditions, stable and effective government requires, in the long run, democratic institutions; that much seems clear from recent history. No doubt, the more earnest and extensive the deliberations leading up to a democratic enactment are, the more likely the enactment is to be an authentic expression of popular opinion (and what else could democratic preference mean?). It does not follow that judges should genuflect to strong currents of public opinion before those currents express themselves in positive law. Reflecting lawyers' concern for process (though he has an unlawyerly

disdain for technicality), Ackerman insists that the popular will, to be accorded constitutional status, have crystallized after due deliberation. But due deliberation is not a guarantor against error, or worse; he acknowledges this, as we shall see, in discussing a hypothetical constitutional amendment stamping out religious freedom. So the grounding of his populism is not epistemological—it is not (like Holmes's version of "monism") the idea that, given ideal conditions for the formation of an educated and reflective public opinion, that opinion is the closest we can get to truth. Ackerman's idea is that, provided something like these ideal conditions is satisfied, the judges should bow to public opinion right or wrong. Why should they? Ackerman offers no answer, and in fact his principal defense of the dualist theory of the Constitution is unconnected with political theory; it's merely that dualism is the theory of the framers of the original Constitution. This is an odd defense for *him* to offer, first, because it is "originalist" in character, and he is anti-originalist, and, second, because it is anti-dualist. It allows the framers of the original Constitution to determine the constitutional significance of all subsequent events.

A further objection is that Ackerman's theory asks too much of the judges. It doesn't ask them just to interpret documents, or to decide cases reasonably, but to determine the "meaning" of amorphous historical "moments." Maybe that formidable bit of jargon, "multigenerational synthesis," is apt after all—as connoting the remoteness of what Ackerman wants judges to do from what they are able to do. It is difficult enough to interpret texts in light of historical events without having to interpret the whole of American political history before you can decide a case. Unless, of course, Ackerman has given us the definitive history, bringing interpretation to an end. He has not. His book is a work of genuine scholarship, but it is not a work of discovery; it is a work of interpretation. It does not exhibit its badges of soundness or propose a mode of verification. Until it commands a consensus among historians and constitutional scholars, it will not provide a usable guide to judges.

Still another objection to making dualism the theory of our constitutional law is that some niceties are nicer than others. Such illegalities as attended the adoption of the original Constitution and the Reconstruction amendments took place in the turbulent wakes of major internal wars. And what was adopted, in both cases, was a text. The New Deal was not a product of war, and did not produce a constitutional text. It produced collectivist federal legislation and a liberal judiciary that proceeded to remake constitutional law.

Ackerman might reply to all these objections that he is describing, not applauding, our constitutional regime; that his analysis is positive rather than normative. Early in the book, he discusses a hypothetical constitutional amendment: "Christianity is established as the state religion of the American people, and the public worship of other gods is hereby forbidden." He would uphold this amendment "as a fundamental part of the American Constitution," on the ground that in "dualist America" it is "the People who are the source of rights"; there can

be no appeal to a higher law. But he does not like the amendment, of course, and he regards its potential legitimacy under dualism as a shortcoming of dualism. Later in the book, when he is discussing the entrenching of rights, he makes clear that, to this extent, he wants to go beyond dualism. He wants to entrench our present Bill of Rights to head off the Christianity amendment and like horrors, which despite his faith in the people he thinks sufficiently (if not highly) likely to warrant an ambitious (though by the logic of his analysis futile) project of formal constitutional amendment. But he describes this project of transcending dualism as "Utopian." Dualism is not Utopia, but Ackerman regards it not only as the best positive theory of the Constitution—the best explanation of the Constitution we have—but also as the best normative guide to judges who interpret our Constitution: the best normative guide, in other words, for the here and now. Which I greatly doubt, for the reasons indicated earlier.

Ackerman could still be right that dualism best describes the structure of the Constitution and the practice under it. Yet this I doubt too. He casts the judges as interpreters of revolutionary moments. There is an alternative story, which has nothing to do with monism or rights foundationalism, which is not mentioned by Ackerman, which is very simple, and which is more convincing. The same forces that shape the thinking of statesmen (as we call politicians whose efforts produce large and durable changes in public policy) shape the thinking of judges. The nationalism that produced the Union's victory in the Civil War also produced Supreme Court justices who thought that a strong national economy unimpeded by parochial local regulations, such as the maximum hour law struck down in *Lochner,* was more important than justice to blacks, and who shaped the plastic language of the Fourteenth Amendment accordingly. The medley of "liberal" ideas that produced the New Deal produced Supreme Court justices who, naturally enough, changed the focus of constitutional law to the promotion of those ideas. The judges at these various stages were not interpreting a revolution. They *were* the (or rather some of the) revolutionaries. Their place in history is determined not by their fidelity to their revolution but by the success of that revolution—which is why Holmes (who opposed the second revolution and anticipated the third), Jackson, Stone, and Warren are heroes, and Taney, Brown, and Peckham are villains. I exaggerate a little, because judges are sometimes blamed or praised according to narrow professional criteria unrelated to the great sweep of constitutional history—but not often.

I think the simpler story is truer than Ackerman's, and for evidence I point to his unpersuasive efforts to explain leading decisions as interpretations of revolutionary moments. Decided just five years after the adoption of the Fourteenth Amendment, the *Slaughterhouse Cases* (1873) rejected the argument that the amendment protected businessmen from state regulation that interfered with freedom of contract. The court held that the Reconstruction amendments had altered the balance of federal and state relations only in the area of race. Ackerman explains the decision as "initiat[ing] one of

the two fundamental approaches to [multigenerational] synthesis that defined middle [i.e., second] republican jurisprudence. This involved *particularizing* the constitutional principles announced at Time Two in a way that restricted their impact upon the older principles of Time One" (emphasis in original). What

The judges of the *Plessy-Lochner* period were not interpreting the Reconstruction amendments; they were inverting them

Ackerman rather elaborately terms the particularizing approach to the task of multigenerational synthesis is more simply described as rejection of the revolutionary interpretation of the Reconstruction amendments. He explains this rejection in an interesting way. The Supreme Court justices of the Reconstruction era had learned about the (first) Constitution through law books, and the books had built a conceptual structure, a structure of broad principles. These justices had "gain[ed] access to the meaning of the Reconstruction texts in a very different way—through lived experience of the greatest political events of their time," and naturally therefore "to them, Reconstruction was the culmination of something concrete and particular—the struggle against slavery." It was only in the next generation, with "the fading of lived experience and the rise of legal dialectic," that judges raised the Reconstruction amendments to the level of general principle that could engender *Lochner* (1905) and like cases.

Some might think "lived experience" a better interpretive guide than "legal dialectic," but a strong indication that the judges of the *Lochner* period were not engaged in something usefully described as interpretation is their abandonment of blacks. Ackerman, fastening on the infamous remark in the majority opinion in *Plessy v. Ferguson* (1896) that segregation would stigmatize blacks only if they chose to regard it as stigmatizing, argues that the decision reveals the grip of laissez-faire thinking as surely as *Lochner*. But the law upheld in *Plessy* forbade blacks to contract with railroads on mutually agreeable terms. Ackerman does not explain how the Reconstruction amendments could be thought, by an *honest* judge, simultaneously to forbid states to interfere with the freedom of contract of whites and to permit states to interfere with the freedom of contract of blacks. The conventional story is correct. The judges of the *Plessy-Lochner* period were not interpreting the Reconstruction amendments; they were inverting them.

No more were *Brown v. Board of Education* and *Griswold v. Connecticut* interpretations of the New Deal "constitution," or more precisely syntheses of that and the previous constitutions. It is true that in distinguishing *Plessy* the Court in *Brown* emphasized the greater importance of public education in 1954 than in 1868, when the Fourteenth Amendment was adopted, or in 1896, when *Plessy* was decided. But to a lawyer the obvious reasons the Court did this—and they have nothing to do with the New Deal—were, first, to explain why it need not be bound by the legislative history of the Fourteenth Amendment, a history

which indicated that the amendment had not been understood by its framers or supporters to require blacks to attend school with whites, and second to justify overruling a decision on which the South had erected its public institutions. The essentially, indeed disingenuously, rhetorical purpose of invoking the growth of public education is shown by the fact that in the years following *Brown,* in a series of per curiam decisions that offer no explanation for their result other than a citation to *Brown* itself, the Supreme Court invalidated a host of public segregation laws that had nothing to do with public education. And whatever the reason for the Court's mentioning public education, it can hardly have been the New Deal. For while it is true that public education was more important in the 1950s than it had been in the nineteenth century, it had grown steadily over this interval and the New Deal had given it no particular push. So far as I am aware or Ackerman mentions, there was no major New Deal legislation dealing with education. He says, "With the New Deal, the public schools could take on a new symbolic meaning. They were no longer anomalous, but paradigmatic of the new promise of activist government." His timing is off; it had been a long time since public schools had been considered anomalous.

Granted, the New Deal was more than its legislative product. It was also the empowerment of the "outs"—Catholics, Jews, workers, intellectuals, blacks, Southerners. It did have an egalitarian component, one manifestation of which was the appointment to the Supreme Court of men like Douglas and Frankfurter who had liberal views on race. The views of these justices, and the heightened consciousness of racism generated by Hitler and World War II, set the stage for *Brown.* But the decision is not usefully viewed as an interpretation of the New Deal, or of the Reconstruction amendments in the light of the New Deal. One senses that Ackerman is very much a Yale Law School product. For he

It was in the era of lynching and Jim Crow that blacks needed judicial protection the most, and they didn't get it

has New Deal nostalgia, as well as legal realist disdain for legal formalities such as the constitutionally prescribed process for amending the Constitution.

Laws forbidding contraceptives had been enacted in the latter part of the nineteenth century, as part of the purity movement—an expression of Victorianism—and by 1965, when *Griswold* was decided, had been repealed in all but two states. The wave of repeals reflected the decline of Victorian sexual morality and the rise of the birth control movement; both trends antedated the New Deal. It is true is that since the Connecticut law was enforced only against birth control clinics, whose primary clientele consisted of poor and working-class women, the law was inequitable. But the Court did not mention this aspect of it. Nor does Ackerman. He tries to relate the decision to the New Deal differently. He argues that the bigger government is, the more urgent is the need for courts to protect individuals, through the recog-

nition of new rights, from being ground down by it. Under the "second Constitution," people had had robust contract and property rights, which automatically protected their privacy from invasion by the states; the New Deal took these away and by doing so made the right of privacy more important than it had been. This is not an entirely convincing point; if the bigger government empowers groups that formerly were politically impotent, such as blacks, the need of those groups, at least, for judicial protection may be less rather than more. It was in the era of lynching and Jim Crow that blacks needed judicial protection the most, and they didn't get it then—their abandonment by the courts being announced with characteristic forthrightness by Holmes in *Giles v. Harris,* which held two years before *Lochner* that the federal courts would not provide a remedy for the disenfranchisement of blacks in the southern states. In any event the point is wide of *Griswold.* The law struck down in that case was not a manifestation of big government. It was a hangover from the era of small government. And it was not a law that big government had somehow made more oppressive. It is true that if the "second Constitution" had *really* protected freedom of contract, then, indeed, a married couple would have had no need to invoke a constitutional right of privacy in order to be able to buy contraceptives; their constitutional right of contract would have sufficed to enable them to buy anything that sellers were willing to sell them. But no one in the "middle Republic" had thought that laws forbidding the sale of contraceptives denied constitutionally protected freedom of contract.

Such laws were considered comfortably within the police power of the states.

I do not want to exaggerate my disagreement with Ackerman. I agree that we should interpret the Constitution in light of our whole experience, including the dramatic upheavals of the Civil War, Reconstruction, the New Deal, and World War II. I agree that an amendment can alter a provision whose words it does not change (so that the Supreme Court may have been justified in *Bolling v. Sharpe* in holding that the equal protection clause of the Fourteenth Amendment had enlarged the concept of due process in the Fifth Amendment so that it now forbade federal segregation of public schools in the District of Columbia). It is a point that has been made by thinkers as otherwise diverse as T. S. Eliot, who said (in "Tradition and the Individual Talent") that "what happens when a new work of art is created is something that happens simultaneously to all the works of art which preceded it," and Ronald Dworkin, who describes law by the metaphor of a chain novel, in which authors of successive chapters are both constrained by and alter the meaning of the earlier chapters. I agree, too,

that judges are properly (as well as inevitably) influenced by deep and broad currents of public opinion. These are familiar points but they are dramatized by Ackerman's startling thesis.

But the thesis itself seems to me dangerous and wrong, though I reserve the right to change my view on the basis of the subsequent volumes of his trilogy. Wrong because the history of constitutional law since 1868 cannot be convincingly explained as the effort of judges to interpret and preserve moments of revolutionary consciousness. Dangerous because it invites judges to treat the popular will as a form of higher law entitling them to disregard ordinary concepts of legality. That is what Hitler's judges did, as documented in Ingo Müller's important book, *Hitler's Justice: The Courts of the Third Reich* (trans. 1991). They correctly sensed a sea change in public attitudes (for remember that Hitler was immensely popular in Germany until the outbreak of war) and enforced the new outlook with minimum regard for legal niceties. It is worth recalling that what Ackerman deems the informal but legitimate amendment of the Constitution by the New Deal occurred at the same time.

THE DIALECTICS OF RACE AND CITIZENSHIP

Stephen L. Carter

Discussed in this essay

American Citizenship: The Quest for Inclusion, *Judith Shklar, Cambridge, MA: Harvard University Press*

Why Americans Hate Politics, *E. I. Dionne, New York: Simon & Schuster*

On Reading the Constitution, *Laurence H. Tribe and Michael C. Dorf, Cambridge, MA: Harvard University Press*

In the several hundred years since their arrival in America, black folk have spent more time officially enslaved than officially free. As it passes its two hundredth birthday, the United States has not yet shrugged off this unhappy legacy. The nation's historical consciousness too often envisions the struggle for racial equality as something recent, something that began around 1954, when the Supreme Court decided *Brown v. Board of Education,* and quickly succeeded. This vision of the modern civil rights movement as the nation's principal period of racial trauma helps explain why America would rather celebrate Martin Luther King than Nat Turner, would rather honor James Baldwin than Frederick Douglass, and even, I suspect, would rather have students emulating Malcolm X than Toussaint l'Ouverture. As a matter of official memory, the Founders of the Republic remain awash in greatness. Ideally, slavery is something that didn't happen; or if it did, it happened to somebody else and was done by somebody else, and neither the perpetrators nor the victims are historically continuous with anybody now living.

But this uneven historical memory should not be mistaken for entire indifference. Over the past thirty years or so, America has worked hard, albeit in frustrating fits and starts, to eliminate the more odious vestiges of official racism. The undeniable fact that there is still a very long way to go should not be confused with the quite different proposition that no progress has been made, a statement made all too casually on college campuses by students who a generation ago would not have had the education or career opportunities that they have today, but who nevertheless insist on reducing the glorious struggle and martyrdom of the civil rights tradition to a mere sideshow, without significance in the true relations of racial power.

At the same time, it remains true today, as it has through all the nation's history, that millions of white Americans place considerable personal stress on a vital indicator of status: skin color. Generally, and with reason, we who are black see this conscious racialism as antiblack. It is useful, however, to take time to think of it the other way around, not as a diminution of the status of blackness, but as a celebration of the status of nonblackness. Thus does race-consciousness—or its close and oppressive cousin, racism—come full circle, meeting white supremacy: the desire to define blackness as representing *something less* is the same as the desire to define whiteness as representing *something more*. Whiteness can represent something more only if there is another quality—blackness—for it to be something more than. (Some black nationalist rhetoric of racial superiority works in the same fashion, with the adjectives reversed.)

This inversion may seem rather obvious, but it generates a series of subtle yet powerful propositions that Judith Shklar sets forth quite nicely in her recent book *American Citizenship: The Quest for Inclusion*. Shklar wants to know what aspects of citizenship have provided citizens with status attainments setting them apart from others, who are not citizens. What is it, she asks in other words, that made American citizenship so valued, especially in the formative years of the nineteenth and early twentieth centuries? Her answer, based on a wonderful variety of sources, is that the entire history of the idea of *status* in this nation has based itself on differentiating the people who matter from slaves.

Thus Judith Shklar proposes to do what legions of historians (and law professors) have tried and failed to: to find a central place for slavery in the American historical narrative about citizenship. It is not true, she argues, that the nation in its early years defined citizen status based on a European model without the aristocracy; rather, she says, the characteristics of citizenship were determined by their variance from the lot of the slaves. When the American colonists posted their

Judith N. Shklar, author of *Citizenship: The Quest for Inclusion*

grievances against the king, they frequently referred to themselves as being treated like slaves. Shklar points out that for the new Americans, this was not simply the rhetorical device that it had been for the Continental political philosophers on whose work they drew. When the colonists spoke of being treated like slaves, they had concrete knowledge of that treatment; after all, many of them were involved in perpetrating it, and the rest could hardly have been unaware of it. "Rebellious Europeans," says Shklar, "might cry out that they were enslaved, but they had never seen the real thing." Americans, on the other hand, "lived with it in pain, guilt, fear, and hatred."

The notion that the status of citizenship in America has always been defined through its differences from slavery presents something of a challenge to a variety of orthodox views. But it makes a good deal of practical sense. It possesses that rarest quality of historical theories, *plausibility*. The slaves were here, after all. They were here from the nation's inception. Some (on left and right alike) would argue that they are with us still. Shklar, however, is careful not to suggest that she has found *the* answer to the question of how status definitions emerged in the debate over the nature of citizenship. Her claim is not that slavery was the single largest factor, but rather that it was a single large factor and, as such, is often overlooked.

It is true, says Shklar, that the first great account of citizenship—Aristotle's —was also developed in a slave society, but the American vision of democratic citizenship was the first to be propounded in a nation so steeped in egalitarian rhetoric, yet at the same time "so intimately entwined with slavery." In defining citizenship, and defining freedom, the American political philosophers wrote against a backdrop in which they did not have to look far to see the face of oppression: "Americans saw slavery everywhere, especially in any diminution of what they regarded as their rights." So, for example, in the debates over universal manhood suffrage in nineteenth-century Massachusetts, we find opponents of property qualifications for voting lamenting that "men who have no property are put in the situation of the slaves of Virginia."

Shklar focuses her argument on two examples of status indicators: voting and earning. Each of these, she argues, developed in American history as a way of differentiating people who were free from people who were slaves. Thus the campaign for the vote—for unpropertied males, for women—is justified on the ground that those unable to vote are no better than slaves; the campaign for free labor, even for unions, is seen as a way of putting distance between the lot of the manual laborer and the lot of the slave.

Shklar's argument for the role of the franchise in distinguishing the free from the enslaved, while provocative, is the more tenuous of the two. America has no tradition of universal suffrage; on the contrary, the original voting rules were established as clearly aristocratic in character. The federal system was not designed to permit the majority to rule. In fact, it was designed to frustrate the notion of majority rule. The House of Representatives was, in the original plan, the only part of the new government in which democracy was expected to hold sway. The senators (in those days appointed by the state legislatures) and the president (in those days elected by an electoral college elected by the legislatures) were clearly seen as representing the states rather than the people. (Both provisions were later changed by constitutional amendment.)

The reason this history matters is that it sheds some light on the political science of the founding generation. Far from being a symbol of freedom, the vote was a reason for concern: if it could be used, it could be abused. In fact, the limited franchise can be tied to such other innovations as the federal system, with its shared sovereignty between the federal government and the states, and the separation of powers, with its concomitant system of checks and balances. These innovations bespeak a general mistrust of popular judgment; that the franchise was initially limited, nearly everywhere, to white male adults who owned property, might simply represent more of the same, with a dose of eighteenth-century racism and sexism sprinkled in.

True, the Founders were conscious of the slaves. Many of them actually owned slaves—that is, they owned and trafficked in human beings. (For this reason, even legal theorists who believe, as I do, that the legitimacy of constitutional interpretation rests on a fealty to the document's text, structure, and history should be wary of seeming to elevate the *moral* perspicacity of the Founders, for they were not, by and large, particularly admirable human beings.) The convention that met at Philadelphia in 1787 produced a Constitution that danced around the issue of slavery without ever quite resolving it. Some among the founding generation criticized the Constitution precisely for its failure to resolve the slavery question.

Still, even if the franchise was limited principally for other reasons, the possession of the right to vote could yet possess

It is frightening to think that many white people might now think the vote less significant because more black people are now exercising it

psychological significance. Shklar notes that voting as a status indicator had nothing to do with the selection of representatives; it was the ability to cast a vote, not the effect of the vote, that determined who was slave and who was free. (She quotes Frederick Douglass quite poignantly to this effect.) This is a nice point, one that some critics say has been confused in current interpretations of the Voting Rights Act as a tool of ensuring not the right to cast a vote, but the right to cast an effective vote. What the critics may miss, however, and what Shklar's fascinating history may also overlook, is that over time, casting a vote that is seen as useless might make the vote itself feel less and less significant and, therefore, might make the possessor of the voting right feel less and less distinct from the slave, who has no right of self-governance.

This potential frustration does not, of course, attach uniquely to citizens who are black. Groups of white people, too, might become frustrated, even anti-democratic in fervor, if they see themselves as always casting votes that have no meaning because their candidates are always losing. And if, as Shklar's evidence suggests, the right to vote has indeed been justified in part as a means of distinguishing the citizen from the slave, one has to wonder what connection to draw between the yearning to draw that distinction and declining rates of voter participation. Perhaps, as the franchise becomes more broadly exercised, it loses the importance that Shklar attaches to it; but it is frightening indeed to think that many white people might now think the vote less significant because more black people are now exercising it.

In many respects, Shklar's case works better for earning. After all, the principal role of the slave was to labor, and of that labor two things are true, indeed, definitional: first, the slave possessed no choice about whether to work or not, and, second (although there were some exceptions), the slave generally received no wage for the labor. And Shklar very

**E. J. Dionne, Jr.,
author of Why
Americans Hate
Politics**

Paul Hossefros

neatly traces a whole history of references to "earning" as a defining characteristic of citizenship—a proposition that fueled not only a fear for and disdain of slaves, but also an anger at an aristocracy that was seen as enjoying the fruits of labor without having earned any of it.

This respect for "earning" as a concomitant of citizenship cuts in two directions: those who labor but earn nothing are not true citizens, which excludes slaves; and those who earn but do not labor are also not true citizens, which excludes the "idle" rich. Thus much of abolitionism is, for Shklar, an effort to protect wages—after all, if slavery were allowed to spread, wage laborers would lose out in the competition—but so is much of the Jacksonian assault on the aristocracy. Similarly, the appeal of the

WPA and similar programs in the Depression is explained in large measure through the desire of recipients of assistance to work for their money, lest they lose their claim on citizenship, that is, on being different from slaves, who earn nothing; the disdain toward "handouts" and, today, toward many welfare recipients, is cut from the same cloth, and, again, works both ways:

The welfare recipients who are told that they must work at whatever job is available see the specter of slavery and indentured servitude come to haunt them again, returned from a not so distant past. And the persistence of racism makes that fear plausible. To those who want to see workfare made compulsory, the idle poor are no longer citizens. They have forfeited their claim to civic equality and are well

*on their way to behaving like unemployed
slaves, kept consumers who do not produce.*

Yes—but again, one wants to be wary of
taking the point too far. On the other
side, one might counterpose the words
of Frederick Douglass, which Shklar
quotes a few pages before:

*All that any man has a right to expect, ask,
give or receive in this world, is fair play.
When society has secured this to its members,
and the humblest citizen of the republic is put
into the undisturbed possession of the natural
fruits of his own exertions, there is really very
little left for society and government to do.*

Douglass, in an important sense, is here
steering closer to the wind than Shklar,
for without regard to what one thinks of
compulsory workfare, Douglass puts
into words the essential ideological
point: it is not that those who are forced
to work to earn assistance are no better
than slaves, it is, rather, that the key to
citizenship, in the minds, one suspects,
of the overwhelming majority of the
polity, is not only the capacity to earn,
but the desire to do so. There may indeed
be racism in the ready assumption that
many recipients of public assistance lack
the desire to work, but that assumption
should not be confused with the larger
ideological point, that working for a living is something that a good American
should want to do.

These imperfections in Shklar's thesis
should not detract from its explanatory
power. For example, the notion that citizen was defined, even loosely, as the
condition of not being enslaved helps explain, in a nonracial way, one of the more
discouraging phenomena of the nine-

teenth century: the ownership of slaves
by free black folk in the South. How can
it be, many a historian has asked, that
these black people were willing to own
their brothers and sisters? The answer,
perhaps, is that they did not see any sib-
ling relationship: the crucial status distinction was not, as we now think, black/
white, but rather, slave/free. Anyone
who was free and had the money could
own a slave. Of course, as it turned out,
attaining the status of slaveowner did not
shield free black folk from discrimination and, later, white rage, especially after John Brown's raid at Harper's Ferry,
when free black people suddenly found
themselves unwelcome in the South and
so fled north, in the first minimigration.
Perhaps it was not the judgment of the
South that all black folk should be slaves;
still, given that white anger and fear were
directed at all black folk, slave or free, it
seems likely that the desire to escape
from the category of slave was not the
only motivation for establishment of
status.

This leads to the one truly troubling
point about Shklar's theory: she does not
deal adequately with the essential matter
of the blackness of the slaves. Doubtless
it is true, as she suggests, that people who
were free defined that status through
their differences from the slaves, and
surely the fact of slavery alone would
have been enough to spur this effort.
Throughout human history, there have
been slaves, and they have come in every
color; but in America, the slaves were
black. They were enslaved because, as
black Africans, they were seen as not
quite human, or at least not capable of
civilization. So in insisting on gathering
status indicators that proved that they

were not slaves, white Americans were, in essence, simultaneously proving that they were not black, and, perhaps, were more human. The point bears emphasis. It is the state of blackness, not just the state of enslavement, that white people have struggled to avoid: as recently as a quarter of a century ago and, for all I know, today as well, it was actionable libel in the South to call a white person black.

Shklar is sensitive to the role of racism in the definition of citizenship, and she mentions it frequently in her narrative. But in the end, one wonders whether she has succeeded in placing the institution of slavery in its proper place in the evolution of the American account of citizenship, or whether she has instead added another depressing chapter to the continuing saga of the effect on American political and intellectual life, not of slavery, but of race. Perhaps she has done both; and whichever is the case, she has done it well.

•   •   •

Judith Shklar's historical analysis makes fascinating reading when placed alongside E. J. Dionne's scathing critique of contemporary governance, *Why Americans Hate Politics*. The reason that the two go together is that where Shklar wants to argue that the history of status in America has been aimed at distinguishing all classes of people from slaves, largely through powers of voting and earning, Dionne suggests that the politics of the eighties and nineties are largely focused on punishing those who were seen as removing the distinctions.

According to Dionne's book — which might just as well have been entitled *Why Americans Hate the Democratic Party* — what the Republicans understand and the Democrats do not is that most Americans despise the sixties. The high-blown rhetoric, the topsy-turvy values, the rejection of tradition, the lurch toward egalitarianism, all of which continue to be cherished by many liberal intellectuals, are anathema to most voters. It is less that they liked things the way they were before than that they think they have had enough radical change for a while, and, in any case, they are tired of being blamed for everything that is wrong and are tired of learning that the solution to every problem is to strike down another traditional value.

This is strong stuff, and, in today's political climate, will doubtless be seen by many critics as playing into the hands of the forces of reaction. But this particular messenger it would be unwise to kill, for he makes good, if worrisome, sense. His analysis of the sixties, like his analysis of the current political climate, is largely on point. The sixties, of course, is not so much a decade as an idea, and different people will assign to it a different significance. A rough definition of the sixties might be that it began in 1963 with the assassination of the last president who truly spoke in the language of optimism, surged forward with the tide of progressive legislation and campus activism, reached its zenith just before the twin disasters of 1968, and muddled to its end at about the time of the resignation in 1974 of one of the most astute politicians of the twentieth century, who finally lost out to his own venality. A few years later, after a period of national floundering, the exhausted American electorate decisively rejected the politics of liberalism in the Reagan landslide of 1980.

And what is the contemporary legacy of those troubled years? An important part of it, one on which Dionne focuses, is the laissez-faire attitude toward moral responsibility—the celebration of moral tolerance, the opposition to moral legislation—an attitude representing less a liberal triumph than an unhappy legacy that leaves millions of Americans bewildered. For many Americans, it simply does not make sense to be told, in the nineties, that they may not use the power of the state to impose their morality on somebody else, except in the service of an expressly liberal end, such as desegregation or support for organized labor. If one does not happen to support the particular moral ends to which government chooses to bend its regulatory efforts, one will naturally vote for a new government, and being called names for doing so—racist, reactionary, sexist, whatever—is not likely to soften one's stance.

Along this line, I recall what George Will, I believe, wrote about South Africa. The South African government, he conceded, is riding a tiger, and the tiger is doubtless one of its own making. Then he added something like this: "However, the best way to convince the rider to get off is hardly by saying that it deserves to be eaten." Too much of the political rhetoric of the sixties seemed of exactly this style: You are evil, and you deserve what you get. Once upon a time, that was a good way to work up liberal guilt. But

with the triumph of Reaganism in the eighties, not so many people are liberals any more, and not so many of them are inclined to feel guilty just because somebody calls them a name. Sometimes the names might be deserved—perhaps, *pace* Will, the South African government *does* deserve to be eaten—but pointing out that possibility is not nowadays a means for changing many people's minds.

Most of those who were part of the Left in the sixties have long since deserted it

The fixation of its rhetoricians on finding the right labels for their opponents rather than searching for a common ground that might have permitted an even greater leap forward is one of many reasons that the romanticization of the sixties by many on the Left is a continuing puzzle. Another is the simple truth that most of those who were part of the Left in the sixties have long since deserted it; indeed, a large part of the core of the fragmenting neoconservative movement comprises old (or rather New) sixties lefties. (A couple of years ago, one of my students, too young to remember the events he was describing, announced in class that a film would be shown of the era in which students were genuine radicals. He did not, however, offer any information on how many of those genuine radicals are now voting Republican.)

What matters more, of course, is that whatever its status among liberal intellectuals, the decade of the sixties is hardly remembered with much fondness by the majority of American voters. The opinion surveys tell us that most Americans think that something has gone badly wrong in America. For many, I suspect, the sixties stand as a symbol of—dare I say it?—liberal permissiveness, which, if it existed at all, might have reached its zenith then. Indeed, Dionne is surely right to link the widespread sense that America has lost its moral compass with a general suspicion that the sixties was the time when it was lost.

What is worrisome about all this, however, is that probably the principal change in American society in the sixties was the remarkable transformation, in one short decade, of the legal and social status of black Americans. The change in the legal status was monumental: discrimination in employment, in public accommodations, in voting, and in housing all became illegal within a four-year period. Even though there are vast and lingering areas of discrimination in all these fields today, the revolution that was worked by the 1964 Civil Rights Act, the 1965 Voting Rights Act, and the 1968 Fair Housing Act can scarcely be denied. The social status of black Americans changed too, not only because of the civil rights movement and the Black Power movement, but also because, as new opportunities opened, black people moved onto campuses where they had never studied, into jobs where they had never worked, and into neighborhoods where they had never lived. The black middle class left the inner cities and began the slow process of entrance into the American mainstream.

Still, Dionne joins a legion of critics in arguing that the liberal race program, with its focus on affirmative action and other politically unpopular race-specific programs, missed the chance to move toward politically popular nonracial programs that would enhance economic opportunities. "The mistakes of the last two decades," he warns, "have been politically ruinous for liberals and disastrous for the nation."

Ah, but what are the mistakes? Many critics on the right argue that in the rush toward egalitarianism, the liberal race program has made merit irrelevant. Although often overstated, this is not a ridiculous critique—not, at least, from the point of view of many voters, who earnestly believe that black folks are getting jobs or places in college that better qualified white folks have earned. Although there are certainly racists among the opponents of the modern civil rights tradition, the fear that it is aimed at wiping out standards of merit, although in my view often groundless, is hardly racist; on the contrary, it is deeply rooted in a desire for fair play, one that nonracial programs of justice could use to advantage. Dionne points to opinion surveys suggesting that many white voters turned against the civil rights program not because it helped black people, nor because it was perceived as hurting white people, but rather because it helped black people alone. As Dionne puts it: "If the runner forty yards back is allowed to make up the difference, which seems only fair, what about runners who faced unfair but less imposing burdens and are, say, only ten or twenty yards back?" He links this concern for equity to the anti-establishment fervor of a George Wallace (and, nowadays, perhaps a David Duke):

Laurence Tribe, co-
author, with Michael
Dorf, of *On Reading
the Constitution*

The latter group included the sons and daughters of the white working class, the children in the community colleges and state schools who were certainly better off on the whole than blacks but lacked the advantages of the children of the wealthy and the students of the Ivy League. If society was so concerned about making the race fair, such whites asked, why was it not making life more fair for them too?

The point is that it is too easy an out to put down the white flight from the Democratic party to racism. A principal error of the liberal program was the rhetorical assumption that black people alone were in need of assistance—or that the obviously greater burdens that black people faced meant that the principal remedies had to be race-specific. Thus some white people ended up in opposition not because they felt burdened but because they felt excluded.

Since the sixties, our racial politics have spiraled downward, and, in recent years, racial attitudes seem especially to have hardened. But Dionne warns against too-ready acceptance of the view that the voters have punished liberals for doing "the right thing" on civil rights: "[T]he tactical implication of this apologia was that liberalism would revive itself only by doing *less* for blacks in the

More than half of white Americans think, even today, that blacks are lazy and, on average, not as smart as whites

future—by running away from the very achievement of which liberals claim to be so proud." At the same time, he seems uncertain how to move matters forward, adding in evident despair: "We have no better example of how *not* to talk about race than the Willie Horton 'issue,' the ultimate expression of a politics of false choices."

Still, the fact that affirmative action and other race-specific programs have been unpopular should not blind the critic (and does not blind Dionne) to the fact that the programs have made a difference. No matter how controversial the means that brought it about, the massive change in the legal and social status of black Americans was perhaps the most revolutionary aspect of the sixties. So if most of America is hostile to the sixties, the chances are good that most of America has not worked through its feelings about the status of black Americans. Put otherwise, when Dionne talks about American politics as being largely about the sixties, what he is really saying, whether he knows it or not, is that American politics are largely about race.

Judith Shklar tells us that one reason that welfare is so controversial—and is seen as so demeaning—is that, for many Americans, it represents precisely the failure to earn a wage that in the past marked black people as slaves. So when, in the eighties and nineties, politicians condemn welfare, they are in effect playing to an American tradition, not the tradition of hard work for its own sake, but the tradition that holds that only slaves fail to earn a wage if they are able. And then there is that other tradition, too: the tradition that slaves were black. According to survey evidence, more than half of white Americans think, even today, that blacks are lazy and are, on average, not as smart as whites. So hating the sixties is, inevitably, hating the gains that these lazy, stupid people have made. Without the institution of slavery, or at least the toleration of private discrimination, to allow people the luxury of having a group upon which to look down, there is the loss of a status indicator. Much of American politics today is about the struggle over responding to that loss.

Some on the Left answer unhesitatingly that if American politics are about race, then American politics are racist, but rhetoric of this kind misses the point. To explain the success of a David Duke or a Jesse Helms, one need not posit that all of their supporters are actively hostile to black people; one need simply posit that all of their supporters are fearful, resentful, and terribly tired. The political mastery of the emergent welfare-bashing and quota-bashing Right is in the ability to play to the worst rather than the best in the American character, in order to convince white voters that what they are tired of is being made to bear all the costs of bringing the black folks—the former slaves—into parity with everybody else.

Here, however, Dionne draws a frightening insight from the 1988 Bush campaign, Willie Horton and all:

Bush was widely criticized, especially by Democrats and the press, for the kind of campaign he ran. The question that goes unanswered in the criticism is: What other kind of campaign could he have run and still emerged victorious? The answer is that [Lee] Atwater [Bush's campaign manager] was right in understanding that almost any other kind of campaign would have failed.

What is one to make of this? Are American politics—and not just on race—really this corrupt? One thinks back to Shklar's thesis that voting has always been cherished by Americans as an aspect of citizenship because it differentiates them from slaves. Maybe it does—but, increasingly, one has to wonder about the wisdom, and indeed the intellectual effort, with which the franchise is being exercised. This is not a comment on the outcome of any particular election—George Bush did not rely more on slogans or less on substance than Michael Dukakis, he just did so more successfully—but rather on the political world that has developed in the two decades since the end of the sixties. One saw this theme at its most alarming in the Senate hearings on Anita Hill's charges that she had been sexually harassed by Clarence Thomas. Thomas responded by branding the hearings as motivated by racism, a "high-tech lynching"—notwithstanding that his accuser was also black. This

response so cowed Democratic members of the Judiciary Committee that their questioning was almost pointless—but it also resonated powerfully with black voters, a majority of whom, according to instant surveys, lurched toward support of Thomas, less in a judgment on credibility than in a form of racial solidarity for which men evidently remain more eligible than women.

Perhaps there never was a golden age, an era in which politicians talked about ideas and the people considered their votes with care. But we as a nation are better educated than at any time in our history. Fully one quarter of American adults have college degrees. We have at our command systems of communication that are nearly instantaneous. Those who care to can access voluminous information on nearly any subject. Is it really true that slogans and images are the best that we can do in our national politics? Because if it is, then welfare queens and racial quotas will remain in our national rhetoric into the foreseeable future, and the politics of racial resentment will continue to seethe.

There are, however, beacons of hope. President Bush's surprising but firm decision to sign the Civil Rights Act of 1991 in the face of undisguised fury from his right wing is one such. Some opponents excoriate the legislation as a "quota bill," and one reason that the president's decision to sign it was so surprising was that he had long been among them. Others see the act as an indispensable tool in the battle against employment discrimination, overturning Supreme Court decisions that made it harder for plaintiffs to win. Whatever the act's true nature—and that, in the long run, only the courts will decide—the president, by signing it, has largely removed a potentially divisive issue from the 1992 presidential campaign. Another beacon of hope is the landslide victory of Edwin Edwards over David Duke in the Louisiana gubernatorial election—a beacon, it must be added, that is dimmed somewhat by the grim realization that Duke won a stout majority (55 percent) of the white vote. As America's turbulent struggle over the legacy of the sixties continues, we must pay close attention to these beacons, for there will also be much thrashing about in the dismal swamp of racial politics.

• • •

Notwithstanding the 1991 Civil Rights Act, as long as racial politics are carried out as usual, it is unlikely that America as a whole will find itself so infected with egalitarian fervor that it will enact as law many of the programs (even the nonracial ones) that even now could make a massive difference in the social and economic circumstances of black Americans. Even were the political branches likely to be more responsive, it might well be, as Dionne suggests, that efforts to force a form of equality for which white America is unprepared are likely to prove so unpopular as to be counterproductive. In modern America, this is where the courts generally come in, for in popular mythology, they are always lurking along the sidelines, like referees, ready to do justice as needed. When the political branches seem unwilling to listen to a plea for what many consider simple justice, it is not easy to wait around

hoping that they will change their minds. Thus whatever the costs to both democratic theory and practical politics, the courts, at least since the era of *Brown v. Board of Education,* have seemed an attractive alternative for forcing social change.

The trouble is, and has been for decades, that it is not as easy as some might suppose to read the Constitution in a way that is at once consistent with democratic theory and faithful to the ideals of equality. Indeed, it might be said that ever since *Brown,* constitutional scholars have been searching desperately for a theory that will make the Court's decision look like something more than a simple grab for power. The proposition that judges might inhabit spheres beyond which they should not act gets little attention in American mythology, but it is one that should not be forgotten. Judges are not simply advisers: judicial action, no less than legislative or executive action, ultimately involves the use of force; judges, as the late Robert Cover wrote, are people of violence.

Which is where *Brown* comes in. The *Brown* decision culminated decades of careful, painstaking litigation, gradually chiseling away at the edifice of segregation under the direction of Thurgood Marshall in accordance with a design by Charles Hamilton Houston and William Hastie. *Brown* was no sledgehammer; by the time the case was decided in 1954, so many lesser cases pointed the way that the result was a plausible outgrowth of the precedents. Still, the Court's unanimous rejection of the "equal-but-separate" doctrine created in *Plessy v. Ferguson* caused considerable controversy. Legal scholars were disturbed; the authors of the Fourteenth Amendment had clearly meant to leave segregated schools untouched. By what authority, then, did the justices now decide that the framers were wrong and their own moral compasses a better guide for the nation?

This mystery has motivated scholarship on constitutional law for nearly four decades. The *Brown* decision has become an unchallengeable element of the political fundament. Presidents may run on platforms promising to nominate justices who do not believe in the right of abortion, but none would dare promise to try to overturn *Brown.* Yet tying *Brown* to a firm set of constitutional moorings has always been a problem. Laurence H. Tribe and Michael C. Dorf, in a provocative little book entitled *On Reading the Constitution,* want to resolve this and similar dilemmas by suggesting that our theories of constitutional interpretation are the real problem. The process of adjudicating constitutional cases, they seem to suggest, is like adding to a story, which means that it can take many directions. What matters most, they explain, is less the selection of the correct rule to discipline the act of interpretation than that the justices keep the story headed in the right direction—one of those presumptions that works only when one knows what the right direction is.

Tribe and Dorf themselves are good storytellers. Dramatic tension is generated as their villain—the jurisprudence of original understanding, championed, in different senses, by Robert Bork and Justice Antonin Scalia—tries to run rampant over individual rights, and is defeated (or will be, because the story is set largely in the future) by a series of arguments against the coherence and morality of originalism as interpretive strategy. Every act of interpretation, Tribe and Dorf correctly note, requires a choice of interpretive rules. They deny that the text itself generates a set of best rules by virtue of its role as a text, and of course they are right to do so. They are sensitive, moreover, to what it is that sets the constitutional text, and its interpretations, apart from others texts: when the Court says: "This is what the Constitution means," the real-world effect is very different from what happens when a literary scholar says, "This is what *Hamlet* means." The Court governs, and its edicts, even if meant as interpretations of law, actually set national policy. (That's why judges are people of violence.)

Some scholars (myself among them) have argued that for just this reason, the awesome political power that it wields, the Supreme Court must select interpretive rules that narrowly cabin its freedom. Tribe and Dorf, however, have little patience with such an approach. They seem to prefer to do their interpretation in reverse, to begin with the answer and then find the provision of the Constitution best interpreted to support it, or, as they put it, to bear the weight. One can well understand that a legislature must act in this fashion, but to assign such a role to a court (supreme or not) is something of an act of political desperation. In this vision, *Brown* was rightly decided not because the text, structure, and history of the Fourteenth Amendment required it, but because the text, structure, and history of the Fourteenth Amendment are able to support it. Of course, the text and structure of the Fourteenth Amendment might plausibly support *Plessy v. Ferguson,* too—but that is not, for Tribe and Dorf, an important problem. *Brown* is better than *Plessy,* apparently, because it moves in the right direction.

Because they want to deny the possibility of a single best meaning, Tribe and Dorf select the metaphor of constitutional adjudication as a conversation (although they credit the metaphor to Robert Fisher and Barack Obama rather

The dialogue about rights has gone on mostly *around* black people rather than *with* them

than to its originator, the late Alexander Bickel). The Constitution evolves, they argue, as long as the conversation continues.

But dialectical methods have a number of well-known flaws, among them two related ones with which Tribe and Dorf fail to deal: first, the dialectic requires rules for determining not only what counts as an argument but who counts as an arguer; second, the dialectic places at a disadvantage people who simply do not argue as well as others or do not have ready access to the forums in which the conversation takes place.

For black Americans, these are omissions that matter. A principal frustration with the dialogue about rights is that it is dialogue that has gone on mostly *around* black people rather than *with* them. The trouble, then, is that if Tribe and Dorf really want to free the Constitution from all of the baggage of the original understanding and the intent of the Founders, what they would put in its place seems to be a Constitution whose meaning is de-

termined by the moral reasoning of well-educated elites. Is this a form of reasoning with which black people should feel comfortable?

Guido Calabresi has pointed out that the Supreme Court, by preempting moral debate on the issue of abortion, has in effect told immigrants who might be strongly of different views that they are not welcome, not genuine members of the American polity, unless they concur in the vision of abortion as a fundamental right. The elites have made up their mind; there is no need for further discourse, and those who demand it are seen as aberrant, somehow un-American.

In much the same way, most of the debate over race has been carried on around, rather than including, the people of color who are most directly affected by it. Robert Woodson, a sometime critic of the liberal orthodoxy on civil rights, is said to have brought the Fairmont Conference, organized as a forum for alternative (read: conservative) black views, nearly to a standstill when he stood at the lectern and complained that just like the liberals (as he described them), the conservatives were discussing how to solve the problems of the poorest members of the black community without bothering to consult any of those affected by the policies under discussion.

This determination to be part of the dialogue rather than simply an object of it is an important motivation for the scholars who have formed what has become known as the Critical Race Theory movement: it is past time, they declare, to bring the excluded voices of oppressed people of color into the conversation about legal meaning. The thesis on its face is so obviously sensible that there are times when I wish I shared their faith that law professors can fairly be considered part of the excluded; or that the oppressed share a distinct point of view that is not being heard; or that one can decide which voices are entitled to how much weight in advance of hearing what it is that the voices are saying.

But I don't. I am as suspicious of dialogues as anybody else, but I am equally concerned about efforts to declare certain opinions ex ante superior to others. Patricia Williams, a law professor who is prominent in the Critical Race Theory movement, has written that what the battle over voices is about is not whose voice should be privileged, but rather whether any voices should be. The goal of Critical Race Theory, in this vision, is not to supplant one hierarchy with another, but simply to open the field of dialogue to points of view it hasn't heard. I hope so.

I am not ready to think of myself as a Critical Race Theorist, and neither are the members of the movement. I continue to be deeply concerned at the idea that one can judge anything about the worthiness of a point of view because of the background—racial, sexual, social, economic—of the speaker. I am a bit of a dinosaur in these matters: I prefer to assess arguments, not the people making them. My concern about dialogue is simply to ensure that as many people as possible have the chance to be heard. But it is important not to confuse the question of whether one has been heard with the question of whether one has been persuasive.

Still, the critics are surely right to question the moral worthiness of a constitutional dialogue carried on simply among the elites who believe that they can reason their way to the best answers without consulting those affected. This difficulty certainly is not limited to issues of race and oppression. The principal weakness of the dialogic models of constitutional review is not that some voices are excluded, but that, in the end, the same people always get to do the talking. In John Sayles's fine film *Lianna,* the title character, married to a college professor far better educated than she is, at one point delivers herself of a splendid line that runs something like this: "Just because you can argue better than me doesn't mean you're right."

The constitutional conversation that Tribe and Dorf envision is carried on essentially in the service of expressly liberal ends (although they do express some hesitation about the Court's abortion decision, *Roe v. Wade*). The story is moving in the right direction, one might say, as long as the good guys are winning the constitutional battles. Tribe and Dorf, however, fear that the current Court is moving the story in the wrong direction, perhaps even backwards, and, one presumes, the replacement of Thurgood Marshall with Clarence Thomas, which took place after the book was written, will provide more grist for this particular mill.

Still, one ought not miss the possibility that the ascent of a Justice Thomas, like the move of the Court away from the liberal agenda, might, for the Left, be a blessing, and not much disguised either. If the Court is less and less the protector of rights, it will be more and more irrelevant to our national moral conversations, which, save in exceptional circumstances, it should be. I pass here the question of which circumstances are sufficiently exceptional that judicial intervention is necessary. Presumably, every reader has his or her favorites; my claim is simply that they should be few. The more often one believes that the courts should impose the moral rule that one is unable to win through democratic processes, the less one really believes in democracy or, for that matter, in the good will of one's fellow citizens. If one believes that nearly all of one's moral preferences should be imposed through judicial fiat, then one becomes morally a zealot and politically an autocrat.

People at work for progressive causes should be the last to abandon the democratic ideal. One wonders, then, when the Left began so to lose touch with the nation that it imagined that all great social changes could (and should) be accomplished through the judicial process. Perhaps the Left was seduced by *Brown,* misunderstanding both the provenance and the legacy of that decision. For

Courts do not always act best when they do the right thing

Brown, although not always taught this way, was the Court at its best, making changes through small increments, each one changing the law only a little from that which had existed before. *Brown* is seen as a radical departure from *Plessy,* and it was—but the Court, spurred by the legal work of the NAACP Legal Defense Fund, had been chipping away at that particular edifice for two decades

before knocking down what was left in 1954.

Courts act best when they act slowly. The result is that they do not always act best when they do the right thing. To demand, all at once, that judges simply do justice—keep the story going in the right direction—is, finally, to invite a reaction from those not ready to change so fast. That is the reaction that has recently so battered the Supreme Court with a string of unashamedly ideological appointments. The open and obvious litmus tests for nominees are disastrous for the ideal of an independent judiciary, but the "we-have-the-votes-so-do-the-right-thing" mentality with which many on the Left celebrated the work of the Supreme Court in the sixties and seventies was just as disastrous for the ideal of democratic dialogue. After all, even if, as Tribe and Dorf suggest, the society should keep its stories going in the right direction, it hardly follows that it is the judges who must be the writers.

The point is emphatically not that all change must be slow, or that the possibility of reaction is a reason not to try. The point is only that the ease with which reaction can be generated when courts act in ways that are unpopular reveals the weakness of the judiciary as an agent of social change. If Tribe and Dorf are right about the direction the country should go, they should of course choose to litigate when they can—but most of the time, they should skip the courts and take their case to the people. The American people, of course, are not easily swayed, and sometimes the inborn resistance to change that seems to be a concomitant of the inborn suspicion of authority in general and the government in particular looms like Everest in the path of a social movement. The People—let's give capitalization where capitalization is due—have about them a great inertia.

But just as a body at rest tends to remain at rest, a body in motion tends to remain in motion. If one can just get the people moving, they will move more forcefully, if also more sluggishly, than any court possibly can. They do not, however, move over a perfect surface: social and economic friction, sooner or later, will bring them to a halt. At such moments—we are in one now—forces on the other side will try to push back. If all the good guys are busy down at the Supreme Court, filing petitions and arguing cases, the effort to push back will be fairly easy, especially because a lot of people, angry that the Court is telling them what to do, will already be looking for that little push. The reason that one ultimately can circumvent the Court is precisely that it doesn't change direction easily. The natural pigheadedness of the judiciary is its strength, but also its weakness. And that, too, is a reading of the Constitution.

• • •

All of which leaves us with the following peculiar result: If Shklar is right, then the most important aspect of American citizenship is the avoidance of the trappings of slavery. If Dionne is right, then the people who see themselves as bearing the costs of the removal of those trappings get mad enough to ensure that the people who have reduced the value of their sta-tus indicia will pay for what they have done. In an electoral democracy, making them pay means replacing them. This means that as long as racism is widespread, the political branches cannot be expected to act for very long in the cause of black freedom. So unless Tribe and Dorf are right in their confidence in moral conversation, progress is impossible.

The trouble is, Tribe and Dorf are right about dialogue but wrong about courts. Their method of reading the Constitution simply means that educated elites get to settle all the moral questions. The people of the United States in whose name the Constitution is written essentially get left out of the argument, at least if they want to argue for the various illiberal positions that Tribe and Dorf reject. Among those left out are the majority of black Americans, most of whom, surveys show, agree with large parts of the conservative social agenda.

Besides, we live in E. J. Dionne's political world; the ascendant Right has picked off the liberals on the Court one by one. So hardly anybody with the power to do anything about it agrees with Tribe and Dorf anyway. No matter how attractive one might find their vision of constitutional adjudication, it lacks contemporary political relevance. The Constitution that Tribe and Dorf envision is not the Constitution as read by its authoritative interpreters, the justices of the Supreme Court of the United States.

Does this mean that progress is impossible? No, because even though Tribe and Dorf are probably wrong, Dionne may also be wrong—not in the broad sweep of his argument, but in the essential pessimism of his vision. Yes, there is widespread racism in America, and, yes, American voters have largely turned their animosity on the forces deemed responsible for the massive social upheavals of the sixties. But that is not the same as saying that no progress has been made, or that the time-line of racial progress, despite occasional wobbling and dips, does not generally trend upward. For even if a majority of white people (as surveys show) continue to accept the myth of black intellectual inferiority, the majority is smaller than it was thirty years ago—and, more important, surveys further indicate that whatever the racist stereotypes that most white people still accept, huge majorities reject the model of entrenched discrimination that the stereotype was once thought to entail. There is still a very long way to go, but progress has been made. True, we have lately seen a retrenchment, but today's harsh economic conditions that have contributed to the recent flaring of racial resentment cannot (one hopes) continue forever. Perhaps America is less hostile than confused, and, as Dionne tells us, terribly tired.

But race clearly continues to matter, an ominous signal if, as may be most important of all, Judith Shklar turns out to be wrong. Perhaps she has her status attributes inverted. Perhaps the key point is not that Americans defined citizenship in a way that excluded the attributes of slavery, but that they defined the attributes of slavery in a way that excluded citizenship. Enslavement was not simply an unwanted status; it was a status assigned to people of a particular color for blatantly racist reasons. Black people

were not despised because they were slaves; they were slaves because they were despised. This bold fact must make us ever wary, for the despising of black people, even if diminished, continues, as we rush toward the new century.

The difference in the degree of racism between our era and eras past is a difference that matters: if racism decreases, the incentive to draw the citizenship lines in a way that keeps black people in thrall will decrease as well. Thus our politics might not be quite as virulently antiegalitarian as Dionne seems to think. Besides, race might have been most of the sixties, but it wasn't all of the sixties. So perhaps what white Americans hate about the sixties is not the forceful elevation in the status of black Americans; perhaps what they hate instead is the rest of what they built.

This is not to say that most white people necessarily *like* black people, or, for that matter, that most black people like white people; racial hostility smolders, and, sometimes, bursts into flames. But attitudes or motivations matter far less than actions, and the degree of racism that persists matters less than the number of opportunities that exist. At this moment, the pie is not growing, at least not very fast; still, our slice of it is far larger than in the past. Traditional forms of racial discrimination turn out to be inefficient. American society, although just starting to recognize the fact, simply cannot afford any longer to exclude talented, ambitious people on the basis of color.

So perhaps the fact that there is no longer so forceful (or successful) an effort to draw the lines of basic freedoms in a way that excludes black people is evidence that there is less desire than there once was to exclude us—not because white racism has disappeared, but because tolerance is able to exist alongside it, and, sometimes, to trump it. Perhaps white people are more willing than in the past to have black people share in the American dream, as long as they are satisfied that black people have earned their share. Some might bristle at this notion, asking how white people dare to judge the black people the nation has so long oppressed, a perfectly fair question. But I propose a different response: as we survey the moral detritus that the sixties left, is it clear that we who are black should *want* a piece of that dream?

Maybe we should—not because the dream is itself the ideal, but because it holds within its confines the seeds of change. "But suppose I don't want it," asked Langston Hughes in his sharp little poem, "Question and Answer," "Why take it?" His answer was simple and firm: *"To remake it."*

IS GOD NEUTRAL?

V. Y. Mudimbe

Yahweh said to Moses, "Why do you cry to me? Tell the children of Israel to march on."
—Exodus *14:15*

I am frightened because I have some experience of the awfulness of violence.
—Desmond Tutu, *Archbishop of Cape Town*

Theology today is inductive and empirical in approach. It is the ever-changing struggle to give expression to man's response to God. It is always inadequate and provisional. Variety is to be welcomed because no one approach can ever do justice to the transcendent reality of God.
—Maurice Wiles, *Regius Professor of Divinity, Oxford University*

These books offer a new vision of Christianity in the Third World. Each testifies to the basic tenets of Christianity while providing a radical new perspective whose roots go back to the 1960s and 1970s—that of a religious practice which, according to Paul de Meester, has moved from a ministry strictly centered around transcendence to a new one more concerned with the concrete existential conditions of humans. Despite obvious divergences, there is a common thread of reference uniting these various contributions: a critical rereading of the Bible enabled by what has been called "liberation theology." The recent collapse of Soviet Marxism has, indeed, raised questions about the pertinence and credibility of these intellectual and sociopolitical policies—since, at least in the United States during the Reagan administration, "liberation theology" was perceived as a means of fostering an international Marxist agenda. Yet the problems addressed by these books—poverty, marginalization, exploitation—are not going to disappear. It is obvious that these types of study will continue to foreground them, thus giving a voice to the voiceless.

Preach Liberty by Steve Bachman, a practicing attorney in the United States born in 1951 and raised in Indiana as a Lutheran, undertakes the task of reclaiming "the Bible for the people." It explicitly opposes "the interpretations of right-wing television and radio preachers" for whom "the Bible has become no more than a justification for the mistreatment

By Pierre & Gilles

St. Pierre Marie Chanel

of children, the subordination of women, and the undermining of prospects for peace between nations or the survival of the planet." The rationale of the argument springs from an alternative reading, which focuses upon "liberating figures" such as Moses, seen as an inventor of "boycott and general strike," King David, seen, at the beginning of "his career, as a Hebrew Robin Hood" and, indeed, Jesus, seen as a hero "executed by the authorities for political agitation." The themes for each chapter reconceptualize carefully chosen biblical verses and passages. They include headings such as "Egalitarianism," "No Social Pretense," "Peace," "Public Decency," "Respect for the Environment," "Respect for Women," "Respect for Minorities," "Respect for Justice," "Social Justice: Against the Exploitation of the Poor," "Social Justice: Affirmatively Aiding the Underprivileged," "Social Justice: Assuring Fair Practices," and "Righteousness over Ritual." Bachman's project seems, in short, primarily didactic. It outlines ways of resisting racist and sexist interpretations of the biblical messages. However, this very intellectual resistance might itself constitute the weakness of his project. The task is to explain how a biblical text can be found to justify every will to power and truth, be it colonialism, Nazism, racism, sexism, or, indeed, Bachman's "progressivism." The author responds:

Our concern with Biblical politics has focused on the matter at another level. For this work, the politics of the original writings is less interesting than the politics of the final assemblage. For some 2,000 years what we know as "the Bible" has been consulted as a moral authority, by groups as diverse as first century mendicants, 10th century European barbarians, 17th century Puritans, and 20th century African-Americans. It is now a part of our culture. The point of Preach Liberty *is simply to note the extent to which certain fundamentals of our culture ground themselves in basic values such as decency, equality, generosity, and social justice. In this epoch of aggressive greed, it is too easy to forget that these values form the foundation of a moral culture.*

Thomas Christensen's *An African Tree of Life* demonstrates, in the words of his publisher, "how mission involves not only a 'bringing-to' a people, but a 'discovering-of' those deep symbols in human culture and God's creation which, in the light of the Gospel, draw humanity to Christ. This book . . . explores the stories and rituals of the Gbaya people of the Cameroon and the Central African Republic. These deep symbols are typically centered, not in the esoteric or exotic, but in the familiar and everyday. Christensen focuses on the especial importance of the peace-bringing tree of life—the *soré* tree—central to the lives and worship of the Gbaya."

Christensen was educated at the Lutheran School of Theology in Chicago, and received a Th.D. from the same school in 1984. At the time of the publication of *An African Tree of Life*, he was associated with the Ecole de Théologie in Meiganga, Cameroon. He defines himself as "a bicultural Christian . . . fascinated by the limiting but also limitless ethnic and cultural ways in which the one gospel of life and salvation . . . keeps coming to ever new expression among us and in the midst of all people." His book gives a detailed description of the symbolism of the *soré* tree, considered among the Gbaya as a sign of peace and as "a doorway opening up a new possibility for life with other people." In a perfectly ethnophilosophical manner, Catholics and Lutherans in Cameroon have seen in the *soré* symbolism a synecdoche of Jesus. Christensen explains how the *soré* functions as a referent with different levels of symbolic meanings: concrete, insofar as the tree and its leaves are considered as the best means "for making a new village, for cooling murder, or for reconciling two villages"; operational, particularly in ritual contexts, where, from the concrete to the abstract level, the *soré* establishes codes for interpreting (through analogies and similitudes) "the ever-fresh creativity and freedom of life"; finally, a positional level which, according to Christensen, "refer(s) [the *soré*] to the totality of cultural elements in Gbaya society and illustrates that its meanings may vary in different contexts."

After an introductory chapter on "deep symbols we share on the run" (which conjectures on the *soré* tree as "A New Naming of Jésus"), Christensen begins by comparing what Christianity offers with what it gains in the Gbaya settings. The first six chapters analyze how the meaning and processes of Gbaya meals rationally lead to the significance of connected rituals, sacrifices, purification, and cleanliness rites. Then follow four sociological chapters on growing up in Gbaya society; the Gbaya dance of *habi* or initiation; the rites of reconciliation; the case of Karnu who resisted French colonialization and who, in African versions of his resistance, is depicted as a "prophet," in European versions as a xe-

nophobe. The last three chapters of Christensen are more theological and are concerned with topics such as the symbolism of the *soré* tree, the Gbaya Naming of Jesus, and theology as the Way to Missiology.

There is in Christensen's project a commitment: to put together arguments for cultural coincidences; namely that there are, in the Gbaya tradition, signs indicating the Christian revelation. Thus the author locates in the Gbaya tree of life both a particular case and an image of the Gospel's message. In this intellectual process, which draws on the classical method of looking for *Evangelii praeparationes,* that is, searching for stepping stones of Christianity, what might be obscured is the reality of the conflicts that exist between cultures and between different interpretations of fundamental events and symbols.

In *Nicaragua's Other Revolution,* Michael Dodson, a professor of political science at Texas Christian University, and Laura Nuzzi O'Shaughnessy, an associate professor of government at St. Lawrence University, address precisely this issue of interpretive conflict. They focus on the relationship between the traditional Christian Church and the Prophetic Church, religion and revolutionary struggle. The study as a whole situates itself at the intersection of Christianity and its "capacity to shape political life," especially in relation to the challenge of development.

In the first part of the book, Dodson and O'Shaughnessy analyze the "Nicaraguan revolution" and its antecedents, dwelling on "the religious roots of North American politics," and present what they consider to be "patterns of political development in the Americas," their general project being to account for differences and specificities. They assert, for example, that "the two halves of the Americas do appear to have a great deal in common in their historical development. . . . In practice, however, their colonial experiences were sufficiently different to lay the basis for a historical relationship plagued by misunderstanding."

The second part offers an elaborate analysis of "the nature of the Catholic Church and its historic impact on society and politics in Central America," unfolding two conceptions of the church: a traditional one, which emphasizes the importance of the *Magisterium,* and, since the Vatican II Council and the Medellin Conference, a different understanding of the church as "a historical community of believers, or the *people of God.*" The traditional view tended to give precedence to the institutional hierarchy as an embodiment of the church and the faith. The second had democratizing implications, and inevitably led to a greater participation and responsibility of the "people of God" in the church and an antithetical postulation favoring the disinherited and the poor. As a matter of fact, even though the newer view "did not imply a rejection of the *Magisterium* but rather an insistence that the hierarchy take account of, be accountable to, the entire community of the faithful," it divided the church into two factions: a traditional, hierarchical church, on the one hand, and, on the other hand, a popular, grass-roots church. The Sandinistas in Nicaragua accommodated this newer vision in their politics and aroused the ire of the institutional church and of the rich.

The tension between the two views raises a fundamental question: what is the church? Dodson and O'Shaughnessy respond by simply presenting a case study. The third part of their book powerfully articulates the contradictions arising, directly or indirectly, from this tension in Nicaraguan society. The confrontation is not only about a religious, orthodox geography opposing a new imagination and its references. What is at stake is an immense struggle concerning power and the possibility of alternatives by reference to the credibility of a dominant discourse and its normativity. The Sandinistas lost, as we know. However, the question about the nature of the church remains and is of concern for numerous believers in many countries. In all the Third World, it appears to be linked to tasks of development and the promotion of the human dignity of the poor and the exploited. Dodson and O'Shaughnessy rightly note that the Medellin Conference "called the churches to be servants of the people. This implied that the religious authority of the churches would be a function of their faithfulness in pursuing the integral development of the people rather than in preserving the continuity of their ancient and venerable institutions."

Jean-Marc Ela, a Cameroonian Catholic priest, articulates this new option from an African viewpoint in *My Faith as an African.* One would have expected to find the author, who holds a doctorate in theology from the University of Strasbourg and a doctorate in sociology from the University of Paris, in a university chair or teaching at a major seminary instead of the northern Cameroon, an extremely impoverished area where he has been living and doing pastoral work for more than ten years among the Kirdis. It is a challenge he has chosen, witness for the exploited:

I find myself in a northern region affected by a state of invisible slavery, as the older priest, Baba Simon, explained on the night of my arrival. My first impression was that the people of the high country among whom I would live for many years are not merely rejected and bereft of decision-making power; they are also totally defenseless and deprived. The mountain peoples are poor because they have been exploited and oppressed for generations, not because they do not work.

What kind of Christianity should a black priest actualize among the poorest of his brothers? Ela deals straight with his convictions:

Faced with this situation [the exploitation of the peasants in northern Cameroon], I had to free myself immediately from a certain number of constraints in order to get a fresh perspective on the problems of my mission. I did not feel called to become the manager of a form of decaying Christianity, bound up in its doctrine and discipline, so I decided to keep my distance from a model of a church designed elsewhere by people who do not know the conditions of the mountain peoples. I had to refuse the false security available to someone who moves into another's house. . . . In order to capture the meaning, I had to live in insecurity. That led to radical questions: "What is the cutting edge of the gospel that can be most directly accessible and meaningful for these people? How shall we live our faith, and thus create around us a desire for the living God? Don't we have to convert ourselves before preaching conversion to others?" Everything impelled me to abandon the traditional Christian questions and patiently let another language of the gospel burst forth from the life of the people.

My Faith as an African comments on this quest and the problems it implies. How does one revalorize polluted beliefs and revise and refound political fables about salvation on the authority of the Christian revelation? Ela, as Simon E. Smith puts it in the foreword to this English version, "takes us by the hand into village Africa, helps us feel the painful reality behind the statistics of exploitation, and shares with us the pragmatic grounding of his conviction that every authentic inculturation of the Christian faith is conditioned on the liberation of the oppressed." Ela's strengths reside in this sometimes iconoclastic ambition.

Part one of the book, "Reawakening the Wellsprings," is a kind of spiritual autobiography that first presents Ela's itinerary and unveils his significant discovery of the "sacrament of community"—"where people aspire to escape from misery and captivity, we must move from catechism to revelation." He also reflects on the possible connections between African ancestors and Christian faith which, from the background of a reconstructed African symbolism, wants to reformulate the issue on how to live in Christ, the role of sacrifice and the styles of Christian celebrations, veneration of saints and preaching the Gospel, in an African context. Next, he meditates on how to tell "the story of God's Revelation" and inculturate Christianity in both the African memory and the present. This section concludes with programmatic pages on the "future of local communities" in which Ela questions the power of the clergy and reconsiders the issue of leadership in Christian communities.

Part two, "Faith at the Grassroots," concretely illustrates the author's advocacy for the poor by discussing, from a biblical and Christian perspective, health issues, the economic exploitation of the Kirdis, and liberation theology's demands. God is not neutral, asserts Ela, since "the 'locus' in which God is experienced lies in the promise of a liberation continually renewed"; moreover, "The presence of misery and oppression is a basic form of the 'sin of the world' that contradicts the kingdom of justice inaugurated by Jesus of Nazareth." In the last part of the book, Ela "missiologizes," from an interpretation of the Gospel and the calvary of the poor, the spirit of African Catholicism in the 1980s and the new requirements for "speaking about God."

By now, one fact has been established: we no longer need to discuss the principle of the possibility or legitimacy of an African theology. The principle has been established. Appeals have come from the magisterium itself, inviting Africans to assume their own responsibilities for building a theology incarnated in the living thought of the men and women of our continent.

. . . .

The recitation of formulas is no longer important to us. What is important is that we try to extricate the contemporary meaning of the Word of God and of the plan of salvation, beginning with the historical understanding that Africans have of themselves and of the world.

Ela's analysis is impressive, solidly grounded in the Scriptures and, even, strictly under canonical control. He quotes profusely from the Bible and pontifical documents. He might be, and radically, in favor of a reconversion of the classical understanding of what the church is. Nonetheless, he affirms himself a faithful son of the church, even though he does not hesitate to raise delicate questions about the pitfalls of Africanization. In any case, he explicitly questions some official policies of African Catholicism:

A liturgy using indigenous music might cause Africans to forget that they are human beings under domination. Expressing their calvary through the rhythm of their own music gives them the hope of celestial happiness—as happened through Negro spirituals in America. When Christianity was implanted in Africa, something important happened at the same time: while the converts were distracted by the Bible thrust into their hands, their land was stripped from them.

. . . .

The rhythm of drums and balaphons within our churches cannot shelter us Africans from the threats of the "weapons of food" brought to bear on peasants crushed by the dictatorship of peanuts, cocoa, and cotton. The famine of the Sahel appears to be not so much a natural calamity or an outcome of climate as a result of a policy of oppression and domination over peasants and herdsmen.

Ela's commitment to the cause of the poor is inspiring. The substance of the book—which carries forward the preoccupations of his preceding publications

African Cry (1986), *Voici le temps des héritiers* (1981), *L'Afrique des villages* (1982), *La ville en Afrique noire* (1983)—reflects a number of major points also present in the more recent study by Dodson and O'Shaughnessy on Nicaragua. In brief, it is faith and faithfulness to the church that make these intellectual enterprises possible. From a strictly agnostic position, one might wonder why this dependence on an institutional church should be needed in order to conceive and commit oneself to a task of development. Is development unthinkable without Christianity? Can theories of development be based on something other than the church's connections? Why should theology colonize sciences and techniques of development?

The ambiguity of theological projects cannot but lead us back to an essential question: how are we to comprehend the credibility of Christianity in the Third World? The late Michel de Certeau, a scholar and a Catholic churchman, notes in *The Practice of Everyday Life* that "the credibility of a discourse is what first makes believers act in accord with it. It produces practitioners. To make people believe is to make them act. But by a curious circularity, the ability to make people act—to write and machine bodies—is precisely what makes people believe. Because the law is already applied with and on bodies, 'incarnated' in physical practices, it can accredit itself and make people believe that it speaks in the name of the 'real.' " In this sense, a receptive reader of liberation theology understands that the Latino-American experience and scholarship of Michael Dodson and Laura Nuzzi O'Shaughnessy, as well

as the knowledge and intellectual generosity of Jean-Marc Ela's *Faith of an African,* are, essentially, even in their signs of revolt and impatience against the church, witnessing to it, to this institution that gives both meaning and hope to the contradictory expectations of the "people of God."

The Missionary and the Diviner by Michael C. Kirwen exemplifies the preceding analysis. The book, according to Laurenti Magesa's introduction, "tackles what is perhaps one of the most central concerns for African theology today. What, from a Christian perspective, is the worth of the pre-Christian divine self-manifestation in Africa?" It clearly inscribes itself in the problematics of the African theology of inculturation. Michael C. Kirwen, a Maryknoll missionary in Tanzania since 1963, relates a personal experience that might recall the spiritual itinerary of Jean-Marc Ela. The only difference between the two, and it is a major one, is that Kirwen is a white American missionizing in Africa and Ela is a black African doing the same job among his people. Yet their testimonies coincide perfectly and the exploration they witness to in the name of Christianity seems similar. Kirwen writes:

> *Over the more than twenty years that I have lived in Africa as a missionary, I have been deeply affected and changed by my African friends. I have not been 'converted' from my Christianity, but I have come to understand and live my religion differently and better through what I learned from them. Many of my African friends actually converted to Christianity; I would be ashamed if this had not also meant that they appreciated more*

fully their own African beliefs, so that they became better persons.

The book is a pedagogical tool: an introduction to a present-day practice of missionizing in Africa. Kirwen converses with a diviner–witch doctor on such subjects as the idea of God, the source of evil, divination, and remembrance or resurrection. The dialogues are contextualized and favor an explicitly pluralist epistemology. They claim to follow "the conversational style . . . [of] a Luo diviner from Nyambogo Village in North Mara, Tanzania." But the whole thing is a montage: "the diviner featured in the book is a composite figure," but "the settings and scenes in the book are descriptions of actual places and events," and "moreover, the conversations reported . . . are based on actual discussions; they are not contrived." On the other hand, let us note that the author insists on the peculiarity of his dialogical method:

(The) words, judgements, and observations (of the diviner) were drawn from live research sessions, which I—together with my students and African informants—conducted with a variety of African religious leaders over a ten-year period from 1974 to 1984. . . .

The commentaries that I have appended to each chapter seek to delineate the important issues and dilemmas arising out of the conversations that are relevant to the Christians of the Western world. This kind of reflection represents a type of reverse mission in which traditional African theology challenges, judges, and enriches Western Christian theology.

The book has been praised in Tanzania. "Well-researched . . . recommended reading to any serious-minded pastoral agent, and to transcultural theologians," writes Joseph T. Agbasiere from the Gaba Pastoral Institute. "Kirwen has skillfully combined a deep knowledge of Christian theology, his many years of productive pastoral work in Tanzania, and a systematic and tireless search for empirical explanations to the complex co-existence between Christianity and African indigenous religions," adds B. A. Rwezaura from the University of Dar es Salaam.

One would tend to trust these specialists despite the fact that the method used by Kirwen draws its strength from concordist techniques that seem to confuse the *documents* of revelation, the *vouloir dire* or message of gods given to two radically different traditions, and the *vouloir entendre* or the perceived meaning that founds the beliefs of Kirwen and his African interlocutors. The montage, at any rate, has produced an essay which is, in reality, fiction. It could have been molded as well into a novel, and its credibility and force would not have been transformed. In effect, both the essay and the potential novel would be situated at the point where social and religious African beliefs and practices intersect with the poetic imagination and theological techniques of Michael Kirwen.

Paul de Meester's *Université et Conscience Chretienne,* modestly subtitled as "Pages from a Professor's Notebook" testifies also to a theology of inculturation, and in an original way. The book consists of quasi-autobiographical essays that develop as meditations on a variety of topics such as the African university, education, ideologies, the study of classics, a trip to South Africa, the Virgin Mary, death, etc., all of them under the umbrella of a challenging entry: the goodness of human beings and the suffering of peoples. Paul de Meester, presently the chairman of the Department of Classics at the University of Lubumbashi in Zaïre, is a Belgian Jesuit who has been living in Africa for more than thirty years, serving as pastoral agent and university professor. His book is simultaneously an endless production of an identity (African, Jesuit, Christian) and a reflection on cultural, social, spiritual, and textual corruptions and the avatars of an intellectual activity in Mobutu's Zaïre. Autobiographical meditations can, as proved here, illumine the heterogeneity of procedures and scandalous networks that can progressively deprive a human milieu of its motivations and hopes. Modest, unpretentious, de Meester's book signifies perhaps mainly a longing for a purity that is challenged every day by the mediocrity of some people and the bad faith of others. Here is a significant pronouncement, and one of the strongest from the essays: "The needs of the poor have priority over those of the rich; the freedom of the weak has priority over the liberty of the powerful; the integration in the society of marginalized people has priority over the preservation of the order that excludes them."

Challenge and longing for purity are expressions that could also be used about *Trapped in Apartheid* by Charles Villa-Vicencio, an associate professor of religious studies at the University of Cape Town, South Africa. Archbishop Desmond M. Tutu considers the book to be "a devastating indictment of the so-called English-speaking anti-apartheid churches." Allan A. Boesak's backing of the book is straightforward: "This is more than just a very good book. It is a call to conversion."

Trapped in Apartheid has two parts. The first is a sociohistorical and theological study of English-speaking churches in South Africa; the second, a sociological and theological analysis that focuses on two themes: the first being Religion as domination and rebellion, and the second, a liberating Ecclesiology. The thesis (which, paradoxically, might be seen also as the conclusion) is as follows:

> Concerned to preserve its place and influence in society, the dominant church has rationalized the demands of the gospel, heeding the demands of the rich and powerful rather than the cries of the poor and oppressed. Theologically compelled to show charity and given to dealing kindly with those who suffer most, the English-speaking churches have nevertheless refused to contradict the dominant social order or reject the legitimacy of the state; thus they find themselves trapped in apartheid.

In the first part, the author attempts convincingly to associate sociohistorical evidence of the churches' practices with the political and economic constraints that controlled them. Chapters 2 ("Imperialists and Missionaries") and 3 ("Gold, Politics, and the Churches") address the scandal of "missionaries [who] were simply not able to distinguish between the message of the gospel and the cultural baggage of imperialism." They problematized the contradictions of churches that, on the one hand, in the name of theology, condemn apartheid and, on the other hand, did not "attempt to consider an alternative economic or political program." From this background, the two chapters of the second part forcefully argue for a conversion. They are both politically committed and "prophetic." The first brings together Karl Marx's critiques of religion as a "compensatory factor" and Max Weber's theory of religion as an option for a "social renewal." The hypothesis redescribes a classical proposition: theology cannot be dissociated from its social context and thus if "ecclesial structures which are shared with the dominant classes, are also dominated by these classes, it follows that ideas and programs of action representative of the poor are invariably found in the margins and on the edges of church structures." The second chapter, one of the most central in Villa-Vicencio's study, elaborates a liberating ecclesiology as a theological imperative, coming from a close reading of basic Christian texts. With competence, Villa-Vicencio rethinks and reformulates the "mystery of God," "the mis-

sion of Jesus," "the power of the spirit," "the worship of the Church." He then concludes by invoking the "memory of Jesus" ("who identified himself with sinners, publicans, prostitutes and rebels— marginalized peoples") and celebrating "a Christ whose presence continues to be made known in those whom Matthew 25:31–46 defines as the least important people of society."

" 'Too little, too late' is not an inaccurate description of the role of churches in South Africa," states the American theologian Charles E. Curran, in *Transition*. Probably, from this viewpoint, *Trapped in Apartheid* might remain a testimony.

These studies in theology are indicative of a new era. We have come a long way from the theologies of conversion and salvation (whose objectives till the 1940s were still to destroy everything pagan in order to implement Christianity) to this new epoch. Cultural differences and voices that were distorted or silenced can now be seen or heard confronting the gospel. More importantly, it is the nature of Church itself that is thrown into question.

COMMON KNOWLEDGE

A New Oxford Journal

Common Knowledge represents a commitment to go beyond established disciplines and, more importantly, beyond the factions at war in the literary and scholarly world. The idea that intellectual life is composed of "issues," and that issues are shaped like battlefields or game boards—with "sides" that one must "take"—is at best obsolete and impractical. *Common Knowledge* seeks to refine a new skepticism—a postmodern, postwar doubt of claims to knowledge and authority—that presents no obstacle to solidarity.

Common Knowledge publishes work in cultural studies and intellectual history that redefines divisive terms and figures of the past and present in ways that make expanded sympathies possible. The distinguished board of editors feels that it is time to abandon simplistic distinctions—East versus West, Left versus Right, theory versus praxis, modern versus postmodern—and elaborate a basis for practical, common knowledge.

The founders of the journal hope not only to expand common sympathies but explode the conventional format of the journal itself.

REGULAR FEATURES INCLUDE:

Rotating columns from leading names in the field:
Richard Rorty, Adam Michnik, W.V. Quine, Vicki Hearne,
Miroslav Holub, and Paul Feyerabend

"Delayed book reviews"—reviews of long neglected yet
significant works

Reviews of articles from other journals

Fragments, notebooks, letters, and works in progress

Poetry, novels, and verse plays

MOCTEZUMA'S REVENGE

Ilan Stavans

While assimilating, Hispanics, 22 million of the total U.S. population according to the 1990 census and the second-fastest growing minority after the Asians and Pacific Islanders, are behaving somewhat differently from other previous ethnic minorities, including blacks. They are taking longer to learn English, are slower in adapting to the nation's behavioral patterns, have difficulty identifying with the collective symbols, and have championed a method of bilingual education by which they honor their culture and roots. While their working habits leave no question as to their interest in personal self-improvement and social mobility, many are trapped by poverty, drug addiction, out-of-wedlock childbirth, and crime. Government programs to improve their situation have been implemented, with limited success. Only a small number of Hispanics have climbed the social ladder to the middle class. Altogether, a disconcerting reality.

How to explain their tardiness in learning English? What to say about their difficulty with assimilation? Historians, political analysts, and immigration specialists have propounded theories, some eccentric and others quite convincing. The lack of complete trust in any one of them, and the ambiguity of the various administrations in the White House when approaching the issue, may well be part of the problem: while officials endlessly debate a possible solution, Hispanics continue to behave in a manner consistent with their idiosyncrasy.

Among those venturing a theory is Linda Chavez, a Senior Fellow of the Manhattan Institute and an outspoken conservative. A frequent contributor to newspapers and monthlies devoted to national and foreign policy, her views are now summarized in her first book, *Out of the Barrio,* an open attack against bilingual education, an accusation against minority leaders for mishandling Hispanic affairs, and an explanation of why Hispanics *aren't* different from any other ethnic group that preceded them. In eight chapters and an introduction, she offers a proposal to radically transform the government's protection of the Spanish language in the classroom and beyond. She also suggests that the best way

Discussed in this essay

Out of the Barrio: Toward a New Politics of Hispanic Assimilation, *Linda Chavez, New York: Basic Books*

**Linda Chavez,
author of *Out of
the Barrio***

Photo © Bachrach

to bring Hispanics out of the barrio is to stop the senseless comparison between their experience and that of African-Americans. Under no circumstance, Chavez asserts, should Hispanics be treated differently.

Yet the portrait she paints of the ethnic minority is misleading. Although the ground on which her arguments are based is solid and well-researched, Chavez often oversimplifies. She disregards the cultural background and intellectual tradition of Hispanics, reducing their actions to mere statistics and legislative records. As a result, a full understanding of their behavior is overshadowed by numbers and names. And while her proposal to drastically change fed-eral, state, and local legislation is persuasive and may be of some value, it comes late. Chavez's political agenda in *Out of the Barrio* might make sense among a handful of naive Republicans in Washington, D.C., but its timing is far off: whatever road the Hispanic community will take in the near future, Hispanics' attachment to Spanish is already deeply rooted, has been legally encouraged, and is unlikely to disappear miraculously in the next decade.

In this essay I shall address the assets and shortcomings of her book, discuss its structure, and comment on its lack of historical and psychological insight. Because of their diverse backgrounds, Hispanics in the United States cannot follow the same patterns of assimilation other minorities, including the Irish, the Jews, the Germans, the Italians, and even the blacks, have taken before. Although they will eventually adapt, and the stereotypes of the criminal and drug addict will disappear with the help of federal and state funds, it won't happen without generating a profound, irrevocable transformation in the nation at large. The question isn't anymore how to make Hispanics integrate, but how to make the rest of the population accept the collective fate they represent: Spanish in the twenty-first century will unquestionably be one of the nation's vehicles of communication; and the best qualities of Hispanic culture will prevail. My own feeling is that bilingual education is an obstacle in the assimilation process, yet *Out of the Barrio* falls short in explaining why Hispanics are so attached to their mother tongue and culture. Chavez's book never penetrates the Hispanic mind.

First, some general remarks. Chavez, her style leaves no doubt, isn't an engaging writer. She is obsessed with objectivity and straightforwardness. A Hispanic herself and a mother who at some point must have asked herself if her own children deserved, or could benefit from, bilingual education, she nevertheless presents herself as the type of impartial observer who hardly ever includes an insightful personal passage to enlighten an argument and enliven the prose. As a result, *Out of the Barrio* lacks literary power. And although as the author she isn't concerned with high narrative standards, the reader is often bored with repetitive dryness.

The book's structure is untraditional. Instead of starting by addressing Hispanics from a sociological perspective, Chavez enters her topic through the political door, attacking the sort of *bicultural* education they have proudly received; she does this to infuriate her opponents. This upside-down organization is confusing: the question of language is addressed even before the author has explained the cultural background of each of the groups that constitute the Hispanic minority: Cubans, Chicanos, Puerto Ricans, Dominicans, and others from Central America (Nicaragua, Guatemala, El Salvador) and the southern hemisphere (Peru, Colombia, etc.). Chavez leaves the description of who Hispanics are for chapters 5, 6, and 7, as if the Spanish they speak were only an ideological issue, nothing more. But one cannot hope to understand a language without first knowing who its speakers are.

Chavez's introduction is devoted to comparing the African-American experience with that of Hispanics. The opening argument moves around the question: Why are the immigrants from south of the Rio Grande asking for the kind of special treatment blacks received as a consequence of the civil rights movement? *Out of the Barrio* claims that although slavery constitutes an incompatible difference between the two minorities, their recent history (from the sixties on) has striking similarities. The Civil Rights Act of 1964 was a conscious attempt to change the conduct of racist individuals, mainly in the South, against a black population that had suffered centuries of humiliation and violence. In order for discrimination to be forbidden,

African-Americans had to be legally categorized as "disadvantaged citizens" who needed help to achieve a status equal to others. The ideas of equal opportunity and affirmative action that resulted from that legislation were shaped as entitlements that pushed toward desegregation and change. In Chavez's eyes, Hispanics also benefited from these entitlements, but for the wrong reasons. By 1965, this ethnic minority was only 4 percent (some seven million) of the total U.S. population, yet when Hispanic leaders took notice of the huge political triumph made by black people, they fought to extend its scope to their own community. Consequently, they had to fight for a "disadvantaged" status in order to benefit from the war against racism and poverty.

The key issue here is that the economic and social reality shared by Hispanics at the time was very different from that of blacks: while the latter, because of their history, from slavery to the civil rights movement, had a place in the collective consciousness, the former had hardly been noticed at the national level. Chavez is correct, but only partially. The Chicanos, inhabitants of the United States for centuries, officially became part of the Union in 1848 as a consequence of the Mexican War, and constituted an important work force in California, New Mexico, Texas, and Arizona. A small but intellectually active Cuban minority had made its home in Miami, Florida, in the late nineteenth century. And at the time of World War II, a considerable number of Puerto Ricans were already living in New York. Immense waves of Hispanic immigration took place at the end of the fifties and afterward, with the victory of Fidel Castro in Havana and the deterioration of the urban economy and its administration in San Juan. Yet the ground had already been explored by relatives of those families who made it to the east coast and the southern states. Hispanic soldiers, most of them children of poor families, were very much part of World War II, died in action, and were decorated as heroes. Thus, the Hispanic presence before 1960 cannot be ignored. If this ethnic minority fought for the same entitlements granted to blacks after the civil rights movement, it was because, paraphrasing Ralph Ellison, Hispanics were also "invisible" citizens.

To benefit from the entitlements granted to African-Americans, Hispanics, in Chavez's view, had to portray themselves as miserably "disadvantaged." Like actors, they pretended to be what they were not. Were they better off than is commonly believed? *Out of the Barrio* states that while the majority were poor and uneducated Chicanos and Puerto Ricans, with the triumph of the Communist revolution in Cuba in 1959 a million exiles of a different sort made it into the United States—a seventh of the total Hispanic population. Unlike their fellow ethnic-minority members, these Cubans were middle-class citizens with a commendable educational level and an urge to climb the economic hierarchy. To portray them uniformly as "disadvantaged," Chavez claims, is misleading. Yet she fails to understand that the Cuban component, while firmly committed to progress, was waiting for the downfall of Castro's regime. With one leg here and another "at home," their status as newly arrived immigrants is questionable, leaving a considerable margin of doubt as to their day-to-day assimilation. Three decades later, the reality in Havana hasn't changed: they are still eagerly waiting to return and a government in exile has already been selected to replace as soon as possible the Communist in Havana. Thus, their pledge of allegiance remains unfulfilled. On the other hand, in 1965 the rest of the Hispanic population (some six million) either had their citizenship or had lived in this country for a least two generations. And their economic status wasn't at all commendable. The Mexican-Americans were in the Southwest. They became part of the union when Generalísimo Antonio López de Santa Ana sold two-fifths of the Mexican geography to the White House for $15 million. Many were rural workers, at times itinerant cotton or plum pickers, and a vast number lived below the poverty level. The Puerto Ricans, members of a commonwealth since 1898, first migrated to Hawaii and then to the mainland. As Chavez correctly states, World War II and the Korean War, in which more than 100,000 of them participated, were the introduction to a universe beyond their Caribbean island. And although a considerable number ultimately moved to New York in the fifties, their economic situation didn't improve much. Chavez is wrong when she asserts that Hispanics as a whole needed to pretend, to act as if they were poor. The idea itself is offensive.

The entitlements that resulted from the civil rights movement strengthened the ethnic identity of Hispanics, as they did of blacks. A suggestion is made in

Out of the Barrio that this wasn't an awakening but what amounts to the invention of a cultural past. Untrue. With the collapse of the Latin American economies and their huge foreign debt in the eighties, obviously Hispanics in the U.S. now have an envied status vis-à-vis their relatives back home. They have become role models. As inhabitants of the world's greatest power, their money, no matter how little, makes them rich. And their wealth is often used to support families left behind, thus solidifying their ties with the place of origin. But that is different from their own history north of the Rio Grande. Here is an example: the Pachucos, rebellious Chicano youngsters in Los Angeles and elsewhere in California during the fifties, understood themselves as extensions of the Aztec soul: they were neither North American nor Mexicans, but a hybrid—a mixture impossible to define. (Octavio Paz devotes the first chapter of *The Labyrinth of Solitude*, "The Pachuco and Other Extremes"—published in serial form around 1950—to their cultural identity, and Luis Valdéz, the artistic director of Teatro Campesino, has dealt with the issue in his play *Zoot Suit.*) While a more radical ethnic perception of the Mexican-American identity was indeed promoted by Chicano militants active in the civil rights movement—such as César Chavez, Rubén "Corky" González, and even the Robin Hood lawyer Oscar "Zeta" Acosta (author of *The Autobiography of a Brown Buffalo* and *The Revolt of the Cockroach People*)—the background was laid out decades before by the Pachucos and other social types. Therefore, to say that the Hispanic identity strengthened during the sixties, without acknowledging its foundation, amounts to a misconception.

"The Bilingual Battleground," the first chapter of *Out of the Barrio,* is a study of the development, in legal terms, of the phenomenon of bilingual education. Chavez studies the legislation favoring this type of training for Hispanic students with little to no knowledge of English. In what is referred to—à la Swift—as "a modest proposal," she concludes that this special treatment originated in 1960, in Dade County, Florida, where public schools were unexpectedly inundated with Cuban immigrants escaping Fidel Castro at home. Mainly because they were sure to return one day to the Caribbean island, their prerogative was to keep their own native tongue, Spanish, as an integral part of their children's pedagogical environment. Consequently, they fought for "intelligent" laws allowing kids to be taught both languages in public schools. Chavez's finding is symptomatic: bilingual education was not a result of poor academic performance by Hispanic children but an attempt to remain loyal to ethnic roots. It emerged among Cubans as a solution to their life in exile, not as a reality of lower-class Mexican-Americans or Puerto Rican children in California or New York.

Her criticism, nevertheless, is targeted against the incredible boom of laws promoting the program in the whole country. By the mid-seventies and during the eighties, the program had expanded to states like Texas, Massachusetts, and New Jersey, and its scope was truly enormous. Schools could apply for federal funds to implement the bilingual method, but because of legal intricacies and as a result of political battles by astute leaders, government money given to them for other educational purposes was often contingent on the implementation of Spanish courses. The irony is clear: at some point, the state not only favored but compelled schools to develop bilingual education programs, thus granting Hispanic culture a legitimate status in public schools, a status no other ethnic culture ever had before.

My own view is similar to that of Chavez. As a transitional method, the goal of bilingual education is not to lose classroom time in the preparation of immigrant children. By teaching them lessons of math, geography, biology, and so on, in Spanish, while students take remedial courses to improve the knowledge of English, the objective is not to obstruct the intellectual development while a second language is acquired. But the consequences are dangerous and far-reaching. In spite of the "English Only" laws in a few states like Arizona and Colorado, the United States doesn't have an "official" language. English is recognized to be the common vehicle of communication; thus, sooner or later the Hispanic student discovers he is the owner of two identities: one domestic and ethnic, another public and collective. *Out of the Barrio* is against bilingual education because it doesn't lead to better performance in English or in nonlanguage subject areas. Chavez is absolutely right. Offering Hispanics the opportunity, even if transitory, to educate their children in an idiom other than English becomes an obstacle in the assimilation process. In fact, she isn't the only outspoken critic to express such animosity: the Chicano essayist Richard Rodríguez, in his 1983 autobiography *Hunger for Memory,* also attacks bilingual education as a "schizophrenic" method by which Hispanics lose themselves in translation and ultimately fail to recognize who they are within the United States. As a Spanish-speaker who has lived in the United States for six-plus years, for me the disappearance of the mother tongue symbolizes the death of the native self. Yet isn't that what the American dream is about—the invention of another Whitmanesque self, a plural identity common to people as diverse as Haitians and Czechs?

My proximity to Mexican-Americans, nonetheless, is enough to understand the extent of damage already done. Indeed, three decades of bilingual education have more than strengthened the cultural identity of Hispanics. The two TV channels, the powerful dailies in Los Angeles *(La Opinión),* Miami *(El Nuevo Herald),* and New York *(El Diario),* the ever-growing number of university careers of South Americans in North America, are proof of the current state of affairs. Here is a compelling example: the Colombian woman who takes care of my son has been living in the United States for over twenty years without a single word of English. And she doesn't need it. She buys food, pays her taxes, and talks on the phone in Spanish. Why then study English? Cynthia Ozick, author of *The Messiah of Stockholm,* once described Yiddish as the only language whose date of death can be stated with precision: 1939. That, I am afraid to say, is unlikely to be the case of Spanish in the United States. On the contrary, in the next few decades more non-Hispanics will have to learn the language in order not to be left behind culturally.

Why do Hispanics refuse to give up their native tongue? Various reasons must be taken into account. Many don't care to become U.S. citizens, which means that the case of Cubans isn't unique. Like the Italians in the twenties, many other groups (Dominicans, Puerto Ricans, even Mexicans) are here on a temporary basis: as soon as they earn enough money, they shall return to their native soil. And many of those who apply for U.S. citizenship do so to sponsor relatives left behind, which doesn't imply that their civil standing is in any way solid. The geographical closeness of the place of origin, and the fact that many Hispanics run away from repressive regimes that sooner or later fall apart, is also important. North America is first and foremost a safe political and economic haven, and a return home is easy and often inexpensive.

But there is something even more crucial. Hispanics are unlike any other foreigners in that they share with the United States the entire continent. Their historical past is directly linked to that of the British colonies that gained independence in 1776. After Columbus arrived in the Bahamas in 1492, two totally different civilizations emerged: the pilgrims of the Mayflower, Puritans and devoted followers of Protestantism, knew their country wasn't meant to be an extremity of England and Holland but an autonomous, independent reality. Their encounter with the native Indians wasn't as bloody as that of Hernán Cortés and Pizarro in Tenochtitlán and the Inca empire in Peru. The Spanish *conquistadores,* true inheritors of a Machiavellian mentality oriented toward chivalry and honor, entered the Americas by rape and religious conversion. The United States is seen as a success story vis-à-vis the tragic scenario in Latin America, where once the Spaniards departed, other oppressive forces replaced them: the French, the Dutch, the British, and the Americans. Indeed, for those across the border the United States is a victimizer, an evildoer. A famous legend in Mexico, "The Revenge of Moctezuma," suggests that if Hispanics are ever to regain control over their own destiny, it shall happen by infiltrating the aggressor's terrain. One of the last Aztec emperors, Moctezuma, instead of fighting Cortés, regaled him with gifts because of an ancient pre-Columbian belief that the bearded white man was divine. No doubt this was a tactical mistake by the Aztecs, but their revenge will one day take place, so the legend goes, from within the enemy line. Hard as it sounds, Hispanics not only aren't learning English, they are forcing this country to speak Spanish—to turn bilingual. By clamoring to have their language recognized, they are placing the entire nation, in Truman's words, between a rock and a hard place. They aren't here to be assimilated, but to disseminate their culture.

Chapter 2 in *Out of the Barrio* is a discussion of the political participation of this ethnic minority in the national, state, and local arenas. Chavez studies the 1965 legislation, the Voting Rights Act, meant to correct specific regional problems of discrimination (mainly against blacks and Hispanics) by attempting to secure them representative seats. The purpose was to guarantee the right to vote in districts in which a minority constitutes a majority of eligible voters, to ensure they could elect their own leaders. The process quickly reached and even surpassed its political goals. By 1975, Hispanics achieved a gigantic triumph, gaining the right to be included in the Act

In 1988, almost 78 percent of Hispanics voted for Republican candidates

in more than 375 jurisdictions outside the South. The prerequisite, as Chavez justifiably points out, was nevertheless treacherous: in order to be eligible, they had to remain inside the barrio. That is, to secure the right to choose their own representatives, they had to perpetuate their poor living conditions in urban neighborhoods, thus giving away their hope of moving upward.

What the author doesn't explain is the overall voting behavior of Hispanics. In this chapter and in the next, "The Power Brokers," she argues that the Voting Rights Act was cleverly manipulated by a handful of community leaders more interested in themselves than in the well-being of their constitutents. She examines their strategies to intimidate and their closeness to black activists of the sixties. Although her argument is strong and persuasive, she ignores some questions: Why is there a lack of trust among Hispanics in their government officials? How to explain, given their poor condition, their identification with Republican representatives, not with Democrats? Irving Kristol once attempted to explain why Jews in the United States, as members of a powerful ethnic minority totally assimilated into the mainstream, identify with liberal values. Logic claims they ought to identify with the Right, yet their vote in presidential and state elections often shows the opposite stand. Kristol's intelligent observations focus on the ancient tradition of liberal Jewish thinkers, like the nineteenth-century figures Moses Hess and Karl Marx. Something along the same line could be said about Hispanics: the consensus among the type of immigrants traveling north is that right-wing and right-center regimes are better, at least in Latin America, because people live in peace and prosperity, and anarchic forces are subdued. Tradition is again the key issue. Unlike Jews, Hispanics have a hard time identifying with philanthropic causes, with the exception of church-oriented activities. The highly repressive colonial, nineteenth-century, and contemporary governments, as well as a sense of dogmatic Catholic tradition—books like Domingo Faustino Sarmiento's *Civilization and Barbarism,* published in a Chilean newspaper in 1845, and Euclides Da Cunha's 1902 *Rebellion in the Backlands* are outstanding evidence—have taught them to prefer conservative values. (In 1988, almost 78 percent voted for Republican candidates.)

A distinction among the different Hispanic groups is made in *Out of the Barrio* in chapters 5 ("An Emerging Middle Class"), 6 ("The Immigrants"), and 7 ("The Puerto Rican Exception"). Before discussing them, an examination of the word *Hispanic,* although Chavez never analyzes it in depth, is required here. The term achieved prominence in the eighties with the new wave of immigrants from Central America. (*Latino* is preferred among music and TV stars.) Used to refer to Spanish-speaking citizens from Latin America— although Brazilians and Iberians are also included—it works as an equalizer: while Hispanics often find themselves in trouble relating to each other, in the United States the media promotes a self-serving image of homogeneity and uses the term *Hispanic* to refer to all without any distinction.

What follows is a description of the segments that form that group. Cubans have been populating Florida since the early nineteenth century. José Martí, the freedom-fighter and *Modernista* poet, before moving to New York, published a newspaper in Miami for his exiled co-nationals. Among the Hispanics, most Cubans, with the exception of a few who fled to Florida in 1980 with the plight of Mariel, are the most educated, intellectually driven, and well-off. They have the lowest unemployment rate (5.8 percent), and the highest income per capita ($33,500). The second group, the Mexican-Americans, shares with native Americans the status of oldest inhabitants of the area encompassed by the United States. Mexican-Americans are the larger in number: 13.3 million according to the 1990 census, compared to 2.2 million Puerto Ricans, 1 million Cubans, 2.8 million South and Central Americans, and 1.4 million other Hispanics. Although they have produced a rich literature and urban culture, they have the lowest graduation rate, the highest unemployment rate (9.0 percent), and one of the lowest incomes per family. The third group, Puerto Ricans, according to Linda Chavez, is the most troublesome: the lowest in the economic scale within the Hispanic minority as a whole (30.4 percent of families live in poverty), even below the Central Americans who have sought asylum during the eighties in southern states and have just begun to slowly adapt linguistically. While Puerto Ricans' commonwealth status allows them to have U.S. citizenship, their assimilation to the mainstream is a sequence of misadventures. *Out of the Barrio* persuasively explains why: they are entitled to unemployment and Social Security benefits. Those traveling to the mainland rely on the system and get trapped in its web.

The Dominicans ought to be placed alongside the Puerto Ricans because their capital-in-exile is New York. After the Trujillo dictatorship, which brought prosperity to the island under a regime of repression, fell in 1961, chaos and economic uncertainty prevailed. Many decided to emigrate and their subsequent success is admirable: without the help of government funds, a considerable number have prospered quickly. The fourth and final group, consisting of Salvadorans, Nicaraguans, and other Central and South Americans, has a high unemployment rate (6.2 percent), but is well-off in income ($29,300 per capita).

What *Out of the Barrio* fails to study are the linguistic patterns and idiosyncratic differences between the groups. Their Spanish is a hybrid of Anglo-Saxon and Castilian words and expressions, and structurally, their sentences are organized neither according to the language of Shakespeare nor to that of Cervantes. They can speak English with Anglos, but among themselves they use *Spanglish*—a middle ground, half a part of the past, half a part of their present and future.

They will not completely adapt to the American way of life since they are in constant contact with newly arrived Central American refugees; memory and daily endeavors will not allow them to betray their identity. The vocabulary each of these groups uses depends on their particular historical circumstance. Argentinians, for instance, are less the product of the interracial mixture between the Spanish *conquistadores* and the native Indians, and therefore have a more Europeanized Spanish than that of Mexicans, who have integrated pre-Columbian terms and names (Aztec, Mayan, etc.) into their day-to-day communication. In general, Hispanics in Chicago or Los Angeles or New Jersey don't say *mercado* anymore for supermarket, but *marketa;* they don't say "voy a *estacionar* el automóvil" but "voy a *parkear* el automóvil"; "*aplicar* a la universidad" instead of "*solicitar entrada* a la universidad." Their cuisines and religious traditions also differ. But Chavez perceives them as a unity. She never attempts a comparative cultural analysis.

What do Hispanics do to unify themselves as a minority? Unfortunately, the question, as crucial as it sounds, is never directly addressed in *Out of the Barrio*. Instead, "Toward a New Politics of Hispanic Assimilation," the last chapter in Chavez's volume, is a sermon of an answer to the question of their troubled assimilation. That is, she deals with how to adapt the ethnic minority, not how to understand its tradition and weltanschauung. She responds to the questions of tardiness in learning English and the lack of electoral participation of Hispanics by asking the government to change its policies on bilingual education and the

Voting Rights Act. As if by taking another course these immigrants will quickly assimilate; and by denouncing the strategies of their leaders to keep their constituency in the barrios, they will make it into the middle class.

Unfortunately, the book fails to do what's most needed: study the Hispanic psyche and its intercourse with the Anglo-Saxon idiosyncracy. *Out of the Barrio* underestimates the tradition and culture of the ethnic minority Chavez claims to fully understand. A true analysis of the problems Hispanics face while assimilating needs to be founded, not in cold statistics and scientific data, but in an ambitious examination of the cultural patters of behavior: their religious beliefs, their love life, their moral values, their domestic habits, their perception of death and foreigners, their aspirations and history. Perhaps as a result of the literature produced south of the Rio Grande by writers like Jorge Luis Borges and Gabriel García Márquez, the *labyrinth* has become a favorite symbol among Hispanics—a chaotic crossroad of identities, a confusion of the soul. And indeed, the Hispanic soul is a labyrinthine game of mirrors and insecurities, and their daily presence in the United States is a consequence of that game. A study of the adventures of the Hispanic mind in this country is urgently needed. What Chavez fails to understand is that this ethnic collectivity, a sum of different parts, will not accept the prevailing moral and educational rules the way other previous immigrant groups did. While problems like poverty, drug addiction, out-of-wedlock childbirth, and crime among Hispanics are likely to be resolved in the near future with better educational programs (in Spanish and English) and more jobs, the most genuine part of their culture will ultimately transform the United States. And it will do so radically. Hispanics have infiltrated the enemy and are ready to deconstruct its very essence. . . . The revenge of Moctezuma.

THE LAST TEMPTATION OF COLUMBUS

Philip Burnham

Depending on who you talk to these days, Columbus might be anything from the incarnation of original sin to the patron saint of free-market capitalism. The fact is that everyone from the Smithsonian and public television to *Newsweek* and Hollywood is using him to reflect on how far the world has come in the last half a millenium. Not surprisingly, a cottage industry for contact specialists, curators, biographers, quincentennial experts, critics-at-large, and ethnic group spokespeople has been spawned to help employ languishing American intellectuals in search of a combative topic.

I don't mean to suggest that the Columbus story is frivolous. In fact, his visit to the Americas is, in Western perception, the threshold between the medieval and modern worlds. As history is commonly told in North America, no other event in historical time since the birth of Christ is so filled with dramatic consequences. In America's secular typology, Columbus is a mysterious though messianic figure who has much of the same *gravitas* as the later Founding Fathers. Local hagiography reveals that

his halo is only eclipsed by Lincoln's, of whom, after all, we have plenty of photographs, speeches, and letters with which to confirm a grand vision of America. With Columbus its star, the quincentennial has already cornered a decent market share and a festively captive audience.

If we reflect on it, American history is split between the pre- and post-Columbus eras, much the way that the pagan and Christian past in the Old World is divided into periods separated by Christ. The parallel between 1 A.D. and 1492 is a fertile one. Both dates announce that history is radically changed (even reversed) from the fulcrum of a single event: the birth of an infant on the one hand, the voyage of an inspired visionary on the other. The two events insist that we consider the "before" and "after" in radically different lights. The barbarism of the Greco-Roman world is contrasted with the Christian mission to civilize it in the Eastern Hemisphere; in the Americas, the wild undergrowth of Indian prehistory is put to the torch by this messenger of modern consciousness,

Discussed in this essay

Seeds of Change, *Herman J. Viola and Carolyn Margolis, eds., Washington: Smithsonian Institution Press*

Columbus and the Age of Discovery, *Zvi Dorner, New York: William Morrow*

Native American Testimony, *Peter Nabokov, ed., New York: Viking Press* a Genoan free agent and ersatz prophet in the employ of medieval Spain. Christ and Christopher are a peerless pair in the ledger of Western myth.

The quincentennial is a celebration of this sacrament, the divinely inspired birth of the modern West. For the rest of the world, the Renaissance is like a line drawn in the dust, and the "pagans" or "primitives" or "aboriginal peoples"— whatever current usage would have us call them—are simply on the wrong side of it. Even their grand civilizations (Egypt, Mali, Mexico), while celebrated as ingenious, are demoted to the rung of "impressive ancient achievements" in the shadow of what was wrought by the Age of Discovery. The "primitives" remain there still, romanticized in our memory at the same time they're disdained for their backwardness, the subjects of a nostalgia periodically reclaimed by the West like the marshes of an endangered wetland.

In the past year a rash of academic studies and polemics have appeared about Columbus and his legacy, many of substantial value. Most, of course, are private, commercial enterprises. A few, however, have been accorded the more prestigious platform of public domain, whether funded by international public television concerns or sponsored, closer to home, by the Smithsonian. As examples of "official" positions on the quincentennial, these latter are worth examining in detail, especially in a year that will be dedicated to public spectacles. Their multimedia audience will be measured in the millions, a hearing denied out of hand to most writers or performers not invited to eat at the public high table.

• • •

Seeds of Change is the catalog of a major exhibit running until 1993 at the National Museum of Natural History in Washington. The theme of the exhibition is the transfer between hemispheres of five important "seeds" in the wake of Columbus—sugar, corn, potatoes, the horse, and disease. The catalog, rather than a single extended narrative, is a collection of essays, most by scholars with an interdisciplinary tilt. It offers a wealth of information on topics ranging from slave adaptability on Caribbean plantations to the importance of potatoes as a root crop that couldn't easily be foraged by marauding European armies. Encyclopedic in scope, the book includes essays on viniculture, ranching, Native Americans, Hispanics, epidemiological history, slave insurrections, and the wholesale destruction of nature in the twentieth century. It's a tall order, comprehensive in scope if not always generous in providing points of true controversy. The slaves of Montserrat were more likely to practice a conservationist ethic than their masters. Diseases like tuberculosis and dysentery existed in the Americas before 1492. There is much to be learned here, and though Columbus is not a major player in these pages, his presence is everywhere felt as the invisible sower who made the harvest possible.

Anthologies usually pretend to be representative. Since questions of minority political empowerment are important in the quincentennial, *Seeds of Change* has several essays written by and about minority peoples—as it should. Some are successful, others troubling at best. The essays on Caribbean slave cultures by David Barry Gaspar and Lydia Pulsipher are lucid and informative if not groundbreaking, taking the tack that slaves created their own culture independent of the Big House, a position that reflects the dominant research in the field of the past twenty years.

On the other hand, Joseph Sanchez's piece on Hispanic influence is miscast as a piece of ethnocultural apology. In cataloging the Hispanic "contributions" to North America, Sanchez claims some dubious honors, from noting that Aaron Burr was a friend of the Spanish government to boasting that Latin America has "contributed enormously to the economy of the U.S. by supplying a variety of raw materials at low prices." The latter is said without any trace of irony, though to characterize it as a "contribution" is like saying that United Fruit

> **Horse Capture seems to be one of the official Indians of the quincentennial: Smithsonian-approved, USDI-inspected, and unlikely to deliver too dangerous a sermon**

Workers happily toiled so that the melting pot could burn on high flame. The essay might have been fine ten years ago when listings of minority contributions were still the mode. Today it sounds like misplaced bravado, which is, in its sum, a paean to American patriotism.

The Native American reaction is also critical, and one of the essays is by George Horse Capture, a member of the Gros Ventre tribe from Montana. Even if he is angry about the fate of Indian peoples (and he has every right to be), his effort is mixed at best. Though wellmeaning in his critique of America, Horse Capture can be ingenuous to a fault, saying of his years at Berkeley that "the campus teemed with beautiful people of all types." The essay is out of place—part historical overview, part personal reminiscence, part antiColumbus jeremiad, it wanders selfconsciously, adrift from its more scholarly neighbors. Appearing also in Zvi Dor-Ner's public television series *Columbus and the Age of Discovery,* Horse Capture seems to be one of the official Indians of the quincentennial: Smithsonian-approved, USDI-inspected, and unlikely to deliver too dangerous a sermon, even if he did participate in the Alcatraz sit-in of '69.

Seeds of Change is about the miscegenation that occurred in the wake of Columbus, if not at the human level then at the larger ecological one. We get a good variety of metaphors from the various writers, including "blender," "amalgam," and "complex mosaic." And so the Western and Eastern hemispheres did mix, even if North America long attempted to deny it on a human level, from Indian removal in the nineteenth century to antimiscegenation laws for blacks and whites that weren't overturned until the 1960s.

In light of this, *Seeds of Change* advances what has become the new paradigm of American culture, the "mosaic." The old-fashioned melting pot has been discarded because of its assimilationist urge and the mosaic installed in its place in public discourse. Like most paradigms, the image it embodies has serious consequences, as dependent as most of us are on metaphor to grasp abstract ideas, even in the most scientific of disciplines.

What is the "mosaic" that *Seeds of Change* proposes? It is a tableau of "togetherness," and "unity in diversity." It is a powerful symbol for human coop-

1992 may well be declared the Year of the Coffee Table Book

eration, lending itself not only to national consciousness but to worldwide concerns as well. Indeed, the American mosaic would hide a larger one behind its facade, though that is only implied in these essays. "The global village" is its current overseas analogue, an international E Pluribus Unum that has been crucial for the West in implementing various arguments for "economic development" throughout the world.

Any anthology is itself a mosaic, and so *Seeds of Change* crystallizes the very paradigm it avows. In its pages we find a "black" voice, a "Hispanic" voice, a "Native American" voice. Everyone has been represented, we are assured. We have, it is implied, a well-rounded view of the quincentennial, a color-coordinated palette comprising everyone from stuffy academics to the radical fringe.

In effect the mosaic is representative, but what it represents is another question. In spite of its impressive breadth, it may, in fact, not address fundamental issues at all. As noted, some of the essays in *Seeds* seem more like straw men than real debates of current shibboleths. In

two of the minority pieces there is lacking a sense of forceful and cogent analysis that one would expect from these quarters. Then too, the only idea we have of contemporary African-Americans in *Seeds* is a discussion of soul food—interesting, though not very controversial, fare. *Seeds of Change* is a readable and informative book—but it is one with an agenda that hides many concerns of American minorities behind an intellectual pursuit of grand synthesis. Why not an overview of the American Indian reservation? Why not a piece on the diet of inner-city Hispanic kids? For a celebration, these might be too embarrassing. The essays stand to attention in the table of contents like a row of Washington lobbyists a little too anxious to press the flesh.

• • •

A book that complements *Seeds* in its lordly neutrality is *Columbus and the Age of Discovery,* another coffee table primer that provides more details than did the television series on which it was based. In fact, 1992 may well be declared the Year of the Coffee Table Book if this first wave is any indication of what is to follow.

As the PBS series revealed last October, Zvi Dor-Ner (author of the text and executive producer of the WGBH series) is happiest following in Columbus's wake—both spiritually and literally. Though cognizant of the admiral's shortcomings, Dor-Ner takes the story of an ambitious Genoan knocking down the doors of medieval geography and writes it up like a journalist doing an admiring profile of a nineteenth-century robber baron. He was in many ways a terrible man, Dor-Ner admits, but wasn't his vision impressive? His ultimate judgment of Columbus is vintage romantic with hints of chiaroscuro, citing his "insight," his "consuming passion," and "intoxication with discovery." Aw, shucks. Christopher, we hardly knew ye.

The book is structured around a reenactment of Columbus's first voyage, a trip taken by Dor-Ner and companions in replica vessels under the auspices of the Spanish Navy. In the tradition of Samuel Eliot Morison, the treacherous coastlines of the past are recharted through the eyes of a modern sailing buff. So taken is Dor-Ner by seaboard rations and navigational methods that Native Americans don't even make a serious appearance until halfway through the book. We are on what Disney might call a "journey of discovery," a not-so-instant replay in keeping with the current American penchant for historical reenactments ranging from bawdy Renaissance fairs to full-scale Civil War battles.

It's true, as the publicity tells us, that this Columbus is filled with controversy. Only it may not be the controversy you expect. We learn that Columbus *might* have had an affair with Doña Beatriz, the governor of Gomera in the Canary Islands, before shipping out for the Bahamas. Then too, teams of experts have unraveled elaborate theories to argue over the real first landing site—was it San Salvador or Samana Cay? And then there are those who claim that Columbus's remains are buried in the Dominican Republic, while others hotly maintain they're right in Seville where they're supposed to be. These are the disputes of Columbus buffs. Their nature belies the gargantuan claims of the project to confront the real legacy of contact.

Dor-Ner's chapter titles reveal that he too is taken by the spirit of the mosaic: from "A Man of Many Faces" to "The World Made Whole," we're meant to see that this was a complex, tragic event that has finally ripened on a happy, if somewhat discordant, note. Another of his titles, "The Columbian Exchange," has indeed become the unofficial motto of the quincentennial. Like the mosaic, this too is an image of concordance and equality that papers over old wounds and domesticates differing viewpoints in a single vision. In both of these books, the experts go to great lengths to show that European diseases did much more harm to native peoples than European greed and cruelty. This is true, and still unknown in many places. But the repeated assertion of it makes one begin to visualize the Conquest as the result of unconscious biological destiny and nothing more, minimizing the real violence that did occur throughout the hemisphere. This is high-tech synthesis that dangerously verges on apology—"Don't blame us, blame our pathogens." It's something like a Renaissance rereading of *The Andromeda Strain* where the responsible parties remain amorphous and beyond reproach.

With Dor-Ner, a producer of great experience and cosmopolitan breadth, we return again to the problem of resolving what are perhaps irreconcilable differences by fashioning a grand "Answer." The final chapter attempts to capture the essence of Columbus by acknowledging several different perspectives of him. From glorifying to debunking, we get another kind of mosaic.

Its nature suggests that *Columbus* has struck a fortuitous balance, a harmonious composite that should be enough to satisfy all the critics. But there is a troubling theme beneath it all. While *Columbus* acknowledges alternative viewpoints about the Conquest (or should I call it "the Columbian Exchange"?), it offers a barely concealed adulation of the West as a technologically superior civilization. The very structure of the book is, after all, the voyage of Saint Christopher. The spine of the story is the adventure of a great man. In different ways, then, both of these books tell us through the medium of the mosaic, "You've all been chosen to be a part of Team America. We hope you'll play by the rules now and stop that incessant complaining."

• • •

The exhibit Seeds of Change will be on public display for more than a year. The television series *Columbus and the Age of Discovery* has already been given the PBS seal of approval, and reruns are in the offing. While not publicly funded as these are, Peter Nabokov's *Native American Testimony* has as its format a chorus of voices that give witness to contact between Western and Native American cultures in North America. Some of these voices are anonymous, all are native, and in at least a figurative sense, they have the power of a public document "suddenly" come to light. In reading them, one has the curious sense of being an authorized eavesdropper.

Native American Testimony is, like *Seeds of Change,* an anthology, though not one with coffee table ambitions. It offers an antidote to the government-sponsored correctness that characterizes some of its current competitors. The text is an expanded version of a book originally released in 1979, updated, no doubt, to take advantage of the interest inspired by the quincentennial. While surely not the first anthology of Indian voices to be published, it is, to my knowledge, one of the most comprehensive in historical scope.

The documents Nabokov has gathered are mostly primary sources, many, but not all, originating from oral accounts. The "authors" of these accounts are Native Americans, and their subject is everything from tribal stories of first contact with white people to present-day descriptions of life on the reservation. Most important, these are witnesses to cultural conflict, however filtered some of the voices may be by the limitations of memory and the attendant dangers of transcription.

Nabokov gives us what should be an essential element in "celebrating" the quincentennial. After the scholars and experts have had their say, let us hear from some of those whose voices have not been prominent on prime-time TV or in the big publishing houses. People whose names are Percy Bigmouth, Pedro Encinales, Carlos Montezuma, Bennie Bearskin, Ruth Muskrat Bronson. Whether or not what they say is "objective," they bring to bear a human dimension too often lacking in official celebrations, especially those crowded with scholarly research and academic prose.

This is a book for people tired of Indians cowering before priests, or savages speaking broken English, or forest pygmies puffing on cigars and dancing to an old Victrola. There is some cowering, some dancing, and some pidgin—the joy of this book is that not all of it occurs on the native side. We learn of the first Winnebago meeting with the French when the People of Real Speech (as the Winnebago referred to themselves) encounter a strange breed of humans who fire powerful "thundersticks" in the air but don't have the slightest idea what tobacco is. Many of the accounts show the strangeness of contact as told from the "other" side, a rare commodity even in the Age of Information. The book goes a long way toward debunking the widespread and pejorative image of the "ingenuous savage," a mainstay of Western popular culture for the past several centuries.

For a long time we have been overwhelmed by Western versions of contact. We have been told time and again that there are no Indian sources on early conflict because native North American cultures had no written history. This is true in part—the number of early sources may be small and sometimes difficult to gauge as to their authenticity. But it is no less true that first contact occurred in different parts of America at vastly different times, making later written accounts much more common. Then too, oral traditions have to be taken seriously if we're to consider contact in all its richness. Nabokov has gathered Indian versions of many of the same events that we have otherwise become accustomed to understanding by reading explorers' journals, newspaper headlines, and a moldering raft of government treaties.

In fact, *Native American Testimony* is a good primer on Indian-white relations over the past five hundred years. Nabokov's introductions are consistently terse, accurate, and well-balanced. This is not to say his editorial discretion is flawless. He tends to romanticize the role of the French in Canada. He includes a few well-known "surrender speeches" that have already been anthologized to death in mainstream publications. His choice of Mary Jemison's text as an example of the captivity narrative casts Indians in a more favorable light than do most relations in that genre.

Still, the selection of sources is refreshingly eclectic and almost always satisfying. Contrary to what one might expect, most of these are not "pity the poor Indian" tracts or political treatises for radical change. There is sadness, there is humor, bitterness, irony, graceful indignation, and even, at times, a warm nostalgia for periods when Indian policy reached its nadir—as at the end of the nineteenth century. There is an anonymous Apache who laughs about the early days of strange government rations when people ground up coffee beans and tried to make them into an edible mush—when told from the Indian side, it's hilarious rather than condescending. Or Wooden Leg, the Cheyenne who is told by the reservation authorities that he can become a tribal judge only if he renounces one of his wives. There are touching memories of people who hated white boarding schools, and accounts of others who thrived in them only to be held in suspicion by their own families for having succeeded in the white world. Joseph Medicine Crow captures a herd of horses from SS officers in 1945, pastures them at the edge of a wood, and suddenly breaks into a praise song for his Crow ancestors. After reading this book, it is hard to think of Indian people as simply being "Indian." *Native American Testimony* restores to them a human dimension often denied in the popular press, in academic ethnography, and in the official literature of the quincentennial.

This book is a reminder that "consensus celebrations," empirical studies, and historical reenactments are not all that we should recall on this anniversary. Traditionally we have relegated Native Americans to a storybook time, the kind of thinking that has consigned Indian exhibits—along with elephants, mastodons, and brontosaurus bones—to museums of natural history. In *Native American Testimony* a few Indians are let out of the museum. It is a rich and moving experience to meet them.

• • •

Of course, the quincentennial assault has only begun. We have much to look forward to in the coming year, including Marlon Brando as the Grand Inquisitor Torquemada and Tom Selleck as King Ferdinand in a new film on Columbus. Don't forget *mappemundi* greeting cards; a revisionist videotape from the Knights of Columbus; quincentennial bus tours of the Southwest sponsored by the Bureau of Land Management; and the latest item, "Columbus—A Game of Exploration, Conquest, and Trade" at $25 a throw. Consult your local memorabilia dealer for details.

Historical celebrations provide much-needed reflection about important events. The quincentennial may be benevolent and educational in purpose, but it is more than just a meshing of neutral interests. It permits a variety of well-endowed sponsors (e.g., European public television money that largely underwrote the PBS "Columbus") to project a monumental historical encounter in a light ultimately favorable to certain groups. We all know that money talks. The question is, who will decide what ventures are granted "public" right-of-way and how will people who have been traditionally denied access to that medium gain a genuine voice? Who, in short, will be called on to give testimony? Even if we don't know where he's buried, Saint Columbus may have to turn over in his grave a few times before the quincentennial becomes a real forum for debate.

PUBLIC CULTURE

VOLUME 4, NUMBER 1 (FALL 1991)

Looking at Film Hoardings **R. Srivatsan** ◆ Knocking on The Doors of Public Culture **Pradip Krishen** ◆ The Meaning of Baseball in 1992 **Bill Brown** ◆ Becoming the Armed Man **J. William Gibson** ◆ The Function of New Theory **Xiaobing Tang** ◆ Worldly Discourses **Dan Rose** ◆ Voices of the Rainforest **Steven Feld** ◆ Anuradhapura **Wimal Disanayake** ◆ **River and Bridge** Meena Alexander

VOLUME 4, NUMBER 2 (SPRING 1992)

The Banality of Power and the Aesthetics of Vulgarity in the Postcolony **Achille Mbembe** ◆ Take Care of Public Telephones **Robert J. Foster** ◆ The Death of History? **Dipesh Chakrabarty** ◆ The Public Fetus and the Family Car **Janelle Sue Taylor** ◆ Race and the Humanities: The "Ends" of Modernity? **Homi Bhabha** ◆ "Disappeating" Iraqis **David Prochaska** ◆ Algeria Caricatures the Gulf War **Susan Slyomovics** ◆ Mobilizing Fictions **Robert Stam** ◆ Television and the Gulf War **Victor J. Caldarola**

ENGAGING CRITICAL ANALYSES OF TENSIONS BETWEEN GLOBAL CULTURAL FLOWS AND PUBLIC CULTURES IN A DIASPORIC WORLD

PUBLICCULTURE is published biannually at The University Museum, University of Pennsylvania, 33rd & Spruce Streets, Philadelphia, PA 19104-6324. A year's subscription for individuals is $10.00 ($14.00 foreign); institutions $20.00 ($24.00 foreign). Back issues are available. Write, call (215) 898-4054, or fax: (215) 898-0657.

THE FUTURE IS ANOTHER COUNTRY

A conversation with Nadine Gordimer and Stephen Clingman.

Stephen Clingman: Let's start with the most obvious thing: the prize. What has it meant to you?

Nadine Gordimer: Well, my attitude toward it has gone through many changes. It's a major shift in one's life, and I think that any writer who tries to dismiss it in an offhand way, with the suggestion that all art is above any kind of recognition, is not being honest or sincere. But it may be too that my position in getting it has been a double one: it's not the position that every literature laureate finds him- or herself in, so maybe that is the key to it.

SC: And what's the double nature of it?

NG: Well, normally you can go home and quietly go on working, and have a certain prestige in the literary world— and also among people who don't read your books—just like any form of success or publicity. But if you come from a situation such as this one in South Africa—and perhaps in particular at this transitional time—then a kind of spot-light gets turned on the country of the laureate. And it happens only in the case of the Peace Prize winner and the literature winner, I've discovered; the others go quietly back to their laboratory. So that it's been a kind of double experience for me to adjust to it.

In my work, as you know, I've always been a very private person, reluctant to dig into it, to discuss it too much, just wanting to *do* it, and somewhat taken aback when asked how things come about, because nobody believes you when you say you don't really know. And there's a feeling of evaluation, a revaluation, a sense of a lifetime of work that hadn't been fully put together before. I suppose it's a bit like a painter or a sculptor having a retrospective. You're forced to think back over what you've been doing for a whole lifetime.

And then on the other side, there's the strong feeling I have because the country that the spotlight gets turned on is *this* country, it's my country, South Africa. And the particular position that I have here, that I've slowly worked toward, is

**Novelist and
Nobelist Nadine
Gordimer.**

another side of my life. I found a level of expectation from my black comrades that I didn't dream would be there. They felt, and do feel, absolutely delighted and proud of me: I can say that because it's something that comes completely from outside. Because they feel that here's someone that the world recognizes—not in the political sphere, but culturally—who belongs to them. It brings with it a great deal of responsibility that I felt very strongly when I was abroad, because in Stockholm, there's a very active ANC as well as other anti-apartheid movements, some of them consisting mainly of exiles. And they were putting upon me, I felt, a big responsibility that they were perfectly entitled to. Especially at this time with the change of government in Sweden and with a changing focus of interest all over the world—turning away from Africa and South Africa to what was Eastern Europe, what is, geographically, still Eastern Europe—they really felt that this was an opportunity for them to keep some of the attention, through me, on South Africa.

Of course, I was very eager to grasp this opportunity, because I've always had, quite rightly, modest ideas of what my contribution to the struggle for freedom has been here. So here was an opportunity for me to do something that perhaps nobody else could; it fell into my lap like manna from heaven. And there were complications around this from the beginning—for example, my position as Nobel laureate vis-à-vis the government of my country. To say the government of my country is not my government, which is my position, is quite a difficult one in the context of the ceremonies of the Nobel Prize. Normally you are presented to the King of Sweden by your ambassador or by your envoy. But they understood perfectly that this couldn't be the case for me: what a paradox it would be! So different arrangements had to be made there.

SC: What were they?

NG: The arrangements were that I would be presented not by somebody from the South African government, but by the deputy secretary-general of the Swedish Academy. He read the citation and so on. Then there was even the protocol of who sits where at the dinner. So that was got 'round. The ambassador was invited to the annex dinner, so to speak, for the overflow of people who can't be fitted into the big one. So we were literally not under the same roof. And also I had said: I don't feel that I can be represented by the present South African government, but I'm not an apolitical person, and I have strong loyalties and commitments to the future—for me, mainly through the ANC. So I would very much like somebody from the ANC to be there. And I thought that it would be very appropriate if my old friend Wally Serote—who is, in my opinion, a wonderful poet and whom I've known for many years, and who happens to be heading the Department of Arts and Culture in the ANC—came with me, both as my friend and fellow writer and as a representative of my political loyalties and my position within them. So he came along and sat with my family at the official occasion.

SC: Extending the metaphor of family.

NG: Extending the metaphor of family, in African fashion. When I read from my work, he read his poetry; on public occasions we answered questions together, whether they were literary or political.

SC: You were changing the rules of the Nobel as you went along.

NG: Yes, the Nobel people were quite rightly anxious that it shouldn't be made into a political occasion. And so was *I,* because, as I had to point out again and again to journalists, if I'd got it for my political activities, which God knows were certainly never enough to merit it, I would have got the Peace Prize. I also did not get it because I'm a woman, but because I'm a writer. But people look for reasons other than the work.

SC: Something that struck me when I saw you on television after the announcement was that you had a kind of radiance about you—there was a sense of

My background was intellectually so thin, it's a miracle I became a writer at all

innocent delight, there was something in you that was still that young girl from Springs. You were genuinely delighted to get that prize.

NG: Yes, I was delighted. Many writers, once they hear they've been on the short-list, have this longing and nervousness and aspiration every year when October comes around. I swear to you, I have never looked at it that way. And I truly didn't think that I would ever get it. And certainly not once it had gone, very deservedly, to Africa. So I think that this

very pleasant surprise was something that I enjoyed. And I was also made happy by the feeling that suddenly I found out so many other people were pleased that I had won. So that to me, that was a kind of justification. If other people believed in it, then I must believe in it.

SC: Would that young girl from Springs ever have thought it possible?

NG: No. I think that my background was intellectually so thin, it's a miracle that I became a writer at all.

SC: Clearly you've tried to settle the division in your life between your life as a citizen and your life as a writer, as you've put it. But the event must awaken some of those ambiguities and divisions again: am I here to get politically involved? When am I going to get back to my writing? Where is my major priority?

NG: Oh, it intensifies it. This is *my* struggle—not the big struggle. And I have never been, I think, away so long from my writing, aside from obvious things like the Nobel Lecture, over which I pondered and slaved quite a bit, because I'm very slow at writing non-fiction, as you know. But to me that's not my work. And this is the bad thing about the prize: I feel cut off from my work, I feel overexposed—like a photograph where you've come out a white blur, I feel bleached out in many ways. And I know I have to fight hard, now, for space and privacy, but there's no question that I won't do it. And I think we have to learn to say no. I mean I'm getting the most incredible invitations; I don't know why it is that *medical* associations seem to want me to come talk to them. It's got nothing to do with the writing: it's just that your name is there and you've got a Nobel Prize. And I find it very, very odd.

SC: You become a commodity.

NG: You become a commodity. And you become something which the con-

The prize is not going to help you with your next story, or your next book

temporary world is determined to make of us: you become a performer. It's the writer as performer. Not the anonymous person behind the book you've written.

SC: That's one sort of complication. The prize must bring others as well.

NG: Yes. I'm surprised to hear from people that for some writers—or people *think* for some writers—this draws a kind of line under their work. They see it as some kind of end, culmination. I don't quite understand that. Because it is not going to help you with your next story, or your next book. So unless you get it when you have stopped writing and you're tottering into the grave, which has happened to some people, that line isn't drawn. Indeed, there's a big question mark.

SC: That sounds even more traumatic.

NG: But I think one has to ignore that question mark. That's something that has to be put out of the way immediately.

If you're going to start worrying about what people's expectations are, then you might as well forget about the whole thing. It is something that has happened external to the work—as a result of the work, but external to it. And it mustn't change any ideas of what you expect of yourself. It mustn't make you lazy, to think that you can not bother to move on, and it mustn't make you afraid. Because that really is inhibiting to some people. That's taking on a false standard. Now, when the prize is announced, there's always this chorus from here or there, saying: Why didn't A get it, why didn't B get it? But you know I also have a list of people who should have got the Nobel Prize. Some are dead, so there's nothing you can do about it: I think Graham Greene should have had one. I think Primo Levi was a candidate for it, but died, tragically too young. So did Italo Calvino. I think Milan Kundera should have it, and he will get it, no question about that. And then of course there are others. I feel if it comes back to Africa, Chinua Achebe should get it, and I've felt that strongly for years. But I understand that it will probably be a poet next time.

SC: Is there talk of this behind the scenes?

NG: No, well, there's always a lot of talk. *They* don't talk, they're very tight-lipped, the academy, quite rightly, but I think that if you look at the names, it seems roughly to be two years fiction, and then another year a poet. Last year it was Octavio Paz, the year before it was Cela, I think, the Spanish writer. I may say that I've already received two letters from writers in remote parts of the world, saying, please put me forward for the Nobel Prize.

SC: And what about the reception of the prize locally?

NG: Well, apart from the wonderful reception by my fellow writers and others in the black community, it seems that the Nobel Prize means nothing to South Africans—nothing at all. It's of no interest to them.

SC: When I speak to people privately, I find it does mean a lot . . .

NG: Yes, but I mean to the newspapers it doesn't. The *Weekly Mail,* in the "Events of 1991," didn't think it worth a mention, which I find astonishing. Not for myself, personally, but any South African having the Nobel Prize—you cannot believe that this isn't something that would have a mention, in a report on what has happened during the year.

SC: You've talked about the complications that getting the prize carries in its wake, and some have to do with your work as a writer. You mentioned earlier that in the endless interviews you underwent, you had to fight for your status as a writer, not an amateur politician.

NG: Well, this sounds awfully snooty to say, but it comes from the ignorance of the people who interview you, and also their view of what is newsworthy and what their readers or television viewers want to see and hear. So that it's very difficult for them first of all to talk to you of books they haven't read, or perhaps that they've skimmed through. For in-

stance, out of the stories in this latest book of mine, *Jump,* there are at least four that have nothing to do, even indirectly, with this country. But I've come to the conclusion that people talk to you about a book without having read it, because they say, "Your stories about apartheid. . . . " Well, first of all, it's insultingly narrowing, as if you simply had the subject dictated to you by the latest newspaper headline. And after a while it's just plain wearying. You feel impatient, you just want to say: forget about it, I can't answer these narrow little questions that you ask me—this is a complete misunderstanding of why I am a writer.

SC: Most journalists don't follow your work that closely. But it does seem to me that you've reached an interesting stage, where, politically speaking, you've joined the ANC, you've made that commitment, you've joined that world from which you were once separated—a world of strangers, now no longer so strange. And yet in your writing, what's happening is that there is a kind of questioning of the political: there's almost a tension between the fictional and the political. Ironically, when you get the prize, everybody sees you as simply writing against apartheid, perhaps not realizing that things have entered into a new phase for you, as indeed they have for South Africa.

NG: What stems out of this is an even further misunderstanding of why I write, and why I've always written. The general question is asked of me, and by extension other writers here: Once apartheid is abolished entirely, do you think there will still be something for you to write about? It's not always put as simplistically as that, but that is what it amounts to. They simply cannot see that it's completely the other way around. I've said again and again, I started to write, as a child, out of a sense of the mystery of life. It wasn't politics that motivated that. I didn't know what politics was; I came from a home where politics was never openly discussed—political attitudes were revealed in

There is this freedom in fiction that there isn't in fact. The inhibitions go

everyday actions, but I had to grow up before I could interpret these things. But my motivation was to solve for myself, to understand life. Of course, you can look for other factors in my background. If I had had a religious upbringing, or if my parents had had a political faith, then perhaps, if I had become a writer at all, it would have been for different reasons. But I think my becoming a writer had something to do with creating my own structure, to make ontological sense of my being there.

SC: I'm almost tempted to ask, though I think this is the wrong way of putting the question, if there were times when you regretted the political impingement on that need to make sense of life.

NG: No, I never felt that and I still don't. I was attempting to make sense of life, but where? At what period, in what country, in what little mining *dorp* and, later on, in what city? So that the factors which I would have to study and some-

how piece together were intensely political as well as sociological, sexual—everything. You can't separate these things. So I can't imagine that I could regret it.

• • •

SC: Your statement in "Living in the Interregnum" that "nothing I say here will be as true as my fiction" has a tremendous resonance, and yet it's hard to pin down precisely why that is so. What is it, in your fiction, that makes it truer than anything you can say outside it?

NG: Because fiction is a *disguise*. Fiction can encompass all the things that go unsaid among other people, and in yourself—all the complexities that, for reasons of your own human relations, you would never bring out in conversation, in confessional even, or in a factual assessment of any situation. Because fictional characters are so complex, they're made up out of so much experience over a very, very long time, and they're so mysteriously expressive of the peculiarity of a writer's observation, there is this freedom in fiction that there isn't in fact. The inhibitions go. And I repeat that statement again and again because for me it is absolutely true. There is always, subconsciously, some kind of self-censorship in nonfiction, which is supposed to be "true." You say: I think, I believe this or that. But all the doubts and all the crisscrossings that are behind that statement appear in a different form in fiction.

SC: There's also something about the dialogic nature of fiction—not in the sense of characters conversing, but in the sense that you, as a writer, can allow an inner dialogue about something, in which alternative perspectives can be ranged against one another, with no necessary form of synthesis between them.

NG: I think that's another important point. In fact, one is usually looking toward a synthesis: it's part of the obligation, if you're giving a lecture, that you've got to resolve something in the end. But fiction is open-ended. And it doesn't matter when people say to you, what did you mean? There are twenty different interpretations of the end of *July's People*. People write their own ending. I'm happy for them to do so. The kind of conclusion that they come to, the individual conclusion among different people, simply follows—in a way very interesting to me—their own political views, their own image of society, their own concept of racism: what is in them that is racist or antiracist. Even their own ideas of how women behave toward their families. I think I told you that when someone wanted to make a film of this book, there was an argument about the fact that the main character, Maureen, leaves not just her husband, but her children there in the bush, and just goes off. The opinion was that no audience—in America, anyway—would ever accept that any woman would leave her children like this. So that this was a concept of motherhood, a convention of female behavior toward children. It was a stereotype that I wasn't allowed to break.

SC: I think our sense of an ending in South Africa has changed. When you wrote *July's People,* there was a sense that, all right, we were living in the interregnum, to use the phrase that you adopted from Gramsci, but it would come to an end. There would be the big day, and then, somehow, the afterlife would begin. But I think what's happened since the unbanning of the organizations and the release of Nelson Mandela and the others is that the ending hasn't come about in that way. It's a much more protracted and complex experience.

NG: When I wrote that book, we were poised like lemmings on the edge of a cliff, we were teetering on the edge of a cliff. Whether one could pull back from it seemed very difficult and unlikely at the time.

SC: Perhaps we need a different sense of an ending, a different postapartheid view of the world, which may be something quite difficult to fashion.

NG: Yes, in the back of our minds, there was this kind of apocalyptic feeling. And perhaps it was always self-fulfilling; we wanted there to be a kind of big-bang ending, because we didn't want to tackle it ourselves. But now it's so incredible and fascinating to see there's no end to the process. Life itself is a process—it's cliché to say it but it's absolutely true. And if you watched the Convention for a Democratic South Africa, you saw us, literally, pulling back from that cliff edge and talking about it.

SC: Talking of Maureen's "betrayal" of her children at the end of *July's People,* at the New Nation African Writer's Conference, they had a special day on gender, and people were discussing not only a nonracial South Africa but a nonsexist South Africa. So that feminism seems to have arrived in South Africa. You have always said that you were not a feminist writer, and you've given cogent reasons for that. Is that view changing?

NG: Not at all. No reason for it to change. I've never seen—for want of a

To me, so much of this feminist writing is *therapy*

better word—creativity in that way. And I never will. I think you only have to look at my work to see why. But of course it's very difficult if you happen to be a woman. I'm a writer who happens to be a woman; there are writers who happen to be men, but they don't seem ever to be faced with this kind of probing examination, the expectation that there should be something special about it, or limiting, or self-releasing, or whatever. To me, so much of this feminist writing is *therapy*. Women have suffered and are suffering a great deal. They have—you see it, again and again—as have blacks, centuries of a kind of slave mentality, which produces tremendous rebellion, thank God, but also leaves all sort of strange remnants. But in my political activity, it's always been the freedom of the individual within the good of the whole that has mattered. Among these individuals I include women; women have certain special disadvantages. But then, so do blacks. And as a result of having been the oppressors, so do whites.

There was a very interesting moment at one meeting in Stockholm where Wally Serote and I both read. Just before

that, we had been given a lunch at Uppsala, at the university, and there were lots of students there. Wally was right at the top of a long table with about twenty people, and I was at the other end; so we had no kind of contact, but apparently somebody said to Wally: You know, Gordimer is being hailed as somebody who has enlightened people, through her characters, as to the true nature of racism, of what it does to individual human beings, but she's white—what does she know about racism? Now, I didn't know about this remark to Wally, so I didn't know what he said, but after we had both read, and the floor had been opened for people to ask questions, he said: "Before the questions start to be asked, I would like to answer a question that was put to me at the table." Now the whole point of what he said was that I had indeed familiarized myself with racism and taken on responsibility for it. So he defended me in this. But when I reflected on it afterward, it struck me as an extraordinary thing. Because, if you think about it, how can you say that those of us, as whites, who imposed racism, who lived by racism, don't know about it? We know about it, all right—profoundly. I'd never thought about it that way before but *of course* we understand racism. You don't have to be the victim; you can also be the perpetrator.

SC: It's significant that there was this solidarity between you and Serote. When Mayor Dinkins of New York came here, you gave him some thoughts about separatism in the U.S.A. and compared it to the state of race relations in South Africa. You've been to America many times. What is your view of race relations in America right now?

NG: Even if I've been many times, I'm only there for short intervals, so I mustn't pretend to know a great deal, but I think in the last couple of years there's been a deterioration, and that is what I was talking to Mayor Dinkins about. Ten years ago, when I went to America, among the kind of people that I know best and mix with, gatherings would be mixed: there would be black people and white people. Now, suddenly, it's all gone white. The black people that I meet are always in a professional context; in TV studios, there are a lot of people in big positions, executive positions—there are black directors, there are people like Charlayne Hunter-Gault and others. But somehow or other, the old easy social mixing among people who were interested in writing, in painting, in theater, in politics, seems to have gone. There seems to have been a drifting apart or a withdrawal, somewhat like we had here in the seventies.

SC: What of the chances of nonracialism in South Africa?

NG: It's very, very difficult. And standing aside from my own position, vis-à-vis being white among blacks, I think that there's an amazing amount not just of tolerance but of good will, from blacks toward whites. I think it's astonishing, at many different levels, and it's quite inexplicable when you think of what blacks have gone through. This is not a sentimental view—and there are young blacks who feel very bitter against whites—but, by and large, from the leadership right the way down to very ordinary people, there's an amazing tolerance. And I would draw a distinction between tolerance and subservience.

There are very, very few blacks, thank God, who are subservient anymore. And really, beneath the surface subservience there was always a sense people had of their own dignity. And if there is such a thing as a soul, I think that this has kept the soul of blacks alive and is the most

Maybe, as time goes by, the mask that you're wearing becomes your face

precious possession that they have. So given the ratio of the population, the overwhelming majority of blacks, from that point of view I think it's very hopeful.

Then we come to the big question of the whites. I think whites really are the big question. Many whites who were tacitly racist if not openly so are now I think moving away from this—for pragmatic reasons. But who cares? You don't have to have a change of heart to behave decently. Sometimes it can be self-serving and you don't mind. And then maybe, as time goes by, the mask that you're wearing becomes your face, as you realize that other people are human beings and mixing with them is not something that is terribly difficult or painful. But what about the extreme right wing? I know that among politically minded blacks there's a great unease about these people. And you know why—because they seem to be meeting and riding around on horseback with their twisted swastika . . . or saying that they want to carve out their own little *whitestan,* a piece of the country where they can live alone—you know, a fenced-in game reserve for whites. It's not really *them* that one worries about, even though they've done terrible things, shooting people at random and so on.

It's not them. The worry is about the composition of the police force. And I think from the police force there's an extension to the civil service, to the whole infrastructure of the country which is in their hands. So that they fear to lose their jobs, their easy jobs and their cradle-to-the-grave security. And this is something that the English-speaking people allowed to happen through my whole lifetime, because, you know, who wants to go sit behind the counter in the post office, or who wants to be a postman? So that the Afrikaners, the peasants who came to the cities during the thirties, the drought time, then moved into these protected jobs, and it was safe and you jogged along—you didn't make much money but you were safe. And the English-speaking whites, of course, moved out into more adventurous and demanding and rewarding jobs—commerce, the professions, and so on. The result is we've landed up in the hands of these people who are potentially dangerous enemies of a nonracial, majority-ruled, nonsexist society—even if the result of the referendum on negotiations has somewhat calmed fears about the extreme white Right. They turned out *not* to have the support among Afrikaners that they claim.

SC: They are the minority of a minority.

NG: Yes, this is now proven. But they can still cause trouble—sporadic violence.

SC: In the short term, at least. But perhaps a long-term realism will prevail, a sense of the demographic realities. And then we can hope that, as you say, the mask becomes the face.

NG: People often talk as if the preeminent question is how black and white will get on together. That's not really the question. The question is the ghastly backlog in education. And the backlog in housing. These are two tremendous questions. I don't know how any future government is going to meet them. It's going to need all the help in the world and all the patience and forbearance, and it also needs something even more difficult. It needs the liberation movements now to deal with the crisis of expectation. To impress upon people: Don't expect that everything is going to be rosy for you tomorrow, that you're going to have money and a good job and a house and a car.

• • •

SC: What's your sense of the state of South African writing over the last ten years?

NG: I think it's been very up and down. You know, right into the eighties, we had this kind of flowering of what I call political lyricism. It came from young people who were in and out of prison, who wrote passionate doggerel—and some wrote real poetry. And then that somehow died away. I regretted, during that time, that the whole important small tradition of the modern short story being written by black writers just wasn't happening anymore. People have begun to write stories again, but if you look at the very small number of books of stories that have been published, you can mention two or three names and that's it. And what has become glaringly evident, in maybe the last ten years, is that many people are struggling to write in English. They have talent, but, first of all, the education is bad; and second, even if the education were to be good, they are still not writing in the mother tongue. Perhaps you can become a good journalist, but when you want to write with inner passion, you need to be able to draw on your mother tongue. And it has become clear that it's one of the great inhibiting factors.

SC: I remember, during a recent panel discussion, that you and Ngugi agreed, though for different reasons, on the importance of writing in indigenous African languages. But there are other writers in the world, such as Chinua Achebe and Salman Rushdie, who have transformed the English language by writing it from within another culture, changing the shape and form of English itself.

NG: Well, I would separate those two. I don't think Rushdie is a good example. Rushdie has had a completely English, European education, and the different viewpoint from which he writes is a cultural one, but not a linguistic one. It's very difficult to separate them, but it's very important. And his influences are European writers, there's no question.

SC: But not only. There's a tradition of oral storytelling and so on . . .

NG: But the manner of writing, the vocabulary, the way that he uses the fantasy in a sophisticated fashion, owes more to Günter Grass than it does to oral tradition. There's a lot of loose talk about how the English language would be enriched by people speaking it, and the demotic speech of people who use English as a second language, and so on. But I think Chinua Achebe, who happens to be a very wonderful writer, is a very good example of somebody who has an extraordinary ability to use everything, from his own language, from pidgin, from mandarin English. So to think of asking Chinua to write in Ibo—well, I don't think he's ever written in Ibo, but he couldn't write better in Ibo than he writes in English because he writes superbly in English. But there are not many Chinua Achebes around—even among people who have had the same education. I can think, without naming them, of some of our best-known and brilliant black writers here. There are still places where their work fumbles in English, where you feel they really haven't

What's the point of running creative writing schools for people who haven't got a proper grasp of the language?

said what they want to say because they haven't quite the grasp of the language.

SC: So you think the future of South African writing may not necessarily be in English?

NG: I think it will be; I don't think that English will ever be given up, there will always be writers who write in English.

But I think there's a whole second layer of people with talent who will write popular literature, which should be available. It's not just the fact that the writers themselves will write better in those languages than they would in English, but they will also reach a wide public. The work won't be elitist the way it normally is, through no fault of ours; all of us who write in English in this country have a very small readership, whether we're black or white, Indian, so-called "coloured," or whatever, because most people are not truly literate in English. Some black writers say to me that very many are not truly literate in their own language either, because education has been so bad. But there still will be more, many more who are. So if we want to spread literature, and the pleasures of literature, I think there must be an opportunity for people to publish in their own languages.

We've got to change our priorities, too. All these ideas of running writing schools—what's the point of running creative writing schools for people who haven't got a proper grasp of the language? We've got to encourage reading,

American cultural imperialism in this country is terrifying

tremendously, because I believe it's the only way you can learn to write. And, secondly, we've got to somehow bridge the gap between basic literacy classes and organizations, and people who want to use their literacy to write.

SC: For a time during the eighties, there was the idea—perhaps one of the apocalyptic ideas—that there could be a people's culture, a people's literature, and so on. But it hasn't proved to be that easy. In America, popular culture is a derogatory term, it's television or whatever. In South Africa, there was the hope that it could mean something different.

NG: No, but it doesn't; it means exactly the same thing. It means popular culture in the American sense of the word, and indeed it comes from America. I hate to use clichés, but American cultural imperialism in this country is terrifying. If you watch TV, 98 percent of the programs come from America. They are sitcoms, they are "L. A. Law" type of programs, they are completely American. I don't know how you are going to make inroads against this. But I think if people can have open to them, from the time they're children, the pleasures of reading—well, there one has a chance, because there isn't a domination of any particular culture, especially as we do have quite a decent body of our own literature. I think what we ought to do is to concentrate on giving young writers a chance by publishing anthologies, because it's in anthologies that you really begin to feel your feet. The mistake we've made in the Congress of South African Writers is that, in order to please our members, we have published whole books of poems by completely unknown persons. Perhaps ten out of twenty-five poems are any good. The others haven't been worked on, they're just dashed off. So nobody reads that book and it can't command any real critical attention or interest.

• • •

SC: Earlier you said that receiving the Nobel Prize is like having a retrospective. When you do look back, could you pick moments, or particular books, stories, or novels, where you think things really came together? Maybe these are turning points, or points when you think you achieved something in particular.

NG: Well, this is a sensible question, not which is your favorite book? Because I don't think writers have favorite books; and if they do, I don't know why. You may have a special feeling for a book, and that would probably be attached to a certain stage in your life or some kind of private circumstance, or having had a go at something you've wanted to do for a long time but didn't think you could do. So, in that context, I would say that there are a few books that have something special to say to me. I think of *A Guest of Honour,* which in a way was not stylistically innovative, though it's not as direct, perhaps, as some people think. But I have a special feeling for that book. I think two things stand out: first of all, if I look back, I'm very interested in the character of that girl, because if I look at her from a distance, it seems to me that she's sort of the last colonial woman, and that she's linked in some way, to Maureen, the protagonist of *July's People*—a big jump. Maureen deals with things differently and comes from South Africa while the other doesn't; the other is the last of the old colonial people sort of left behind, floating around in Africa.

SC: A sport in the old sense.

NG: A sport in the old sense, yes. So that it's interesting for me to see how, if somebody intrigued me, I worked around it, and then, two books later, took it up again in a different way, quite subconsciously. Also because that book was not set in South Africa, but it had a broader view, and it asked, indeed, the question, what happens afterwards— when the nice, neat, black-white, anti-imperialist, anticolonialist, or whatever-it-is struggle is over. What happens then?

The Conservationist is also a book that I have strong feelings for. Because it's my most lyrical book, and I really just assumed that the reader would take the leaps with me. I don't explain anything. I mean, it's set within the grid of the most complicated racist laws. They just become evident, or they're symbolically evident. You either understand it or you don't. And also because after I'd done it, I realized that I was dealing with the central question that comes up again now all the time: the possession of the land.

Burger's Daughter illustrates the other side. For a long time, I had been waiting for somebody to write a novel which would try to bring to a broad canvas the position of the white Left in South Africa, and the extraordinary dynasty of belief and struggle in these families, and their position vis-à-vis blacks. People wrote so many good factual books about their experiences in prison, or about their experiences in exile, but nobody wrote a novel about it. I felt very inhibited, because I didn't belong to one of those families: I wasn't at all on that level of total commitment and sacrifice. So I felt that it would be somehow presumptuous of me to be the person to write the book.

But eventually, as nearly always happens with me, I forgot that anyone was going to read it and I just wrote it.

SC: When you say inhibited, did you really have to hold yourself back from writing it?

NG: Yes, that book had been going around in my mind—obviously it changed as the situation changed—but I wanted to do it for years. But there I had something that I've always said a writer should never have: I had my eye on who's going to say what about this book that I've written. It was the only book I've ever written where I sort of held my breath, thinking, well now, there will be such opprobrium, and it's going to fall on my head, from the very people to whom I was paying homage in this book. Of course, some of those things did happen. Not—interestingly—from individuals who lead that kind of life, but criticism did come—that I had a damn cheek. There was something analogous to that remark in Uppsala: she's white, what does she know about racism? In this case, she's not a revolutionary Communist, what does she know about this? It happened in some left-wing journals, the *South African Communist* and so on; I was attacked. Recently I met people who were involved in this, and, so it seems, now we're all good friends. But there you are. These things change.

With my last novel, *My Son's Story,* I show, through my character, a lot of division, ambition, infighting within the movement itself, which, though it's not mentioned, is obviously the ANC. So again, I thought—especially with my position then, when I was writing, already close to the ANC—I am doing what a good loyal brother or sister doesn't do, but I forgot about it and I did it. And it has been accepted. Which amazes me. I was fully prepared to have some trouble, but they don't seem to want to deny that there are these problems, as there are in any political party or organization. And from the signs I've seen among fellow writers—people like Achmat Dangor, like Njabulo Ndebele, and others—there's no feeling that we're going to sweep things under the carpet.

• • •

SC: You're someone who's always maintained the right to ask questions in your fiction, but in your politics you've moved to the left over the course of your life. And today, passing from one interregnum to another, there is this question: what is the Left? How do we think about this in the wake of what's happening, not only here but in Eastern Europe?

NG: I say somewhere toward the end of my essay "Living in the Interregnum" that we have to think about a new Left.

There are no pure reasons for political commitment, and perhaps that's good

I cannot believe that all that was progressive and good in theory should be abandoned, and nor would I say that it should be abandoned after seventy-four years. What is seventy-four years in social history? It's not even three generations. So

I was making some kind of appeal to myself and others, that we should think hard—abandoning what has proved a failure, and so much has been. I mean even something that's quite hard to swallow: it seems that you have to have a market economy. That any kind of collectivism goes against something in human nature: people want to have, they want the freedom to work for themselves. You want to strike some kind of balance between that and being swallowed up by one big world under United Fruit or something of that kind . . . all the old bogeys that we had. And I still believe in that, Stephen. I really do. You have to have a little streak of utopianism; you have to be idealistic. Without idealism, politics is a very empty thing. But you must be realistic, to know that you're never going to get there, but that you have to move part of the way. But I think that, for the moment, my inner attitude is quite cowardly, in that I retreat into concentrating on *here,* on what's happening in South Africa and our problems and our solutions, knowing all the time that they're completely connected with the outside world, and that we cannot find a solution that isn't, in some way, going to be worked on elsewhere. But I am in retreat from the whole global question.

You know, there are no pure reasons for political commitment, and perhaps that's good. I mean, what are pure reasons? How does a white born and brought up in South Africa come to reject the white ethos? Why? You can't tell me that it's just some wonderful pointing needle of justice. I think there are all sorts of background reasons, personal rea-

sons. Among Afrikaners, for instance, it's often been mixed up with rebellion at incredible authoritarianism from the father. And a sense, also, that women are so subjected to male authority. There's a whole feeling of wanting to get away from this. And then that broadens into an understanding of what happens to blacks, coming from the political authority. And so the external, objective reason and the internal reason for rebelling come out when people slough off their birth-determined identity and become something else.

SC: It seems, to take up Eastern Europe again, that the one thing intellectuals held on to—having been through a revolution that failed and that was now oppressive—was some conception of the ethical. In a world in which everything else has gone dark, maybe that is something to keep a hold on.

NG: I think so. And when we say the world has gone dark, it isn't because we've been overwhelmed by dictatorships; it's that what we thought of as human advancement has turned out to be rejected by people themselves.

SC: Of course, there wasn't a sense here that those on the left necessarily believed in Soviet communism à la Eastern Europe. It wasn't as if the Left was monolithic.

NG: No, but you do find this belief among blacks, and among the many young blacks who still adhere to the South African Communist party here, even though the party has moved. If you talk to them, they still imagine that this world that was dreamed of in 1918 should come here, this is the form of freedom that these young people have in mind. It's quite frightening.

SC: It is. And it suggests another paradox, which I see in *My Son's Story,* for example, which amounts to a crisis of language—because the language that constituted the language of liberation in South Africa was the language of oppression elsewhere. And we have to come to terms with that.

NG: I don't know how we come to terms with it. Even if you look at the Freedom Charter, the ideas are admirable, but they are so broad, loose, rhetorical, and they derive, truly, from the political rhetoric of 1918. And then what comes in, in its place, among writers? One of the most promising people here is this rap poet, Lesogo Rampolokeng. But now he indulges himself, gets away from disciplining himself as a writer; and he's got wonderful gifts of imagery, to me always a starting point for someone as a writer. He's just letting it go, letting it rap. Which is much easier than refining it, and getting the essence out of it. He abandons the political rhetoric that comes back from the dead past, the old rhetoric of liberation, and his new rhetoric of liberation is rap. Incantation.

SC: But you're suggesting that, if it's done properly, the writing of fiction may have a role to play, politically, by contesting political rhetoric.

NG: Yes, I think it has all the time. I think many writers are beginning to re-alize this: there is a kind of nausea attached to it. But there's also a terrible inhibition among young people beginning to write. If I run a workshop, I like to start off by saying, why do you want to write? A flicker across the eyes, and parrotlike, it comes out: I want to express the oppression of my people. Or, I want to write about what my people suffer. Or, I want to contribute to the liberation of my people. There's hardly anyone who tells the truth, which is, I don't know why. Or, Because there are things I feel that I want to write about. Funnily enough, if there is anybody who has the guts to say this it's usually a woman. To say I want to express my feelings, I want to tell what I know.

I wouldn't say I disagree with Albie Sachs when he talked about the notion of culture as a weapon of struggle and called for a moratorium on that, because I think he's also been misunderstood. There should be a moratorium on didacticism, he's right about that. But I think one has to preface that by recognizing, and I certainly do, that our literature—and by that I would include the theater—*has* been a weapon of struggle. When people who perhaps would never have thought about what happens when kids are shot in a riot here saw *Sarafina!,* the musical play, they understood it in a way that you don't seeing a minute-or-two flash of violence on television. What led up to it before, what happens afterward, is what comes in the theater and what comes in fiction.

So I think that we did have, in literature, a role to play. Even if, like myself, you didn't write propaganda. Sometimes what doesn't appear to be propaganda is a form of propaganda in that it shows people what's really going on.

And they make their own decision about the morality of what was done. Whereas propaganda makes the decision of morality for you and thrusts it down your throat.

SC: So that's a tradition that can continue: literature can still play an important social role.

NG: Well, I think it won't continue in quite the same way. We won't have the bad side of it, which is the inhibiting effect on people. Where if they wanted to write about some incident in childhood, they didn't think it was "relevant." That will go. What will be needed now is something different from that; it will be the courage to do what we've been talking about: to allow the writing to be a critique of society.

SC: The old role, but in a new form and shape.

NG: It's the old role in a new shape. And this is something that's inherent in writing, no matter where, or who is doing it. And it's a subconscious thing.

SC: In a sense now, we're entering another country. Not the past as another country, but the future as another country.

NG: The future is another country.

SC: And a new identity for South African writers.

NG: Well, new subjects opening up. I can't understand why people can be worried that because apartheid will go, there's nothing to write about. I simply cannot understand it.

SC: It's like that piece of idiocy that came out of Washington a few years ago, that history had ended.

NG: Well, I knew God is dead, according to some philosophers years ago, but I didn't know history had died.

SC: Yes, we were told that the future would basically be one big shopping mall.

NG: That wasn't so wrong. Anyway, a phase of history has come to an end. It has changed.

SC: The old certainties have gone.

NG: But, as you say, what are the new ones? Perhaps, if you look back, something can always come out of failed social experiments, good or bad.

SC: That's no consolation to the people who have suffered.

NG: Of course not. There is the sacrifice of a whole generation.

SC: I think these things come around. They'll come around in a new form, perhaps unrecognizable to us.

NG: But you know what the troubling thing is? There's this wonderful idea that we're all brothers and that it's one world. I know that when I was first grown up, there was the idea that barriers were breaking down, barriers of communication were breaking down, and now, indeed, they've all broken down. And we're moving toward one world: we have economic unions here, we have talk about common currencies, all sorts of groupings moving together. But the biggest move ever toward one world, which was the Soviet Union, has fragmented. And, desperately suffering as they are, this is what people want. Then, too, if you look at the incredible civil war going on between the Croatians and the Serbs, it's absolutely staggering. You'd have to believe that people are born in sin, the sin is nationalism that is in them. Do you agree?

SC: Absolutely. When I was in school, we learned that nationalism was a phenomenon of the nineteenth century; well, there's never been a century for it like this one.

NG: Especially toward the end of it.

SC: And it's frightening.

NG: The passions! It's absolutely staggering. People are prepared to lose everything. To die just for their language, their culture, the little bit of power in some little corner of the world . . . it's very difficult for us to understand. Then I think maybe there's another phenomenon. People like us, like you and me, white South Africans, we start off from a position of deracination. We have put out our roots into the soil, the mulch we

hoped we'd help to make, of a nonracial society, so that's something that we feel we can belong to. Our parents, our grandparents, having come from somewhere else, characterized us as aliens, conquerors, whether we conquered anything or not, in somebody else's country. So maybe it's difficult for us to understand this deep nationalism.

• • •

SC: But what opposes nationalism in this country? Nationalism was always the National party—it was the party of apartheid. You've got the African National Congress: so that's nation-building in another way. How do you get outside of nationalism, especially when other options are in crisis?

NG: You're quite right. The ANC chose a name whose implications we don't even think about anymore. But that's because the ANC presents itself, I think quite sincerely, *not* as African nationalist.

SC: Well, it's true. I think it's genuine in that way. Perhaps what that means is that nationalism, like anything else, doesn't always take the same form.

NG: Well, in the ANC we look upon ourselves, black and white, as *one* nation.

SC: And maybe that's distinctive in a world where nationalism divides.

Volume 15, No. 1 is a special issue on the literature of Guadeloupe and Martinique that illustrates the dynamism and creativity of the literature of these two sister islands since the days of Négritude. Composed of critical essays by mainly North American specialists in Francophone literature, this special issue takes an outside approach to works within the Francophone literary tradition. The issue will provide students and researchers, as well as the general reader, with a crucial introduction to contemporary French Caribbean writing.

Published quarterly in February, May, August, and November.

Announcing a Special Issue of *Callaloo*

The Literature of Guadeloupe and Martinique

Volume 15, Number 1
Maryse Condé, Guest Editor

CONTENTS INLCUDE: A Shift Toward the Inner Voice and *Créolité*/ **Ann Scarboro** • Inscriptions of Exile/ **Françoise Lionnet** • Edouard Glissant: Towards a Literature of Orality/ **Michèle Praeger** • Feminism, Race, and Difference/ **Lizabeth Paravisini-Gebert** • A Woman's Voice: Marie-Magdeleine Carbet/ **E. Anthony Hurley** • Antillean Authors and Their Models/ **Danielle Dumontet** • Maximin's *L'Isolé soleil* and Caliban's Curse/ **John D. Erickson** • Patrick Chamoiseau, *Solibo Magnifique*/ **Marie-Agnès Sourieau** • Narrative and Discursive Strategies in *Traversée de la mangrove*/ **Suzanne Crosta** • Studies in Caribbean and South American Literature: A Bibliography/ **Kathleen M. Balutansky** and others.

Callaloo—A Journal of African-American and African Arts and Letters
Charles H. Rowell, Editor

HIPHOPRISY

A conversation with Ishmael Reed and Michael Franti.

Bill Adler

Ever since it first surfaced some fifteen years ago, rap music has been as divisive within the black community as without. The music will force a listener to declare which side he's on. Are you a b-boy or a buppie? Are you "down with it," or are you too damn old?

But in addition to its delineation of a class division and a generation gap, rap has also defined a kind of culture gap. With a couple of notable exceptions, the great black writers and poets of the contemporary scene have treated rap like a stepchild. This "ig-ing" of rap compares unfavorably with the examples of, say, Langston Hughes and LeRoi Jones, whose love of the "street music" (and the art music and spiritual music) of their heydays animated both their creative and critical writings.

Accordingly, I got in touch with novelist/essayist/playwright/poet Ishmael Reed to see if he might be interested in interviewing a new rap group called the Disposable Heroes of Hiphoprisy. I'd read his books, seen him interviewed about the music in a television documentary devoted to the Oakland rap scene,

and knew of his crusade in recent years to rid the network news of racist bias against black youth (a campaign conducted under the aegis of the Oakland chapter of PEN). I thought that if Reed and Hiphoprisy's Michael Franti had a chance to sit down together, they might indeed find something to talk about.

I also knew that Franti, virtually alone among present-day rappers, had the requisite intellectual range. Now just twenty-five years old, he and his partner in Hiphoprisy, Rono Tse, formed Hiphoprisy out of the ashes of a band named the Beatnigs, a postpunk "industrial" outfit that recorded one album for Jello Biafra's Alternative Tentacles label in 1988. Franti had turned to music after dropping out of the University of San Francisco's basketball program in favor of concentrating on his education. In this he was following the advice of Dr. Harry Edwards, who noted that professional sports tend to chew up and spit out their black heroes with systematic regularity and that, as the saying goes, a mind is a terrible thing to waste. This notion of the disposability of black achievers recurs

with some frequency in Hiphoprisy's debut album, *Hypocrisy is the Greatest Luxury* (4th and Broadway Records), the songs of which form the spine of the following discussion.

• • •

Ishmael Reed: How did the disposable Heroes of Hiphoprisy come to be?

Michael Franti: I was brought up to be a young, gifted, and black athlete, and that's really all that I was thinking about

when I went to school: just be a basketball player. And when I got to school, I found that the myth of sports, particularly for the black athlete, is a complete fallacy: you're there for one reason and that's to generate interest and income for the school. So obviously, the idea of Disposable Heroes comes from my own life personally, as a young black man coming up and being told, "Okay, best thing for you to do, since you're six foot six and you're black, is to play basketball." And I said, "Okay, I'm good at it. I practice at it. I work hard." And you get to a

Ishmael Reed and Michael Franti, in Oakland.

James McCaffry

certain point where you begin to understand that sports are perpetuated by the myth of the successful black athlete who is a millionaire, who is held up to all black people as a role model. On the way up everybody tries to do it, but you become a disposable hero at a certain point. You have your day in the sun, you get to whatever level you can, and then you're thrown on the scrap heap because you're disposable, your purpose has been served. That's what the first part, Disposable Heroes, is about.

So, five years ago, I started hooking up with a lot of young artists who were working in the theater and started combining African drumming with metal objects that we found out at the shipyards because we didn't have instruments or a place to rehearse, playing on metal things, and then just doing poetry and dance to it.

Hiphoprisy has to do with the hypocrisy of trying to be an artist of conscience in an industry that has no conscience. The question is, in your own life, what are you doing? What are you doing as an individual?

IR: Your songs indict consumer goods, designer cologne, and other luxury goods. But it's hard not to be implicated in what you critique. A poet on Pacifica Radio had a line that I thought was most telling. She said that she felt like a cell in the body of a serial murderer. Do you sometimes feel that even though you're indicting the system, you're part of it?

MF: Oh, yeah. I think about this every day because I have a child. How am I going to justify to my son, ten years from now, what I was doing while I was

on tour for two months? Was I out talking all kinds of crazy stuff, about holding my dick and being a rapper? Or was I engaging with issues that, I could tell him later, are ones that I would want *you* to understand; issues that I feel are important, values that I would want *you* to have in your life and hold as important? It's just a matter of responsibility, and the name Hiphoprisy deals with the fact, that inevitability, that there is hypocrisy in all of our lives.

IR: You said Hiphoprisy.

MF: Hiphoprisy—it's the hypocrisy of hip hop music, because there is a lot of political hip hop music now.

IR: What about Paris and NWA? They seem to be socially committed. On the other hand, I understand Eazy E of NWA joined some elite section of the Republican party. What does that say about the ethics of some of the rappers, not to mention some of the young black filmmakers? I heard, for example, John Singleton say in an interview that he was in on the decision to include violence in the trailers for his film, *Boyz n the Hood,* and he justified it by saying that was the only way to get the kids in to see a serious movie, and then they'd find out it had to do with more than violence. But I thought that was a very cynical marketing move. Why shouldn't you expect that violence would break out in the theaters, after people see these trailers?

MF: Ice Cube's in the movie, and it was supposed to be a movie about the problems of young black men, and the lack of fathers and role models. And then Ice

Cube comes out and does a St. Ides beer commercial. Like the week after the film came out.

IR: That explains the hypocrisy. What about the hip hop part?

MF: Hip hop is basically in the African tradition of talking over a rhythm. And you know hip hop music has all of the traditional elements of African storytelling: of braggadocio, of dissing, of humor. . . . And it's a contemporary version of that storytelling. It started off with deejays just using a drum machine and sampling other records. They didn't have instruments—you know, it's expensive to buy instruments these days and you just make do with what you have.

IR: What do you say to critics—I've heard this from mostly conservative critics who like jazz—that hip hoppers are artificial, that they plagiarize, they use stuff from other sources . . . even though when somebody plays a jazz solo, they may plagiarize: everybody sounds like Charlie Parker, you know?

MF: Well, it's not plagiarism. It's taking something from one context and putting it into another context and creating another work out of it. It's collage, an audio collage. And collage is an African art form. I notice even in your books, in *Mumbo Jumbo,* you're taking images out of different contexts and putting them together.

IR: Absolutely.

MF: But at the end of the day, it makes sense. And that's what hip hop is doing.

You know, recently people have made comparisons between hip hop music and jazz music, and the thing that I find similar about hip hop music and jazz music is their ability to change. Jazz music has the ability to change its format completely. You can go from bebop to cool jazz, electronic jazz to what is now almost like classical jazz, which is the preservation of jazz, but it has this ability to change. And it's the same thing with hip hop: it has the ability to change—different styles, different paces, different emotions. In a sense, it reminds me of the Jes Grew phenomenon in *Mumbo Jumbo.*

IR: I think rap is part of the same process. I was trying to discuss this process—Jes Grew—that some writers had pointed to as something that other African Americans used to create a new form. I think rap is certainly in that tradition. I'm also struck by the music that you select to go along with the literature. The choral music in "Satanic Reverses" is really a haunting piece. What kind of music is that?

MF: It's performed by Kenyan monks. I found a record of the "Kyrie" that they had performed in Africa using traditional African instruments in Catholic mass.

IR: They use Catholicism as a front in Africa. As a matter of fact there's some African religious group that's having widespread appeal in Italy, some charismatic group that the pope is looking down upon. The Africans and African Americans seem to put a twist on forms of everything that comes. They're very absorptive. They are able to borrow materials from other cultures and put their own twist on it. The trombone and the

trumpet in "Satanic Reverses" produce a really chaotic, cacophonous sound. Was that deliberate?

MF: Yeah. The music is chosen to go along with the text. First we come with the rhythm which will best work with what I'm saying, the text of the song. For different songs you try to create a different mood.

IR: You say "we"—

MF: Yeah, Mark Pistol, Charles Hunter, Ron Tse, and I.

IR: And what do you do? You just take music from all different sources?

MF: No. We make most of the music ourselves. We also use industrial equipment, power tools, pneumatic sanders. . . .

IR: That was considered very avant-garde in the 1920s: industrial sounds as music. I'm impressed because a lot of your critics dismiss rap without really listening to it. The kind of stuff that the rap musicians are doing was being done in the 1960s in art galleries: the multi-media sound. One man who is associated with this cut-and-mix technique of audio collage in literature was Brion Gysin. That was considered avant-garde in those days, and now you've taken it downtown and made it international. I think a lot of the critics don't understand the innovations that rap musicians are making.

MF: I think it's not even that they don't understand. I think a lot of critics are *afraid* of it because it is a black thing—a very flamboyant, aggressive, black thing. And a lot of critics just don't want to deal with it—regardless of what you're saying, because a lot of rappers are saying a lot of stupid stuff—they don't want to see a black person, man or woman, who is being boisterous and flamboyant.

IR: Being threatening. Saying some of the things you're saying—

MF: Well, on top of all, in our music, is political content.

IR: It seems they would be more comfortable with the misogynist stuff, even though they pretend not to like it.

Misogyny sells records, but it's important to examine *why* it sells records

MF: That's the thing. You have this group, NWA, with the number one record in the country and it's blatantly misogynist, and not only that, but one of the group was sued for $22.7 million for beating up a woman in a nightclub, a journalist.

IR: But Mick Jagger had a song about how he wanted to get some Puerto Rican girls and how black girls like to fuck all night. He got into trouble with the NAACP. Do you wonder if sometimes white criticism is used to market white artists?

MF: Who's buying the records? Now, it's mostly white kids. Something like 80 percent of rap is being bought in the white community now. But it is important that we address the misogyny that is in the music. I don't think that we can just sit back and say that this is just a reaction by the white media. . . .

IR: But why don't the white media see misogyny in Peter Gabriel's "I'm Your Sledge Hammer" or Hall & Oates' "Maneater"? They seem to condone it among white artists.

MF: I think that misogyny sells records, but I think it's important that we examine *why* it sells records. The reason that it sells is that young people who are buying the records, young males in particular, are fed this stuff in the media every day, in films and in television: males are the dominant gender, women are sex objects and are treated as sex objects. This is not just in rap music. This is in *all* music. This is in all TV, this is in all film. Black artists have been particularly put down for this and, with a lot of rap artists, justifiably so. But I think that it's important that the media and the consumers themselves just don't buy the records. If you feel it's misogynist, don't buy the records.

IR: The work you perform is very politically sensitive. You know, you have compassion for women, compassion for gay people, you're against censorship: all the right stuff. Do you really believe this? Is it genuine?

MF: Yeah, I believe it.

IR: How did you come to this? Having a child?

MF: Having a child is part of it but also, see, I'm a person of mixed ethnicity, and in rap music there was this whole move-ment of Afrocentricity, which I found to be very confusing and misleading. First of all, as you were saying, most black people in America are of a mixed ethnic heritage, either by choice or by rape or whatever. But also our culture is a mixed culture. We are not just black or white, you know. A lot of what is positive in our society is a result of the amalgam-ation. You know we can't just trace it back to a primeval source and say: "This is a specific African trait, and this is a Eu-ropean trait. And all African traits are good and all European traits are bad." So when we talk about Afrocentricity, it's a problem for me. Although I identify with being an African-American person, because that's how I am treated when I walk down the street, I began to reflect that, well, I'm all these other things, too. Should I be ashamed of that fact? Or should I try to come to grips with the fact that we live in a multicultural society and I am a multicultural person myself? On top of all that, I was adopted and raised by white parents. And so the whole idea of coming to terms with my identity was one of examining who I am and making a decision to accept certain things about myself. To the extent that I accept who I am as a person, I can establish my eth-nicity.

IR: Well, you know the Afrocentrics, on the other hand, say that they've been smeared by the media.

MF: I would agree with that. But I'm saying that a lot of it in the hip hop world is misleading: it's like a super-black trip.

IR: Why do you think that African-American people distort their heritage? For example, we know that most African-American people have Native American ancestry. We have Asian an-cestry. My father looks like a Filipino American. I have Irish ancestors just as you have, and I can prove it through ge-nealogy. The African heritage is only one of our heritages; there is also the Euro-pean father, the African mother, and the Native American mother. Black men co-habitated with Native American women after the male population was decimated as the result of wars conducted by the U.S. government against the Native Americans. Many African intellectuals view African Americans as a group dis-tinct from their own. I'm studying Yoruba now—but I'm always amazed at how African writers and thinkers dismiss the current back-to-Africa romanticism, and say that these people who call them-selves Yoruba priestesses and priests are not really interested in the hard details of West African culture, only their ability to cite the attributes of a few gods. And they make some sharp remarks about Swahili. The favorite Afrocentric lan-guage is Swahili, but that's the Arab slave trader language. It has a Bantu syn-tax but an Arab vocabulary. It's as ironic as English being the language of Euro-centrism, when the English have never identified with Europe. But back to the question why you think African Amer-icans deny the European and the Native American heritage.

MF: I think a lot of people don't know

about it, first of all, and I think that we live in a white culture and we are oppressed by white people all the time so. . . .

IR: So we define ourselves in the manner in which the whites define us?

MF: In the song "Socio-Genetic Experiment," I pose the question: "Did I piss in their gene pool or did they piss in mine?"

IR: Let me ask you about this miscegenation thing. I've been reading some

Don't you think that the white neo-Nazis and some of these black nationalists should unite, so as to save on overhead?

black artists in the younger generation who have come out against miscegenation. They think that miscegenation is a horrible thing. And it reminds me of the obsession of the Nazi movement. I read some of the American Nazi literature, for example *The Turner Diaries* by Andrew MacDonald, which is a bible of the neo-Nazi movement in the United States, and this is a big obsession. Every other page there's all this stuff about white women and black men, all the way through. Don't you think that the white neo-Nazis and some of these black nationalists ought to get together, to unite so as to save on overhead? They could, for example, share computer costs.

MF: Some black people agree with a lot of really extreme white fundamentalists. They're like: "We want to have a separate state. We want to have a separate economy." And they would agree with someone like Tom Metzger of the White Aryan Resistance (WAR), who would stand up and say white people should be with white people and we should preserve our way of life.

IR: He says that he has met with black nationalists and they agree with him. And they attend each other's rallies and things.

MF: I think it's almost suicidal to take that stance because we're so multicultural.

IR: And they themselves miscegenate. The black people who are saying these things themselves miscegenate and have European ancestry.

MF: Where do you draw the line? I'm a pretty light-skinned black person. Should I only be with somebody of my own specific light skin tone?

IR: Don't you think it's maybe about three hundred years too late to talk about a pure race? After all this cohabitation and miscegenation?

MF: Yeah! I mean, what is a pure race? We're *all* descendants of Africa . . . so when we talk about a "pure" race, it's not a race issue, it's really a cultural issue. I was reading Chinua Achebe's book, *Things Fall Apart*. And that's about someplace where everybody is black and marrying out of the culture is devastating. On campus at the University of California, Berkeley, there's such a division between white students and black students . . . and somewhere in between are the mixed students. They've actually formed a group there to have sort of a dialogue and a support group for mixed students who don't feel like they should have to choose. Like, if I'm not just black or just white, I shouldn't have to choose —I should just be able to be who I am.

IR: Look at the problems that nationalism is causing all over the world: the Serbs and the Croatians are fighting each other because of nationalism. Maybe nationalism was good in a former time, but now maybe it's too late for the world to be involved in all these squabbles.

MF: The world's too small to sustain this. It's almost suicidal.

IR: Let me ask you something about the politics of your album. It seems like a case of issue overload sometimes. I mean someone might accuse you of wallowing in Politically Correct Heaven here, and I'm just going to be the devil's advocate. Like you have the song, "Language of Violence," about gay bashing. What do you say to people who believe that all these different issues and members of these different groups you're sympathetic to shouldn't get as much attention as the real impoverished in this country, the people out on the streets.

MF: What happens is you get Compassion Fatigue after a while, you know. And then it becomes: what should you do first? Should you deal with the lowest person on the rung or do you deal with, like, what's here? I've always said you should deal with the six inches in front of your face, which is the surroundings that you live in, and that's what I write about. The song that's in the context of gay

bashing, I don't ever really specify in the song whether the guy is gay or not. It's irrelevant whether he is. I just say that he's *accused,* he's *called* gay, and that happens at schools all the time, where somebody who is quiet or slightly effeminate gets accused of being gay, and then all of this stuff can happen. But that song is really about the language, it's about the use of language as a means of dehumanization, to the point where it doesn't matter. You can beat this person up and it just doesn't matter, you know. So at the end I ask a question: "Is this a tale of rough justice in the land where there is no justice at all? Who is really the victim or are we all the cause and victim of it all?" I'm posing the question. The issue of homosexuality is one of the final taboos that is being brought out in the open, you know. But at the same time that it's being brought out in the open, the violence against gays is up. You have the issue of AIDS which, from my perspective, is an issue of persecution against the gay community—

IR: Not the result of their personal behavior?

MF: Well, it's a heterosexual thing, too, and it took ten years for the medical establishment to figure out how widespread it was among the gay population, but if you look in Africa, it's the number one killer in Uganda. I mean, people are going to say all kinds of things about the sexual practices of black people, sexual practices of gays, and I don't think that's the issue. The issue is people are going to be dying, and it's going to be a disproportionate number of those people who are black dying because they're going to be the last ones who are informed.

IR: Do you think you've broken new ground in rap, in that one does not usually expect your wide range of images and allusions to everything from science to popular culture? A lot of rap is one-dimensional.

MF: These are just issues that concern me and that concern a lot of young people today. The reason that you don't see it a lot in rap music is because rap music is an industry. It's what we're talking about in the song "Famous and Dandy." Kids do whatever is the easiest way to get over. If you're poor and you want to be a rapper, you do something that's already been successful. You do a "dissing" rap or "everybody party" rap or whatever because you don't want to take the risk of not having your stuff get over.

IR: You know this is very serious work you do. You don't use broad humor but you use a sort of high humor, which is irony. For example, your line that it's a Christian thing to do, to bomb Iraq (in "Winter of the Long Hot Summer"). Where did you develop the sense of irony—irony as opposed to out-and-out humor, I mean?

MF: Well, in the case of this particular comment, I saw in the news that these soldiers were writing messages on the bombs—"This one's for you, Saddam"—and when the first pilots came back they were talking about the bombing as if it were football: "Yeah, we had them in the first quarter, we scored three touchdowns on them in the first two minutes." And this one guy came on and said, "We lit up Baghdad like a Christmas tree, the whole city was just sparkling like lights."

IR: What does that tell you about the health of the nation's mind?

MF: We've manufactured consent. But when the government is talking about going over to Iraq and dropping bombs and killing, you know, upwards of 200,000 people—let alone those who are going to die from the effects of this war over the next fifty years—it's essential to have the average citizen looking the other way and believing, "OK, nothing happened. It was this clean, surgically executed war." The whole media representation is bullshit.

IR: In your single "Television: Drug of Nation," television is the villain.

MF: I don't think television is the villain. The programming is. In writing and in music you have the ability to write and put your words out to people on a shoestring, basically. If you have a word processor or a Xerox machine or whatever, you can disseminate information. In America, though, television is privatized. So, there's a big question about how it relates to the First Amendment—because not everyone has access to television. It's monopolized by the corporations. Now, if you look at television in Europe, it's very different than what television is in America.

IR: I don't know if you know about our TV news boycott. We organized a boycott out of here, in my house. With a computer and PEN Oakland, which is the Oakland branch of our chapter of PEN International. We organized town meetings in ten cities—and writers all organized that, so that shows that writers at least can influence people's thinking about television—and it ended up in a debate between me and Walter Goodman of the *New York Times,* where he was saying that television is just being accurate when it portrays all the problems of society as occurring in the inner city, in the urban areas, and that if we criticized this coverage, television would not do more, but less of this kind of coverage. This viewpoint is ignorant. Even Tom Metzger of the American Aryan party admits that the typical welfare recipient is a white single mother. Goodman was taking the television executives' side.

Is TV the reflector or the director? Is it mirroring what's going on or *shaping* what's going on?

That was a point of view that they took when they were answering our complaints through the media. The TV execs were interviewed by the newspapers in various parts of the country, who wanted them to respond to the questions raised by our boycott. And some of the executives, at CNN and ABC, for instance, were trying to explain where we get this overwhelming coverage of all the illegal or illicit activities of society taking place in the inner city. And they were saying either that that's just the way it is, or that they just do what the police tell them to: they just follow drug busts in the inner city instead of in the suburbs because that's where the police make their busts, which is not accurate. But your indictment is strong; you're saying not only is it a health problem, but it's sort of a way of programming the consumers.

MF: In the song I ask, at one point, "Is TV the reflector or director?" It's posing the question, is television mirroring what's happening in society or is television actually *shaping* what's going on in society? And from my perspective, and that of my group of young people, television is where we get *all* our information from the time that we are born. The perceptions we see on television of ourselves, and of the rest of the world, are the ones that shape our consciousness.

IR: You mentioned the Willie Horton advertising campaign in the song.

MF: I thought it was complete racist nonsense. I think that the whole approach has been to play on the fears of conservative voters in the elections. There's an election year coming up again, and we see in the media more and more of this talk about quotas, racism, affirmative action, the garbage with Clarence Thomas. And, just as in '88, the conservatives are trying to play on the fears of white America: "If you don't get Bush into office, you're going to have niggers running up on your doorstep. You're going to have this revolving door policy of prisoners leaving and not serving their proper sentence and coming out to haunt you in the streets."

IR: *Black* prisoners . . .

MF: Raping your women and assaulting your children and stealing your car.

IR: You call them conservatives, but they seem to have only one issue, and that's having to do with blacks—black quotas, illegitimacy. So even multiculturalism is viewed as a black conspiracy.

I doubt whether these people have ever read Thomas Hobbes. But are they true conservatives or are they just using conservatism as a cover for racism? I mean, there are a few conservatives who are unpredictable, like James Kilpatrick and William Safire, who criticized the Marion Barry bust as a case of entrapment. "Never had the United States government stooped so low," is the way he characterized this bust.

MF: There are conservatives who are conservative by doctrine, and then there are conservatives who are that way by convenience.

IR: Do you see conservatism and the opposite, call it liberalism, as being mutually exclusive? For example, there are a lot of people who support so called left-wing issues. I myself support massive aid from the government to aid people who can't help themselves, or the working poor, which is like the old Republican program. That's Lincoln. You can't think of anybody who used more massive aid to relieve the suffering of the working poor, the slaves in the South, than Abraham Lincoln. But at the same time, I feel that the part of the city I'm living in would be a better neighborhood and area if some of the people were more responsible and self-reliant. Do you see this new conservatism, as opposed to the traditional leftism of the African-American leadership, leading to some kind of synthesis? Can a new third way emerge out of this dialogue between the Right and black Left? Because there are good sides to both arguments.

MF: What I feel should happen is that we should be self-reliant, yes, and I feel that

we should take more responsibility. But I feel that every footstep we take in taking more responsibility should be matched with dollars by the federal government.

IR: Let me agree. The extreme left is saying that African-American people, Hispanics, just average people in any group have no control over their destinies and that the government should just give them a blank check. And on the right wing they're longing for some kind of former agrarian state when you went out and grew your own crops and neighbors helped to paint your house and all that stuff. And it's a romantic idea because now we have high-tech industries and people have been displaced because big manufacturers are taking their jobs abroad and looking for cheap labor in other places. Now, I noticed a lot of conservative critics loved the Matty Rich movie *Straight Out of Brooklyn*. I'm not questioning the motives of this filmmaker, but he does seem to be preaching the idea that the inner city is some sort of jungle, a Darwinian situation, and that only one or two people can make it out. I live in the inner city and I see a lot of people making it. I mean, the average black kid is not into this stuff—drugs, guns, crime, etc. So why is the right wing pushing this view so heavily?

MF: I think it's convenience. Just like the Clarence Thomas thing: "We want to show this black man who comes from poverty, picking himself up by the bootstraps." Anybody can do it, and if you don't do it, it's because you're not working hard enough.

IR: I've noticed also from reviews of the

new crop of plays and film and even some of the music that the critics seem to have bought into black nationalism. In other words, they treat the African-American community as if it were a separate nation, sovereign and responsible for itself, that therefore should generate its own economy, as opposed, say, to viewing the African-American community as a colony which is exploited from the outside.

MF: They always compare us to other groups who have come to this country, but what they leave out is the systematic disruption of the formation of a true autonomous nation. First of all there were millions of us killed on the way over here, in transit, and then when we got here they took away all of the cultural elements that made us strong. And so you have this group of people who have never been able to get on their feet. You're telling them to pull themselves up by their bootstraps and they don't even have boots yet. One of the problems I have with television stems from the fact that so few programs are produced by black people with black characters in them. Obviously, with a show like *Dynasty,* everybody knows it's surreal, because you have a thousand other shows about white people. But when you have a show like *The Cosby Show,* to me and you, that's surreal. But because it's the only show of its kind, it's presented to White America as being the Way of Black Folks.

IR: It also paints the fantasy that African-American people have arrived, that these problems existed in the old days, but they don't exist now.

MF: It's the same thing with these films. There hasn't been a steady stream of black films. Every now and then there's a little upsurge of a few films, every fifteen years or so, but there's not enough. So when you have a film like Matty Rich's, which deals with a black man beating his wife, you don't have anything else to balance it out. You don't have another film that deals with another type of black family.

IR: We did one—Steve Cannon, Walter Cotton, and I. The title is *Personal Problems,* and it was directed by the late Bill Gunn. We can get it shown at museums, at the Whitney, but we couldn't get it on network TV.

MF: That's another thing about the black films. If you look at the titles of black films that are being put out to all of our country, they're from a very small perspective of the black experience. They're all about the same thing basically.

IR: Your song about *Amos 'n' Andy* comes in here. Let me ask you: don't you think that you'll find Amos and Andy in all groups and that rather than being stereotypes, they're archetypes?

MF: Yeah. On the liner notes to that song I talk about the fact that *The Amos and Andy Show* was developed by white people in the '20s, and when they brought it on the television in the 1940s they had to find—it was after World War II—black characters who would play the racist roles. And at the time those were the only roles that were available to black actors in television and in film. Today, in the proper historical context, I personally find the show funny.

IR: A lot of black people do. But you're not supposed to say that to whites. When I was growing up, for black people, that was the favorite show.

MF: I can appreciate it in its context and I can respect the actors for their comedic genius, understanding this is a racist program. But for the majority of people in America, when they see it, that's their impression of black people.

IR: I'm just playing the devil's advocate here, but in *Amos and Andy* you have a variety of people. You have middle-class blacks, upper-class blacks. They and middle-class and upper-class whites are always the butt of the jokes in the show, sort of like the Marx Brothers. And it had the trickster, George Stevens, and this gullible Andy Brown and Amos, who was a hard-working cab driver and family man. Now, there's more variety in that than in some of the stuff you see in movies today. Some of these films made by some of the young black filmmakers don't have as broad a view as that. So what does that tell you about where we've gone?

MF: We've gone backwards.

IR: There are relentless criticisms of society in your work—and you don't seem to be imprisoned by rhyme, the way some people do, people who are more concerned with the form than the content. And you obviously do a very ingenious job of mixing the music with your group. At the same time, when I look at this work, I'm depressed because there is nothing but corruption and dread in your view of society. It's very bleak. Now if you were put in a position where you could change some of these things, what would you do? How would you make it better?

MF: You know, revolution always has this connotation of "Let's get a gun and go kill the president" or whatever. But if you look at what happened with the Indians in Guatemala, they had a revolution, but it didn't occur until liberation theologians came about and were able to tell these oppressed Indians: "God does *not* want you to be this way. Even though the Catholic Church has been telling you for the last several hundred years that God has preordained you to be a slave, that's actually not the case." And once the Indians came to that revolution of thought, they were able actually to engage in meaningful struggle. Now, I think that any armed struggle in this country is going to be just squashed, as we've seen time and again.

IR: So you're looking at the revolution in consciousness.

MF: I'm talking about revolution in consciousness. I think young people in particular are just inundated with this other type of rap music, and it's just about "everybody have a party." But I think that with us, rap is one way we can get a message across. Somebody said that listening to this record was like reading a Dostoyevski novel. And in fact the record company was proposing to market it by saying: "If you read one book this year, let it be this record."

THE RACE IS ON

A conversation with Shelby Steele and Julianne Malveaux.

A few short years ago, Shelby Steele was a rather obscure literature professor at San Jose State University. But the 1990 publication of his collection of essays *The Content of Our Character: A New Vision of Race in America,* his appearance on a PBS special, and the reviews that accompanied his essays catapulted him into the limelight. His message—that white racism isn't the only problem blacks face, that inner psychological barriers are also a problem—has been widely discussed and debated. In essays that are both intensely personal and sweepingly general, he coins phrases like "race fatigue" and "integration shock," and concludes that because he's tired of dealing with race, the rest of us must be, too. The mainstream media has embraced him and his message eagerly. He has been acclaimed as "one of the most important writers in the country today" and as "the perfect voice of reason in a sea of hate," as the *Los Angeles Times* has it.

Before I spoke with Shelby Steele in San Jose, I'd read his work and disagreed with much of it. I wondered about his "new vision" of race, much of which is

old ground visited by scholars like Thomas Sowell, Glenn Loury, and Walter Williams. I was struck by Steele's angst, his willingness to probe the inner workings of his mind and then to project them on other black people. And I was puzzled by some of the contradictions in his work, the extent to which he wrote in a personal vacuum, oblivious to history or social science.

The contradictions I saw on paper were magnified when I met Shelby Steele face to face. On the one hand, he is a self-described hothead who takes no stuff, especially on matters of race. On the other hand, he is an angst-ridden scholar whose vision is based on his detailed analysis of feelings. Our meeting started on a genial enough note, but our conversation quickly became so spirited that voices were raised, tabletops slapped, and silverware rattled. I challenged him, probed the content of his essays, and he responded with a passionate belief in his message. I came away from our dialogue surprised at his verbal fervor, something that clearly did not come through in his writing, puzzled at the intensity of his anger at the "civil rights establishment," and utterly frustrated at his trust—to my mind, naive—in the American system.

•   •   •

Julianne Malveaux: Let me start by asking about your work in the literature profession. What did you write your dissertation on?

Shelby Steele: I wrote three novels.

JM: Were they published?

SS: One was.

JM: What was the title of it?

SS: I forget. It's been a long time.

JM: Who published it? Where might one find it?

SS: Some of my fiction is in *Black World;* if you want to take the time to read that you've got more stamina than I do at this point. I used to write for *Black World.*

JM: What do you teach at San Jose State?

SS: Afro-American literature, creative writing, African literature, twentieth-century American fiction.

JM: And what kind of publications have you done in that area? What did you write before you started writing about race?

SS: I've written a lot on African writers, a couple of things on Ralph Ellison, some on the New Black Theatre, and some criticism.

JM: Why did you write *The Content of Our Character?*

SS: It seemed to me that people have not, for a long time, examined the underlying assumptions about race in America and haven't checked them out with reality. People weren't really talking, just communicating through our rehearsed positions. I felt oppressed by that since my reality felt different. Over time, irritation built up and I started writing.

JM: What kind of reaction did you expect from this book?

SS: Obviously, I knew I was going to start some stuff, but that was a good discipline for me because then I knew I had to go back and check it out, mull it over. I tried to write very modulated, reasonable, well-written essays, not to come out throwing punches. I did know there would be a reaction.

JM: Some of the people I've been talking to have said you've gotten the play you have because you wrote what white people wanted to hear; how do you respond to that?

SS: Well, I hear that all the time, and I had no intention of writing what white people wanted to hear. If you operate under that limitation then you're not ever going to find out what you think. One of my pet peeves is that blacks are far, far too concerned about what white people think about them, and worry about that to a point that we don't say what we really think nearly enough, and I think it has really hurt our dialogue in the black community and locked us into public

Julianne Malveaux

Jim Dennis

postures I think can publicly hurt us. We ought to stop this obsession with worrying about what white people think. It's a waste of time: who cares?

JM: Well, white people are calling many of the shots. I think it's relevant to be concerned with, not necessarily what they say, but certainly what they do! Especially as their actions relate to wages, employment, politics.

SS: We can't talk about white people as a monolith any more than we can talk about black people as one. If white people are going to be enemies of blacks then they're going to do it whether or not Shelby Steele is around.

JM: You talk a lot about black inferiority, and say we are too worried about white people. It seems to me that when you talk about inferiority, because so many of the examples you use throughout your book are personal, you are really talking more about yourself than the rest of us.

SS: No. I think it is absolutely impossible to be born in America as a black person and not to be stigmatized with your race, to come from a culture that has endured that stigma for 350 years and not to have internalized it to the extent that one will consciously or unconsciously have a certain anxiety about race whether you feel inferior or not. I think it's an underexamined and powerful force in black life.

JM: I think it depends on your experience. My generation was burning buildings when yours was leaving. I don't have any peers who feel inferior. I think you are speaking for yourself.

SS: No, you keep getting these studies that show things like four-year-old black children picking the white doll instead of the black doll. They have already been stigmatized, they have felt the brunt of race and internalized it to some extent. I think every black in America has it. I don't call it a feeling of inferiority, I call it an anxiety about inferiority.

JM: This is one of the generalities in your book that frustrates me. Devoid of footnotes or a knowledge base, you just assert that people have this inferiority anxiety. Based on your experience?

SS: Where does knowledge come from? I think I see something here. I truly believe that it's there. I think your resistance to the notion of it is proof that it's there.

JM: No, I just find it totally out the box. My resistance is that I don't see it.

SS: How could it not be there? How could you be a "nigger" in American and not have stigma?

JM: Basically, because I'm not a "nigger."

SS: But you are called one.

JM: Certainly not to my face. I'm called a whole bunch of things. But, again, what I see you doing is using yourself as a laboratory to come to some conclusions. You are taking your personal

Shelby Steele

©1990 Ari Mintz/New York Newsday

angst and imposing it on a race.

SS: W. E. B. Du Bois, what did he do? What did James Baldwin do?

JM: I know you're not comparing yourself to these brothers.

SS: What did any of them do? What does a writer do?

JM: Reading you, you pick up some of what you like and dislike, some of your passions, some of your fire, some of the things that turn you on and off. Looking at that I really would say that this is an anxiety-ridden man. I was fascinated by you, certainly.

SS: That's the job of the writer—to look into some places where others don't choose to go. Any writer worth his salt should be able to do that or you wouldn't make it as a writer. What writer do you know that's not like that—that's any good? Show me a literary writer who does not have some psychological sense of the way the world works, some sense of what goes on beneath the surface. That's the job of that kind of a writer. That's my job. If I can do it, fine; if not then I'm out of work.

JM: To what extent are your views a function of the fact that your wife is white?

SS: I think my views are a function of having lived an integrated life, and I think it's been a blessing to me because it's given me a perspective that I never would have had had I lived a more isolated life, racially. I think it's been a very expansive experience, showing me things that I otherwise would not have had a chance to know.

JM: Why are you such a fan of integration?

SS: I'm not a fan of integration; I don't advocate integration.

JM: You don't? In your epilogue you talk about, you know, getting into the mainstream . . .

SS: Damn right! Get into the mainstream. Goddamn right! If you're not in the mainstream, you're dead! Jews are in the mainstream, they have a culture and a community. The Asians are in the mainstream, they have the same. What's wrong with being in the mainstream? You are in the mainstream. I'm in the mainstream. If you get out of the mainstream where are you gonna go?

JM: You say you're not a conservative?

SS: Absolutely not!

JM: Your book reads like a fairly conservative treatise.

SS: If you write a book or if you make a statement in which you say something that might be interpreted as critical of black life—Bingo!—you are a right-wing neoconservative. So no one will look at your actual politics after that.

JM: Well, what are your politics?

SS: I see myself as a classic liberal, always have been and still am. I've never voted Republican in my life; I voted for Jesse Jackson the last two opportunities I had to do it. I believe very much in government programs to help blacks and poor people in general to develop. I think Head Start ought to be expanded. I think that there ought to be programs that intervene even earlier in life, in infancy,

People say I let white people off the hook. I want to see where this hook is, what all these white people are on

that teach parenting skills to single mothers. I think there ought to be a Marshall Plan, as the Urban League calls it, that goes into the inner city and helps these people to help themselves.

JM: You don't say all that in your book.

SS: That's what I believe. On the other hand, I also believe that we need to take more responsibility for ourselves.

JM: One of the problems with you and the other folks running around saying black folks ought to take responsibility for themselves is that you imply we take no responsibility.

SS: I don't think that we do, no. Do you?

JM: We could do more, but to me when people come out with "black people need to take more responsibility," I'm reminded of our history, which has been a history of taking responsibility. No one has come up with a perfect program, but . . .

SS: I would suggest that we not wait for it. People say I let white people off the hook. I really want to see where this hook is, what all these white people are on. So guilt ridden that they're handing out money for programs. I don't see it. The truth of the matter is, we're going to have to do it ourselves.

JM: I think that most people believe that. I think, at the same time, that we do a simultaneous thing. I think we have to agitate even as we take responsibility.

SS: I agree with you 1000 percent. I think we have to fight on two fronts; we have to continue to fight racism because discrimination is still a problem. At the same time, we've got to go forward.

JM: You minimize the effects of racism in your writing, but now you're acknowledging its existence and importance.

SS: I think that racism is a problem, as I say in the book. On the other hand, I have seen blacks move steadily forward in this society that is racist. Both things are true, so why deny one?

JM: I don't think that anybody is denying the progress that exists for some black people, but progress hasn't happened for everybody, and I don't think that the reason is this notion of inferiority or psychological issues, but the institutional dynamic of racism.

SS: Can you explain institutional racism? When I went to college in 1964 in Iowa—a white Iowa campus where we got called "nigger"—if we went downtown they wouldn't let us in the barber shops. This was back in the days when it was still a segregated world. I'm talking about heavy-duty racism. You knew where to go and where not to go. You had professors who were clearly angry that you were there. Every one of us graduated from college . . . every damn one! Today, you got every kind of support group—writing labs, black studies programs, black student counselors, black deans of student affairs, black student lounges, black student unions, Afro houses, everything—and you got a national dropout rate of 75 percent. Now, you going to explain that by white racism?

JM: I think a campus experience is qualitatively different when there are five black students than when there are five hundred. The more of us there are, the more threatened whites feel.

SS: When I was a freshman there were about eighteen of us in a student body of about one thousand. When I graduated there were about sixty of us. We were clearly a presence on campus, but we didn't have people sending us a secondary message that we needed special services. We were told we had to work harder.

When black kids go to these largely white universities, there is real integra-

Nothing explains an 80 percent dropout rate— no goddamn racism under the sun . . .

tion shock. The amazing thing is that those kids, who often come in with the same test scores and grade point averages as their white peers, within a semester or two are performing at a lower level. There are studies at universities that have been replicated all over the country—the more white friends a black student has, the higher his grade point average is. The fewer white friends a black student has, the lower the grade point average. There is among those students a cultural failure. Nothing explains an 80 percent dropout rate—no goddamn racism under the sun . . . that would have to be apartheid or something. A full six years after admission, a national figure, only 25 percent of black students have graduated. Six years after admission, black students are five times more likely to drop out than white students. The numbers are horrible. It's shocking. Blacks have the lowest GPA by a full point of any group in America except for reservation Indians. It is a culture that is killing off a generation because it's a horrendous situation.

JM: You don't feel that white racism has anything to do with it?

SS: White racism, white racism, white racism, everybody wants to keep saying. I'm telling you I went to school when there was white racism. All I've tried to do in this book is look behind that curtain of white racism. I'm not saying it isn't there, I'm just saying let's see what else is there. I've been at universities for twenty years now, and they are willing to bend over backwards to try to make black students happy.

JM: I don't know of any universities willing to bend over backwards!

SS: They go out of their way, what more could they possibly do? How many more black student lounges can they have?

JM: Come on. You're nitpicking. Theme houses play a positive role, just like women's studies centers do. They give students a place to feel comfortable, a place to retreat from battle.

SS: I would rather you say retreat from integration shock.

JM: No, that's your term. And is that what's wrong with a theme house?

SS: I think theme houses are a boundary. I think there is some fear there. You can't erect boundaries and somehow void the fears that are inside of you.

JM: What about affirmative action? Is that a boundary, too?

SS: Affirmative action is a straw issue. What we need from this society is intervention that goes from Head Start, preschool, first grade, so that we are educationally developed and can make it into those institutions on our own and demand that they treat us fairly.

That costs money, it takes effort and a commitment on the part of society. Society buys its way out by saying, "I'll let you"—magic wand, problem solved. And if you can't read anywhere near the level of the white kid sitting next to you, you get discouraged and two semesters later you're gone.

The numbers show that preference is not doing anything for us, twenty years of it, and we're further behind. Affirmative action isn't the answer.

JM: Affirmative action opened doors. Do you think they'd have opened on their own?

SS: The point is they are open.

JM: They didn't just open, something happened to make them open.

SS: We passed the 1964 Civil Rights Act that demanded that they be open and it gave us legal redress if they weren't. If we found discrimination we could sue. When I moved to the University of Utah for my doctorate program [Salt Lake City, Utah] and a landlord didn't want to rent to me because I was black, I took his butt to court and won. I think too many blacks don't do that, so racists think they can get away with it. These crackers should be in court all the time and a message should be sent—"If you do that you're going to court"—and you would clean some of this stuff up. Too many times we walk away from it and don't use the rights that are available to us.

JM: Your interest in racial justice certainly doesn't come across in your book.

SS: Well, I'm a civil rights baby, I grew up in the movement. I sat there and saw my father get his jaw broken trying to integrate a park in South Side Chicago. I believe profoundly in civil rights. If someone reads my book and says I don't believe in civil rights, this is someone who wants to take a swing at me because they don't like other things I've said. I have accepted that racism is a problem. I get into hassles, fistfights, shoving matches about it all the time.

JM: When was the last time?

SS: Let me tell you the truth, in Santa Barbara, about eighteen months ago, I

If you get in my way because I'm black, I'll try to wipe you out, I'll try to hurt you

got into a shoving match with a homeless man, a young dude, healthy looking, who asked me for a quarter, and when I said no he called me a "nigger." And I had a stick, too; I was going to wear him out. He had to run. I don't play with that.

I am a "black nigger" from the South Side of Chicago. I grew up in a tough world and had every kind of racism, grew up fighting the Polish people in the South Side. It was a tough world. I know what it's about. I'm not a cool guy, I'm a passionate guy and I just don't take that shit. Anybody who knows me knows that I don't take that. I am the kind of person who would always fight a situation like that, and still am. It's not a thought, it's a reaction. At the same time, I understand that I have to live my life, to move forward with my life, certain goals and ambitions that I have. I have to pursue those, and if you get in my way I'll try to wipe you out. If you get in my way because I'm black, I'll try to wipe you out, I'll try to hurt you. You have no right to be there and I won't sit still for that. You don't get in my way, no problem, I'll move over. What's contradictory about that?

We [black people] have no capacity to even talk with each other honestly about this, we just lie all the time.

JM: Who lies?

SS: The dialogue in the black community is full of too many lies because we're not after the truth—we're just playing this game of racial politics with white people; we're trying to chalk up points against them and they're trying to chalk up points against us, and so you can't say that because the white man will get a point on his side. Even though it's true, you better not say it because he'll take that stuff and run with it. Everybody in America is playing racial politics, and all they want to know is whether what I've done gives them a score on their side or whether it gives a score to the other guy. That's all they care about. They don't care about the truth. Nobody ever really reviews my book. They don't really look at the evidence.

JM: You have a very cynical view of the world.

SS: I have a very accurate view of the world.

JM: Of course, you would think that.

The Repeating Island: The Caribbean and the Postmodern Perspective

Antonio Benítez-Rojo
Translated by James E. Maraniss

"Benítez-Rojo's book ... will be an indispensable source for scholars and critics who venture into life, art, and literature of the chaotic Caribbean."—Julio Matas, *Cuban Studies* 328 pages, paper $15.95, library cloth edition $45.00

C. L. R. James's Caribbean

Paget Henry and Paul Buhle, editors

"These penetrating studies throw much-needed light both on C. L. R. James and the Caribbean worlds about which he cared so much.... Required reading for all who would like to understand James's varied work."
—David Barry Gaspar, author of *Bondmen and Rebels* 288 pages, paper $16.95, library cloth editon $45.00

Not Slave, Not Free: The African American Economic Experience since the Civil War

Jay R. Mandle

"An original and substantial contribution to the economic history of African Americans in the United States."
—Lou Ferleger, University of Massachusetts
152 pages, 41 tables, paper $12.95, library cloth edition $29.95

The Atlantic Slave Trade: Effects on Economies, Societies, and Peoples in Africa, the Americas, and Europe

Joseph E. Inikori and Stanley L. Engerman, editors

"This is cutting-edge, state of the art history-economics on the Atlantic slave trade."
—Vernon Burton, University of Illinois
423 pages, paper $14.95, library cloth edition $45.00

Duke University Press

6697 College Station
Durham, North Carolina 27708

GENERATION X

A conversation with Spike Lee and Henry Louis Gates.

Henry Louis Gates, Jr.: The Malcolm X project has been in turnaround, in development hell, for two decades. Not for lack of talent, either. James Baldwin and Arnold Perl, David Bradley, Calder Willingham, Charles Fuller and David Mamet were attached to the project as writers at various points. What's the real reason this movie was never made—until now?

Spike Lee: I just think the studios were scared of the film. And the rising popularity of Malcolm, coupled with the box office appeal of Denzel Washington and myself, is what made it economically feasible for them to invest in the project.

HLG: So the reports that there were script problems aren't really to the point.

SL: That had something to do with it, but I just felt that they were too scared. You have to remember that for many of those years, the Honorable Elijah Muhammad was still alive, so that was another deterrent. And the bad blood between the Nation of Islam and Mal-colm's camp has subsided over the years. I don't think it's an accident—the film's being made now by Denzel and myself. I think we were the people all along who were meant to do it.

HLG: David Bradley says they didn't keep firing the writers because the scripts were wrong; they fired them because the *story* was wrong.

SL: I would agree with that. Malcolm X was basically disputing the American dream. And if there's one thing Hollywood is about, it is selling the American dream. So Malcolm X is at odds with the images that Hollywood has always been about.

HLG: On the other hand, he *is* the American dream: rags to riches, figuratively speaking. The self-made man. Very much like Benjamin Franklin's autobiography or Booker T. Washington's—

SL: Pulling yourself up by the bootstraps, self-education.

Denzel Washington during the filming of "Malcolm X"

©Steve Sands/Outline

HLG: Right.

SL: Yes, but there are many different stories like this, with many different ethnic backgrounds. The story they choose to tell is always John Doe, Horatio Alger. It's never been about people of color.

HLG: How do you think about the relation between the film and the facts? For example, Bruce Perry's 1991 biography disputes some of the standard, canonical episodes of Malcolm's story. Like the 1929 fire that destroyed the Lansing, Michigan, house: Perry claims it was probably started by the father, Earl Little.

SL: Why's he going to burn down his house with his family in it?

HLG: And he's skeptical about the 1965 firebombing of Malcolm's house: Was it the Nation of Islam, or was it Malcolm, which is what Perry suggests?

SL: I know guys in the Nation who *told* me the Nation did it. They own up to that.

HLG: And he doubts the activity of the Klan in Nebraska and Michigan. He even disputes the way Malcolm's father died. Say Perry's right on some points, wrong on others. In a subtler way, any form of narrative history involves falsification or distortion of some kind; you're always shaping the facts to fit a narrative framework. But in the case of Malcolm X, there's an especially heavy political freight to carry. You got a taste of this kind of thing in the controversy over the historical veracity of Oliver Stone's *JFK*. The point is that while the *Autobiography* stands as a generally truthful work, individual episodes, some pretty basic, are disputed or controversial. And my question to you, as a filmmaker, is, does that matter?

SL: It does matter; I think that's something every filmmaker or writer has to deal with when you're dealing with someone who has lived. I think Oliver Stone's *JFK* is a great movie. What he did in *JFK* is what he did in *Born on the Fourth of July*. And I think the most important question you have to ask is, what is the *intent*? Our intention is not to tear down Malcolm; for us this is an act of love. And in those cases where we had to change names, change events, or make three or four characters into one, well, I don't think that's distorting the Malcolm X story. You have to realize we're not making a documentary, we're making a drama. Ella Collins is not in this film; Farrakhan is not in this film; you don't have Reginald introducing him to Islam in this film. So you've got the same problem as a filmmaker adapting a vast novel to the screen. You can't include everything; some things you switch or turn around. But you always have to ask artists what their intent is, and this film, as I said before, is an act of love. I know there are people who will say: this film is false because Malcolm didn't do such-and-such . . . and Denzel is too light-complected, and even though he dyed his hair red, that's not the color that Malcolm X's hair was. I mean, those little things do not detract from the overall work. Let's look at the body of the film, the overall sense of it.

HLG: Is this a "Malcolm" for our time?

SL: Individual viewers will have to make up their own minds. One of the reasons we've gotten static is that Malcolm was so many people. Everybody has their own Malcolm who is dear to them, and their Malcolm fits their own personal and political agenda. So everybody claims him in whatever period of life he was in at that particular time. All I can say is: I was the director, I rewrote the script by James Baldwin and Arnold Perl, and I will take full responsibility. I will say that this is the Malcolm I see.

HLG: Spike's Malcolm. But is Spike's Malcolm the Malcolm before Mecca or after?

SL: We show them all. That's why this film is an epic, that's why it's three hours: we want to show the total evolution of what made him, we want to show the three or four different people he was along the line. People tend to have one view of Malcolm, but he had many different views over his life, he turned completely around several times in this life. We leave it up to the audience to pick and choose which one they agree with, but we want to show all the Malcolms.

HLG: Do you have a favorite?

SL: I like them all—even when he was a

hustler. I can see what steered him that way: having seen the state commit your mother, the family broken up, your father killed. All these things led him to the course he took. I try to keep him together as one person, and all these things, you might say, are spokes in the wheel that made him. I know for sure Warner Brothers is trying to stress the Malcolm *after* Mecca, when he stopped calling white folk blue-eyed grafted devils.

HLG: That's the split everyone sees in him. But does this post-Mecca Malcolm, this more embracive figure, appeal to you, given your own sensibilities?

SL: Yes. I think that Malcolm came to a point where he saw that we're all brothers. And what he had done, through the Nation of Islam, was something he felt very bad about. I think that Malcolm felt personally responsible for every person who joined the Nation because of him. And you'd get arguments with people like Farrakhan, but Malcolm was the one that broke with the Nation of Islam. That doesn't negate the power and greatness of Elijah, but it was Malcolm who gained the Nation the attention of the world through the media. He was the fiery orator, and Elijah Muhammad simply did not have the speaking skills. You know, I had a meeting with Farrakhan. And it's funny, they don't even *care* what we do with Malcolm. All they cared about was how Elijah Muhammad would be portrayed in the film.

HLG: How is he portrayed?

SL: We show him as a very brilliant man—a man who taught Malcolm, and

then put Malcolm out there and gave him a chance to become the person he was. But I don't think he was a divine man; he was a human being, and we bring up the whole thing about his secretaries. He had a weakness for young women, and my view is, that's fine—except that he never owned up to it, and anytime these women would get pregnant, they were

Malcolm post-Mecca *is* the one where he evolved the most

banished from the Nation. Nobody knew who the fathers were; they were kicked out.

HLG: You mentioned that Warner prefers a certain Malcolm. How did that manifest itself, and how did you deal with it?

SL: They just make suggestions; I have final cut. I know what they're trying to get at. At the same time, they have a point. Because I think that Malcolm post-Mecca *is* the one where he evolved the most. That is not to negate what Malcolm did when he was in the Nation, aside from those theories that white people were grafted by the evil scientist Yakub and that there's this wheel spinning above us that's going to destroy the world. Even in those days, he was speaking important truths about oppression and resistance, and at a time when no one else had the courage to say the things that Malcolm was saying. These were things we all knew were true, but none of us in the past had the spine to stand up and say.

HLG: You talk about having final cut,

but one way people attack you is to say that in the final analysis, he doesn't *really* have final cut.

SL: Those ignorant motherfuckers haven't read my contract. I have final cut on all my films: that means I decide what goes in, what stays out of the movie. That's it.

HLG: Should we think of this as, in some sense, the film adaptation of Malcolm's autobiography, rather than an independent historical chronicle?

SL: The Baldwin-Perl script was adapted from the autobiography by Alex Haley. But the problems with it were in the last third of the script, where the split with the Nation occurs. They were really, I felt, walking on eggshells, tiptoeing over a lot of stuff—again, at the time Elijah Muhammad was still alive, there was a lot of bad blood still between Malcolm's camp and the Nation—and they really didn't deal with the split, and how Malcolm was killed. Since then a lot more information has come and we've really been able to develop the last third.

HLG: What sort of additional research did you do in order to capture a bygone era?

SL: That's where you have to use your production staff—Wayne Thomas, production designer; Ruth Carter, who did costumes; Ernest Dickerson who shot the movie; various other art directors; and a whole art department. Tons of research was done. I myself did a lot of reading and talked to people who knew Malcolm. I went to Detroit and talked to Malcolm's brother and Omar and his sister Yvonne; I talked with people at the Organization of Afro-American Unity like Peter Bailey, Earl Grant, Benjamin 2X, Kathleen Misslesharp, who was a captain at Malcolm's Temple Number Seven. I talked with William Kunstler, Betty Shabazz. Charles Kenyatta, Percy Sutton, Rob Cooper, Alex Haley, Dr. Omar Ozan, who wrote the letter that opened up the door for Malcolm when he went to Mecca, because people in the Nation were not considered true Muslims. I tried to use all these people who were there with Malcolm, who knew him.

HLG: What's your relation to the Nation of Islam? During one of the many controversies connected to this film, you were quoted saying that a nonblack director like Norman Jewison wouldn't be able to do justice to the subject. By that logic, what about a non-Muslim director?

SL: I think it's got to do more with race than religion. There was so much research that had to be done, and the people you had to speak to for the most part were black: I don't think they would have opened up to anybody white. Now, in all my films since *Do the Right Thing*, we've used the Nation of Islam for security on the set, and we used them again on *Malcolm X*. But there was one point where they had gotten the word from Chicago to pull out. And they stuck with us. They flew out to Chicago and we had to sit down with Minister Farrakhan and it was smoothed over. But Chicago still

put the word out that they're going to keep their distance, they're going to wait till the movie comes out.

• • •

HLG: There's a sense in which people already talk about a "Spike Lee movie" as a genre: there's a peculiar mixture of humor, politics, sensuality, drama, elements that constitute a distinctive sensibility in your own work. And, after all, these are films that you conceive, write, direct, and produce yourself, on your own, in a sense. *Do the Right Thing* wasn't based on a Pat Conroy novel; *School Daze* didn't originate on Broadway. In that generic sense, then, is this biopic *Malcolm X* really a "Spike Lee" film?

SL: I think it is. It's a challenge, because it's the first film that I didn't originate. I had to respectfully deal with Malcolm X but still see if I could put my personal stamp on it. But I think we've been able to do that.

HLG: How?

SL: I had to walk a tightrope, but you can still tell that I directed this film. I still feel it's a personal film like my other films. It was paramount to us that Malcolm would be a human being—we didn't want him to be a Jesus Christ figure, you might say. We wanted him to be complex, wanted him to have shades of gray, not be all black or white. Of course, you can write material like that, but in the end it comes down to the actor, and Denzel gives a tremendous performance as Malcolm.

HLG: Why would you risk so much on a film so fraught with controversy from the git-go? Why roll the dice on this, instead of going the way you were going?

SL: I had to take the opportunity. People ask me all the time: do you think about the pressure, about what's at stake with this thing? And I realized you can't think about it, because if you do, you'll be paralyzed. Denzel and I have a running joke that both of us are going to have to leave the country when this film comes out.

HLG: Why is the life of Malcolm, Spike Lee's Malcolm, needed right now?

SL: It's needed for the same reason that Malcolm was needed when he was alive, and even more so today. One of the things that Malcolm stressed was education. Well, we're just not doing it. It's such a sad situation now, where male black kids will fail so they can be "down" with everyone else, and if you get A's and speak correct English, you're regarded as being "white." Peer pressure has turned around our whole value system.

HLG: Since the late sixties, "authentic" black culture had been equated with street culture, or urban vernacular culture. It wasn't always this way.

SL: Wynton Marsalis talks about this all the time. It's really crazy. Matty Rich, who made *Straight Outta Brooklyn,* was attacking me by saying: "Spike comes from the middle class, Spike is the third

generation college educated—I didn't go to college, I didn't go to film school, I'm from the streets . . . "

HLG: I'm pure, I'm authentic.

SL: "I'm pure, I'm ignorant." I mean, that's nothing to brag about! This is exactly what I'm saying, where intelligence or education is being looked down upon. And that's stupid. Ignorant.

HLG: If you were a Martian, landed here, and wanted to know about black culture, and went to see the movies made over the last year, with that as the source of your knowledge of who black people are, what do you think you'd conclude? How is black culture represented?

SL: If a Martian landed here and had to imagine what black culture is, based upon recent black cinema, it would conclude that all black people lived in ghettos, did crack, and chanted rap. There was all this talk about the nineteen black movies that came out last year. If you look at them, their subject matter is basically limited to two genres: they're either comedies, or inner-city homeboy revues. Well, this year, there's only nine black films coming out. Do the arithmetic. It's not a good sign. And there's a whole lot more to black culture that just isn't reaching the screen.

HLG: I saw the results of a survey they conducted in various black schools in Washington, D.C., where they asked students to list things they consider "acting white." And one of the things on the list was going to the Smithsonian Institution. I couldn't believe it—when I was a kid, going to the Smithsonian Institution was like going to Disneyland, or better. You could listen to your heartbeat, see space capsules. Then you realize that a certain amount of romantic black neonationalism is tied into this attitude we've been discussing, which is a real problem for me. Is your movie going to counteract that?

SL: You see Malcolm educate himself; you see him going though the dictionary, copying every word and definition, A to Z. You see him striving to better himself, to educate himself, to talk correctly, to stop swearing and stop other people from swearing . . .

HLG: There's a kind of buppy nationalism that does seem to be waxing strong these days. I recently remarked, in a college seminar, that there are limits to identity—that you don't usually wake up in the morning and say to yourself, thank God I survived the night as a strong black man. And one of my students raised his hand and said, "*I* do." So I said, "Tell me about yourself; where'd you go to school?" He said, "Exeter, sir." I said, "The State rests." But what you find, often, is that there's a generation for whom Malcolm is purely a symbol, rather than somebody with substance, and that's so whether on the streets outside this building, or in Harvard Square.

SL: That's something we hope to address in this film. You have to realize there's a lot of reeducation that has to go on. I guess the first step is their wearing a cap or T-shirt with a slogan. But hopefully that's only a first step. Then you hope that it starts to be more, and deeper,

than this cosmetic bullshit. For a lot of people, that's where they're at: they wear an X hat, they've got the Malcolm X T-shirt—and maybe it's better than wearing Batman or Bart Simpson, but it's going to take more than that. The hat or the T-shirt isn't going to get you far. You know, people like shortcuts, so if you want to show you're "down," it's like, you don't have to question anything, because you have this T-shirt or this hat.

HLG: Why do you think there's been such a resurgence of interest in Malcolm X, especially among black youth? You see this "Malcolmania" in rap music, posters, baseball caps, a flood of new books, and, of course, your movie as well.

SL: I think Chuck D., with Public Enemy, and KRS-One, with Boogie Down

The whole turn-the-other-cheek business isn't getting anywhere in black America. That's why people aren't walking around with a *K* on their hat

Productions, have to be credited with really giving black youth Malcolm through their lyrics. It began there and it just started to build from here. Even more than that, though, the issues he talked about haven't gone away. If they had, there wouldn't be a need to listen to what he had to say anymore. Conditions have even gotten worse. That's why he's more popular now than he's ever been.

Louis Farrakkan, as a national spokesman for The Honorable Elijah Muhammad. In 1964, Farrakhan wrote in *Muhammad Speaks* that "the die is set and Malcolm shall not escape. . . . Such a man as Malcolm is worthy of death."

Archive Photos

down and turn the other cheek. The other day, there was a bias case where some white teenagers set on a black kid and painted him white. The next day, some black guys retaliated—fucked with some white kids and painted them black. So the whole nonviolent, turn-the-other-cheek business just isn't getting anywhere in black America. That is one of the reasons why people aren't walking around with a *K* on their hat.

HLG: James Baldwin said, and James Cone says this, too, that around the times of their deaths, Martin and Malcolm were, religion aside, virtually identical with respect to their viewpoints on the racial situation. Think that's true?

SL: Yes, they definitely had made overtures to each other, to find common ground where they could work together. I think they always had the same goals, just took different routes, and by both taking different routes, there were some words between them—each would speak on the other's tactics. But I think at the end they really saw that they had more in common than not.

HLG: What about the need for heroes? I think one of the reasons Malcolm's so visible on the streets is the lack of heroes. Does your Malcolm emerge as a hero?

SL: Very heroic. I think Ossie put it best in his eulogy: he said Malcolm is our shining black prince.

HLG: Why are we seeing "Malcolmania" and not a "Martin-mania"? Why isn't Martin sexy?

SL: Well, Martin was more mainstream. Black youth today are not going to sit

HLG: What audience is this film primarily directed toward: are you trying to educate black America or white America? Given the complexity of the subject, can one film do both?

SL: Yes, I think all my films have done both. I've always found it interesting to view my films as having two different audiences, one black and one white. We have enough stuff in there that everybody gets something out of it.

HLG: That's a hard balancing act to pull off.

SL: It can be done. Everybody can get an education out of this film. This film's about America, and all Americans can learn from it. Like Malcolm, we're taking a global view of this film: it's not just about the United States, we're thinking about the world. And there will be people who'll want to see this around the world.

HLG: But, to go back to the running joke between you and Denzel, you run the risk of alienating people once you go beyond the manipulation of symbols. Certainly it happens when you start to separate truth from falsehood, wheat from chaff, saying: no brother, the Jews did not invent slavery, the degree of melanin in your skin doesn't correspond to the degree of humanitarianism in your heart, and the Egyptians did not levitate the Pyramids and fly around in airplanes, whatever the Portland Baseline Essays claim. Now, you've sometimes been called a griot. One of the things that most Afro-Americans don't know is that the griot was always estranged from his community, always a marginal figure, exiled at his death, even buried separately from the rest of his community, because he was the person who was supposed to call a spade a spade. He was the person who was supposed to say, these are the veils you have before your eyes.

SL: This is something that's difficult to deal with, because we all want to be united as a people, and we've really been divided on purpose from the beginning, back when they made sure nobody spoke the same tongue on the slave ships. So there's always this decision to be made: should I speak out because what's going on is false, or should I keep my mouth shut? It's like the whole Clarence Thomas–Anita Hill thing. Or the whole thing between me and Baraka. I know there have to be differences, case by case; sometimes maybe differences should be talked out behind closed doors, other times, maybe it has to be done publicly. So there's this fine line, between going for the truth, while, at the same time, you don't want to make it seem that black folks are fighting black folks.

HLG: The trouble is, we're 35 million people—and that's just the ones that the Census Bureau counts . . .

SL: I know there's not one unified black thought. So there's always that issue of who determines who's black and what's black, and what's black enough. Who appointed Amiri Baraka the grand pooh-bah of black culture?

HLG: He did.

SL: Himself. There was no general election, though. On the other hand, I see people getting mad at you for saying Leonard Jeffries is full of shit. And they can say, you're just as bad as the white press that's attacking him. What people have to understand is that your questioning of his stuff doesn't come from hate or animosity. It has to do with truth. Whereas the guys at the *New York Post* and people like that are just pure racists. So there has to be a distinction made, and even though we're black, we still have to be allowed to disagree. Now, sometimes, the question comes where the disagreement's going to come. Are we going to go out in public, where we just have two black people fighting all the time?

HLG: A battle royale.

SL: A battle royale in full view of white people . . . or are we going to take these disagreements behind closed doors and see if these disagreements can be worked out.

HLG: Sometimes I've found, though, that black people don't take each other seriously until it hits the public.

SL: That's true.

HLG: And then you're stuck. But just as the charge is leveled at various black writers and intellectuals, people will charge that the white establishment created you. The line is that you're a product of *them,* that black people didn't elect you spokesman, so where do you get off talking like one?

SL: That's true. I've not been elected by black people as a spokesman, I've never positioned myself as a spokesperson for black people. The white media always designates who they feel should speak for black folk. This year we decide this is the person: when something happens that concerns black people, we're going to call this person for their reaction. I've never set myself up to be a spokesperson. At the same time, some things need to be spoken about, and I do have access to the media, and I'd be a fool not to exercise that on occasion.

HLG: It's also one of the ways a persona is created. It seems every marketable filmmaker concocts a legend about himself. Van Peebles became both the Left Bank pavement *artiste* and the outlaw with a tattoo on his neck, daring one to cut on the dotted line if you can. . . . What's Spike's legend? Surely the last thing you want to be known as is a New York urban bourgeois who not only, God forbid, went to Morehouse, but graduated from Morehouse, too.

SL: What I've been able to do is make a persona that people can believe in to sell the films. I started in the position where I'd done some low-budget films, and you know that the studios were not going to put a lot of promotional money behind that. I had to be the one to stand up on a soapbox and say: come and see this film, come and see this film, come and see this film. And so that's really how it started. And that ties in with the commercials with Mars Blackmon, for Nike and Levi's.

HLG: You don't see a tension between these two things, the artistic and the commercial.

SL: Nowadays you got to sell your product out there or nobody's going to come. And if nobody sees your movies, you won't be able to make another one.

HLG: This is your first film with Warner . . .

SL: And last.

HLG: Why's that?

SL: I've done three films before with Universal Pictures, and I just have better relations with the people there—Tom Pollack, Katie Silvers, Sandy King, Skip Jacks. I've not had that relationship at Warner Brothers. At Universal they left me alone: they understood what I was trying to do, they gave me money, and I went ahead and made my film. That really hasn't been the case at Warner Brothers. The reason I made it at Warner is that they owned the property. Universal would have loved to make this film, but they didn't have the property.

HLG: How was the financing with Warner?

SL: It's a $32–33 million movie, but Warner Brothers only put 18 into this film. And Largo bought the foreign rights for 8; so it's 6, 7 million over budget. But that $32–33 million figure was what our original budget was from the beginning. If we had held out and said, we're not making this film unless you give us $32–33 million dollars, the film would not have been made. So we went in, knowing that somewhere down the line, we'd have to find some extra money. But we had to get the film made then: it's been two decades, and we had to seize the opportunity.

HLG: With a budget this size, you've got a bigger crew, more locations, historical details: how was the adjustment?

SL: It was a big adjustment, because none of us—Ernest Dickerson, myself, Ruth Carter, Wayne Thomas—none of

us had done anything on this scale. This film is vast, a three-hour epic. It involves a lot more people, a lot more sets, a lot more locations, a lot more decisions to be made . . . more money at stake, a longer shoot. A longer shoot means more fatigue.

HLG: Will you stick in this budget range, or go back?

SL: I'll go back. The budget depends on the story. This was a $33-million story.

HLG: You've said before that the amount of control the studios exert is in direct relation to the amount of money they put up. Were there more suits on the set this time, more of a sense of studio control this time?

SL: No, they rarely came to the set. Their attitude was this: we're putting $18 million into this and not a penny more; anything that's over budget, the producers are going to have to cover, and we don't care. So they didn't hang around.

HLG: Another aspect of the production that's gotten press in the trades is the well-publicized argument you had with the local Teamsters Union, which you described as "lily-white." You said you didn't want to hire from their pool. How was that finally resolved?

SL: It worked out. We got a black teamster captain for the first time in the history of their union, and we made them hire a lot more black teamsters. Of course, it's just a drop in the bucket. What's funny is that once we started to shoot, about halfway through, Eddie

Murphy started to film; and instead of hiring more black people, the union wanted to take half of our blacks and distribute them to Eddie Murphy. Well, we said, hell no. If Eddie wants more blacks, then you've got to hire more blacks for Eddie, let more blacks into the union.

HLG: Did they do it?

SL: Not right away. But this is something that Eddie has to deal with.

HLG: On another point of contention: some people have described the flap that Amiri Baraka manufactured as the railing of a failed populist against a successful one. That is, here's someone who would also like to engage the popular consciousness the way that you've succeeded already in doing. What's your own take on the Baraka thing?

SL: I think Amiri does love Malcolm. At the same time, I think there's some jealousy in this. I think he looks around today and he's seeing young black people doing stuff, enjoying access to the media, access to the people. I mean, how many

People say, you should meet with Baraka. I mean, fuck him

people can you reach as a poet or playwright? How many people ever saw *Dutchman?* Ten thousand at the most? How many people saw the movie? I think that gets to him, the fact that we have access to so many people, and we're making money at it. And it just came at the wrong time. What's really sad is that

you'd think the people before you should be glad that somebody comes up who's successful, and who's only building on what they did. It's like the old, bitter black ball players who looked down upon Jackie Robinson, because Jackie was the one that got the shot and it just so happened that they were born ten years too early. Well, don't knock Jackie because he was the first to get picked. That's how I saw a lot of that, with Baraka.

HLG: Do you feel an obligation to reach out to the older generation?

SL: I reach out to the people who want to reach out to me. Why should I reach out to Baraka? People say, you should sit down with him, you should meet with him. I mean, fuck him. If he has such a wealth of knowledge about Malcolm, why has he never written a book about Malcolm X? Why has he never written a play about Malcolm X? Why has he never written a screenplay about Malcolm X? Now, once I start doing something, he starts talking about it. What did he do before? Nothing. I said in *Newsweek,* all these people, all you great students of Malcolm X, I'm going to give you my Federal Express account number; send me your papers, send me your transcripts, send me your manuscripts about Malcolm X. I didn't get shit. They didn't *do* shit. They're just running their mouth; they hadn't done any scholarly research, they hadn't done any work at all.

HLG: Baldwin said that when white people attacked him, that just got his blood up; but when black people attacked him, that just made him want to cry. Could you talk a little about what it's like being trashed by black people?

SL: I don't think that just because you're black, you can take the attitude that you're beyond criticism, beyond being trashed. I think, for the most part, black people have been too lenient on black artists. If a black artist goes around doing stuff that we feel is an affront to the people of the race, we should stop buying their records or seeing their movies or whatever it is. But we never realize our economic clout the way we should.

HLG: But that's what people like Baraka are trying to do to you, get people to boycott your movies. . . .

SL: With Baraka, the vast numbers of black people don't know who he is. He can scream all he wants, people are not really going to heed him.

HLG: Still, is black criticism more painful than white?

SL: I think Public Enemy said it best in that song, "Every brother ain't a brother." You might think because someone's black that right away they're going to like your work, but it's not true. Among film critics, that guy Armond White, who writes for the *City Sun,* never likes anything I've done. Is it different? It is different. But you can't assume that because you're black and they're black, automatically they're going to love your work. In the end you have to please yourself.

HLG: Still, in a marketplace where the crossover audience matters so much, what reality checks are there to preserve the "integrity" of a black production, or does such a thing exist?

SL: I think it's up to the creating force. I think that as a black person there are things you can do that will naturally bring in white folks to your work, whether a TV show, a record, or a movie. But at the same time, you don't want to water down your work, or make black folks pay for your efforts to attract this crossover audience. With people like Lionel Ritchie, there's a constant decision about what kind of audience they want to bring in. Black art has always had that dilemma. If I do choose to cross over, will I alienate my black audience? In a lot of cases, artists have gone for the crossover market, totally left behind their black audience, and once the white folks got tired of them, tried to come back to the black folks. Too late, often.

HLG: Too late, yes. Film history is littered with flashes in the pan: the black

A lot of guys making films today don't have any craft, and they're proud to say so

message films of the forties, Belafonte in the fifties, the blaxploitation era of the late sixties, early seventies. What have you done to render yourself flashproof?

SL: Flashproof means having a body of work. With *Malcolm X,* that makes six films over the last seven years. We need to grow and to get better, because there's so much to learn in filmmaking.

HLG: As to the movies themselves: what do you want them to be remembered for, and earn money for? Much as critics know what they mean when they talk about a Ford film, a Hitchcock film, and so on, what will a Lee film be remembered for?

SL: I want to be remembered for honest, true portrayal of Afro-Americans. And bring our great richness to the screen. Black cinema hasn't produced its Duke Ellington or James Baldwin yet . . . but if we stick to it, we'll make sure this isn't just a trend. And if we look at things for the long run, I think this will happen.

HLG: How do we keep it from being just a trend?

SL: By trying to be the best filmmakers we can be. By learning the craft. By having a love of cinema. Not being in it just for the money, for the glory, or the number of pretty asses you can bone when you're casting your films. That's what it's going to take. It was a love of music that enabled Duke to do what he did.

You got to have that love of whatever it is you're doing, the craft of it. And you have to go and spend time in the woodshed. John Coltrane, Wynton Marsalis, they practice five, six hours a day. They're not bullshitting. A lot of these guys making films today, they're bullshitting. They don't have any craft, and they're proud to say it: "I didn't go to film school, I never made a film before." Most of the time it ends up looking exactly like that. It looks like crap.

There are so many stories to tell. Hollywood—for the most part, their shit is dried up. Theater, too. I mean, there has to be a reason they're doing Shakespeare for the ten millionth motherfucking time. No other new white writer ever? Just this dude Shakespeare? Or Chekhov's *Cherry Orchard*—how many times do you have to do that shit? I know there's such a thing as a classic, but to me that stuff is dead. And our stories have not really been told. Think of all the novels that have still to make it to the screen: *Song of Solomon, Bluest Eye, Their Eyes Are Watching God*. It's like virgin territory.

Oxford

BILL ADLER is the author of *Tougher than Leather: The Authorized Biography of Run-DMC* (New American Library, 1987) and *Rap: Portraits and Lyrics of a Generation of Black Rockers* (St. Martin's Press, 1991). He also does independent publicity for the Disposable Heroes of Hiphoprisy.

DAVID BRADLEY, a professor of English at Temple University, is the author of the novels *South Street* and *The Chaneysville Incident*.

PHILIP BURNHAM, a former Fulbright Scholar in American studies, is a journalist based in Washington DC. He has taught literature at the University of New Mexico and Cheikh Anta Diop University in Dakar, Senegal.

STEPHEN L. CARTER is William Nelson Cromwell Professor of Law at Yale and author of *Reflections of an Affirmative Action Baby*.

STEPHEN CLINGMAN edited and introduced Nadine Gordimer's collection of nonfiction, *The Essential Gesture: Writing, Politics, and Place*. His study *The Novels of Nadine Gordimer: History from the Inside* is being published in a second edition with a new prologue by the University of Massachusetts Press (Bloomsbury in the United Kingdom).

MICHAEL ERIC DYSON teaches in the American civilization department and the Afro-American studies program at Brown University and is the author of the forthcoming collection, *Angles of Vision*. He is a frequent contributor to *The New York Times Book Review, The Nation, Tikkun,* and *Z Magazine.*

STANLEY FISH is the author of *Surprised by Sin, Self-Consuming Artifacts, Is There a Text in This Class?* and *Doing What Comes Naturally: Change, Rhetoric, and the Practice of Theory in Literary and Legal Studies,* among other books.

HENRY LOUIS GATES, JR., is director of the W.E.B. Du Bois Institute for African American Research at Harvard University. His interviews with Ted Joans and Eldridge Cleaver appeared in *Transition* issues 34 and 36.

JULIANNE MALVEAUX, an economist and syndicated columnist, is the editor, with Margaret C. Simms, of *Slipping through the Cracks: The Status of Black Women.*

W. J. T. MITCHELL is editor of *Critical Inquiry.* His books include *Blake's Composite Art* and *Iconology: Image, Text, Ideology.*

V. Y. MUDIMBE is the author of numerous works of fiction, poetry, philosophy, theology, and philology, and is himself the subject of several book-length studies.

RICHARD A. POSNER is a U. S. Court of Appeals judge for the Seventh Circuit and a Senior Lecturer at the University of Chicago Law School. His recent books include *Cardozo: A Study in Reputation, The Problems of Jurisprudence,* and *Sex and Reason.*

ILAN STAVANS, a Mexican novelist, scholar, and columnist, is completing *The Stranger Within,* a book of reflections on Hispanic culture in the U. S. His books include *Imagining Columbus: The Literary Voyage* and a bilingual edition of *Sentimental Songs* by Filipe Alfau.

SHELBY STEELE is the author of *The Content of Our Character.*

Manuscript submissions

Manuscripts should be sent to the Editors, Transition, 1430 Massachusetts Avenue, 4th floor, Cambridge, MA 02138, and should be submitted typed, double-spaced, and in triplicate. Unsolicited manuscripts can be returned only if accompanied by a self-addressed stamped envelope. In general the journal follows the recommendations of The Chicago Manual of Style. *For specific instructions on style contact the editorial office.*

Book reviews

All copies of books to be considered for review should be sent to Transition, 1430 Massachusetts Avenue, 4th floor, Cambridge, MA 02138.

Advertising

Correspondence regarding advertising should be sent to Transition, Journals Department, Oxford University Press, 200 Madison Avenue, New York, NY 10016.

Subscriptions

Subscription rates for new series volume 2 (1992) are $24.00 for individuals and $48.00 for institutions. Outside the U.S. please add $14.00; for air-expedited delivery, add an additional $8.00. Single copies and back issues are $8.95 for individuals and $15.00 for institutions. Outside the U.S. please add $4.00. Subscription requests and change-of-address notifications should be directed to the Journals Fulfillment Department, Oxford University Press, 2001 Evans Road, Cary NC 27513.

Microform

Microfilm and microfiche inquiries (for both previous and new series) should be directed to University Microfilms Inc., 300 N. Zeeb Road, Ann Arbor, MI 48106.

Photocopies

The journal is registered with the Copyright Clearance Center, 27 Congress Street, Salem, MA 01970. Permission to photocopy items for internal or personal use of specific clients is granted by Oxford University Press provided that $.05 per page/per copy is paid directly to the CCC for copying beyond that permitted by the U.S. Copyright Law.

Requests for permission to photocopy for other purposes, such as general distribution, resale, advertising and promotional purposes, or creating new collective works, should be directed to Transition, Journals Department, Oxford University Press, 200 Madision Avenue, New York, NY 10016.

Where the outspoken speak out.

In 1961, some of Africa's most provocative thinkers started speaking out in a new magazine called **Transition.** It pulled no punches. The New York Times called it "Africa's slickest, sprightliest, and occasionally sexiest magazine."

Editor Rajat Neogy refused to listen when told by government officials that **Transition** was speaking a little too loudly. He was subsequently sent to jail.

After 50 uncensored, unguarded, and uninhibited issues, **Transition** ceased publication because of political and economic pressure.

Thirty-one years later, **Transition** is back. It's about time.

From Mandela to Mapplethorpe, affirmative action to the politics of AIDS, racial politics in New York to feminism in South Africa, the new **Transition** tackles today's most controversial issues head-on.

Though keeping an emphasis on African and African-American concerns, the new **Transition** has taken on the world. No idea, thought, person, belief, or subject is considered out of bounds.

Today's most original thinkers—novelists, playwrights, poets, critics, film-makers—are saying what's on their mind. And they're saying it in **Transition.**

Chairman of the Editorial Board   Wole Soyinka

Editors   K.A. Appiah
              Henry Louis Gates, Jr.

From the pages of Transition

Wole Soyinka on intellectuals and the big con ■ **Richard Rorty** on prophetic philosophy ■ **Jamaica Kincaid** on cultural erasure ■ **William Finnegan** on Malawi's malaise ■ **V.Y. Mudimbe** on third world theology ■ **Ariel Dorfman** on the vision of violence ■ **Christopher Hitchens** on Lebanon's road to hell ■ **Spike Lee** on Malcolm-mania ■ **Ali Mazrui** on Schweitzerian racism ■ **Ernest Gellner** on nationalism's ABC's ■ **Lewis Nkosi** on the mind of South Africa ■ **Carlos Fuentes** on the *other* other path ■ **Edward Said** on nationalism and the academy ■ **William Boyd** on voyeurism and travelogue ■ **Dennis Brutus** on Mandela's burden ■ **Nadine Gordimer** on postapartheid culture

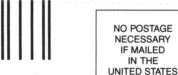

NO POSTAGE
NECESSARY
IF MAILED
IN THE
UNITED STATES

BUSINESS REPLY MAIL
FIRST CLASS MAIL   PERMIT NO. 705   CARY, NC

POSTAGE WILL BE PAID BY ADDRESSEE

OXFORD UNIVERSITY PRESS
Attn: Journals Department
2001 EVANS ROAD
CARY, NC 27513-9902

NO POSTAGE
NECESSARY
IF MAILED
IN THE
UNITED STATES

BUSINESS REPLY MAIL
FIRST CLASS MAIL   PERMIT NO. 705   CARY, NC

POSTAGE WILL BE PAID BY ADDRESSEE

OXFORD UNIVERSITY PRESS
Attn: Journals Department
2001 EVANS ROAD
CARY, NC 27513-9902